Recent Advances in Neuromorphic Computing

Edited by Kang Jun Bai and Yang (Cindy) Yi

Published in London, United Kingdom

Recent Advances in Neuromorphic Computing
http://dx.doi.org/10.5772/intechopen.1003289
Edited by Kang Jun Bai and Yang (Cindy) Yi

Contributors
Ali Mehrabi, André van Schaik, Chandrashekhar S. Patil, Dayeon Jeong, Fang-Yi Gu, Fuming Lai, Girish U. Kamble, Hongyu An, Jinho Jeong, Jin Hyeok Kim, Kangjun Bai, Ki-Yong Oh, Kyung ho Sun, Md Abu Bakr Siddique, Ruizhe Li, Seho Son, Shengfu Tong, Somnath S. Kundale, Tianze Liu, Vidya V. Alman, Yang(Cindy) Yi, Yan Zhang

First published in London, United Kingdom, 2025 by IntechOpen
IntechOpen is the global imprint of INTECHOPEN LIMITED, registered in England and Wales, registration number: 11086078, 167-169 Great Portland Street, London, W1W 5PF, United Kingdom

For EU product safety concerns: IN TECH d.o.o., Prolaz Marije Krucifikse Kozulić 3, 51000 Rijeka, Croatia, info@intechopen.com or visit our website at intechopen.com.

British Library Cataloguing-in-Publication Data
A catalogue record for this book is available from the British Library

Recent Advances in Neuromorphic Computing
Edited by Kang Jun Bai and Yang (Cindy) Yi
p. cm.

This title is part of the Artificial Intelligence Book Series, Volume 35
Topic: Computational Neuroscience
Series Editor: Andries Engelbrecht
Topic Editor: Magnus Johnsson

Print ISBN 978-0-85466-224-1
Online ISBN 978-0-85466-223-4
eBook (PDF) ISBN 978-0-85466-225-8
ISSN 2633-1403

IntechOpen Book Series
Artificial Intelligence
Volume 35

Aims and Scope of the Series

Artificial Intelligence (AI) is a rapidly developing multidisciplinary research area that aims to solve increasingly complex problems. In today's highly integrated world, AI promises to become a robust and powerful means for obtaining solutions to previously unsolvable problems. This Series is intended for researchers and students alike interested in this fascinating field and its many applications.

Meet the Series Editor

Andries Engelbrecht received the Masters and Ph.D. degrees in Computer Science from the University of Stellenbosch, South Africa, in 1994 and 1999 respectively. He is currently appointed as the Voigt Chair in Data Science in the Department of Industrial Engineering, with a joint appointment as Professor in the Computer Science Division, Stellenbosch University. Prior to his appointment at Stellenbosch University, he has been at the University of Pretoria, Department of Computer Science (1998-2018), where he was appointed as South Africa Research Chair in Artifical Intelligence (2007-2018), the head of the Department of Computer Science (2008-2017), and Director of the Institute for Big Data and Data Science (2017-2018). In addition to a number of research articles, he has written two books, Computational Intelligence: An Introduction and Fundamentals of Computational Swarm Intelligence.

Meet the Volume Editors

Dr. Kang Jun Bai is a research electronics engineer at the Air Force Research Laboratory Information Directorate (AFRL/RI). Before joining AFRL, he received his Ph.D. in Electrical Engineering from Virginia Tech in 2021, his M. S. in Embedded Electrical and Computer Systems from San Francisco State University in 2017, and his B. S. in Electrical Engineering from the same institution in 2014. His research interests include mixed-signal integrated circuit design and nanoelectronics devices for bio-inspired computing systems, model emulation for deep learning benchmarks, and the development of emerging applications for mobile edge platforms.

Dr. Yang (Cindy) Yi is a professor in the Bradley Department of Electrical Engineering and Computer Engineering at Virginia Tech. Her research interests include very large-scale integrated (VLSI) circuits and systems, computer-aided design (CAD), neuromorphic architecture for brain-inspired computing systems, and low-power circuit design with advanced nanotechnologies for high-speed wireless systems.

Contents

Preface

We stand at the precipice of a new era, one defined by the pervasive influence of Artificial Intelligence (AI). No longer confined to the realm of science fiction, AI is rapidly transforming industries, reshaping our daily lives, and challenging our understanding of intelligence itself. At the heart of this revolution lies Machine Learning (ML), the engine that empowers computers to learn from data, identify patterns, and make predictions with ever-increasing accuracy.

Powering this evolution are groundbreaking advances in hardware, including neuromorphic computing, which promises to unlock new levels of efficiency and performance by mimicking the brain's architecture. Such advancements are fueled by breakthroughs in emerging memory materials, which offer the potential for denser, faster, and more energy-efficient storage. To further accelerate AI's capabilities, in-memory computing eliminates the bottleneck of traditional data access by processing information directly within the memory itself. These techniques are being implemented on a range of platforms, from Field Programmable Gate Arrays (FPGAs) that offer flexibility and reconfigurability to specialized neuromorphic processors like IBM's NorthPole and Intel's Loihi.

In recent years, the trend towards edge applications promises to further decentralize AI, bringing intelligence closer to the point of data creation and consumption. Imagine real-time medical diagnostics in remote areas, autonomous robots collaborating on factory floors, or smart city infrastructure optimizing traffic flow and energy consumption – all powered by edge AI.

The future of AI is not predetermined but rather a trajectory shaped by our innovations. We can envision a future where AI is seamlessly integrated into every aspect of our lives, from personalized healthcare to sustainable energy solutions. This future will be characterized by more sophisticated AI models, greater energy efficiency, and enhanced security. Looking ahead, the convergence of AI with other emerging technologies like quantum computing could unlock entirely new possibilities.

This book explores such an exciting evolution, providing a comprehensive overview of the current state of AI and offering insights into the future trajectory of these transformative technologies. We'll examine the core principles, the practical applications, and the ethical considerations that will shape the future of AI in the years to come.

Kang Jun Bai, Ph.D.
AFRL Information Directorate,
Rome, USA

Yang (Cindy) Yi, Ph.D.
Virginia Tech Innovation Campus,
Alexandria, USA

Section 1

Emerging Materials and Computing Architectures

Chapter 1

Harnessing RRAM Technology for Efficient AI Implementation

Fang-Yi Gu

Abstract

This chapter details the utilization of RRAM devices as key components in neuromorphic computing for efficient in-memory computing. Beginning with the fundamental mechanism of RRAM and its data storage capabilities and followed by efficient AI implementations with RRAM. This includes discussions on RRAM-based accelerators facilitating DNN computations with remarkable O(1) time complexity efficiency, as well as the RRAM's multi-level characteristics. Subsequently, the chapter addresses challenges encountered in RRAM technology, such as variations, IR-drop issues, and the substantial energy and area requirements associated with DAC/ADC operations. Solutions to these challenges are briefly summarized. Emphasis is then placed on the critical issue of programming RRAM devices, with challenges including cycle-to-cycle variation and energy-intensive processes. Various programming techniques are explicated, accompanied by a comparative analysis of their respective advantages and drawbacks.

Keywords: In-memory computing, RRAM, RRAM-based DNN accelerators, reliability, RRAM programming

1. Introduction

In the conventional Von-Neumann architecture, the separation of memories, logic units, and control units has led to the emergence of the 'memory wall' phenomenon, namely an enlarging divergence in performance evolution between processors and memories. It is reported that over recent years, this trend has become increasingly evident, with processor performance boosted by over 10,000 times while memory performance has seen only modest improvements, around 10 times [1]. In response to this challenge, researchers have turned their attention to exploring alternative memory technologies with superior performance and higher density storage. Nonvolatile memories (NVMs) have emerged as particularly promising candidates, whose superiorities include simple structures, nonvolatile data storage, low power consumption, high scalability, and compatibility with CMOS devices. Moreover, some of them possess the capability of not only storing data but also performing computational tasks.

Filament-type resistive random-access memory (RRAM) stands out as a prominent member of the NVM family, drawing significant interest from researchers and industry alike. Leveraging reversible resistive switching (RS) mechanisms, RRAM is capable of data storage. Beyond its storage capabilities, RRAM exhibits analog behavior, enabling it to perform multiplication computations. Later in this chapter, we will present the filamentary mechanism of RRAM, elucidating its intricacies in a straightforward manner. Additionally, we will explore how RRAM facilitates time-efficient vector matrix multiplication.

2. Resistive switching (RS) mechanism

An RRAM memory cell consists of a metal–insulator–metal (MIM) structure, where an insulating layer is sandwiched between two metal electrodes. The filamentary mechanism uses external voltage applied to the electrodes to control the growth or reduction of a filament to modulate the desired resistance value of the memory cell. The cell can be switched between a high resistance state (HRS) and a low resistance state (LRS), or logic '0' and logic '1'. In the HRS, the filament is disconnected, resulting in high resistance, while in the LRS, the filament is connected, leading to low resistance. Additionally, RRAM possesses multi-level characteristics, which is an essential feature to achieve more compact memory density. This will be further explained later in the chapter.

An RRAM cell begins in its pristine state, with an insulating layer that requires a high voltage pulse, known as the '*forming voltage*,' to create a conductive path. This process, called *electroforming*, prepares the cell for filament modulation using different voltages. To switch the cell from a HRS to a LRS, a *set* voltage is applied. Conversely, to switch from LRS back to HRS, a *reset* voltage is applied.

There are two types of RRAM based on filament composition: *ion-based RRAM* and *oxygen-vacancy-based RRAM*. In *ion-based RRAM*, the filament is formed through the migration of metal ions and the oxidation/reduction of the electrochemically active top metal electrode (anode). When a positive voltage is applied, oxidation occurs, generating metal ions that drift toward the inert bottom electrode (cathode) and reduce to form a conductive filament, switching the cell to LRS. During the reset process, applying a negative voltage oxidizes the deposited metal atoms back into ions, rupturing the filament and switching the cell to HRS. **Figure 1** illustrates the set and reset process of an ion-based RRAM cell.

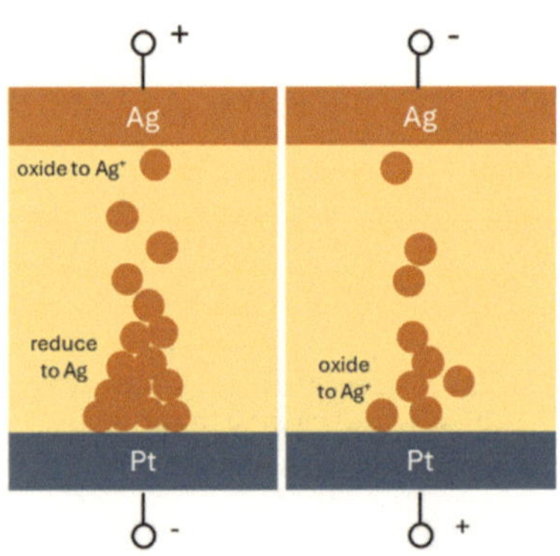

Figure 1.
Set (left) and reset (right) process of an ion-based RRAM cell.

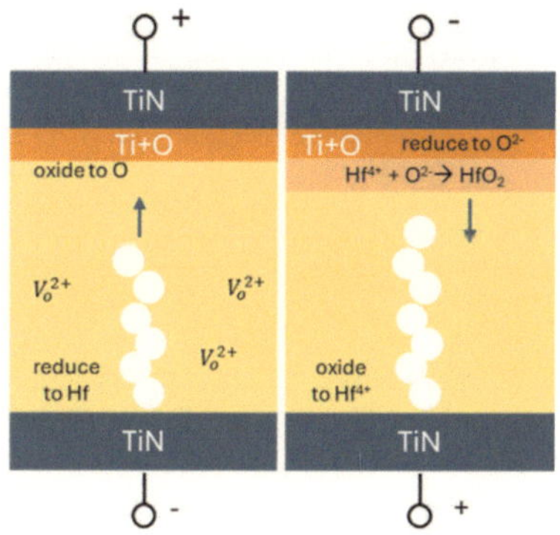

Figure 2.
Set (left) and reset (right) process of an V_o^{2+}-based RRAM cell.

In *oxygen-vacancy-based RRAM*, the filament is formed through the migration of oxygen ions. The electroforming process produces a sufficient amount of oxygen vacancies to initiate the RS—when a high electric field is applied toward the anode interface, the dielectric material in the insulating layer (typically an oxide layer) experiences breakdown, weakening its insulating properties and allowing charge carriers to move freely. During the set process, oxygen atoms within the dielectric lattice are further ejected, becoming oxygen ions (O^{2-}) and leaving behind positively charged vacancies (V_o^{2+}). The drifting O^{2-} can transfer electrons to the anode (oxidize) and form an interfacial oxide layer, which can act as a protective barrier against further oxidation and conveniently serve as an oxygen reservoir. While the V_o^{2+} reduce at cathode and serve as electron hopping sites for current conduction paths, namely conductive filament, allowing the cell to switch to LRS. During the reset process, the oxide interface releases oxygen ions, which combine with the oxygen vacancies within the oxide layer, switching the cell back to HRS. An example of an oxygen-vacancy-based RRAM device is shown in **Figure 2**, which illustrates the RS process of a TiN/Ti/HfO2/TiN RRAM [1]. Two types of oxygen vacancies exist in the insulating layer: HfO^{2+} and Hf^{4+}, which are represented as V_o^{2+} in the figure.

During the process of forming the filament in the dielectric layer, a *compliance current (Icc)*, which is the maximum current allowed to flow through the selected transistor, is enforced on the RRAM device to prevent permanent breakdown, ensuring the device does not enter an irreversible state in which even the highest reset voltage cannot dissolve the filament. The magnitude of gate voltage on the transistor in a 1T1R device controls the magnitude of Icc. The higher Icc is, the stronger the filament is formed, meaning that this LRS state can be stable over longer time, namely longer retention time. However, it also means that higher reset voltage is required to switch the device back to HRS.

3. Efficient vector matrix multiplication (VMM) with RRAM devices

RRAM devices are capable of storing weights as resistance states. When RRAM devices are constructed into a crossbar structure, as depicted in **Figure 3**, vector matrix multiplication (VMM) can be easily executed due to the analog behavior of RRAM.

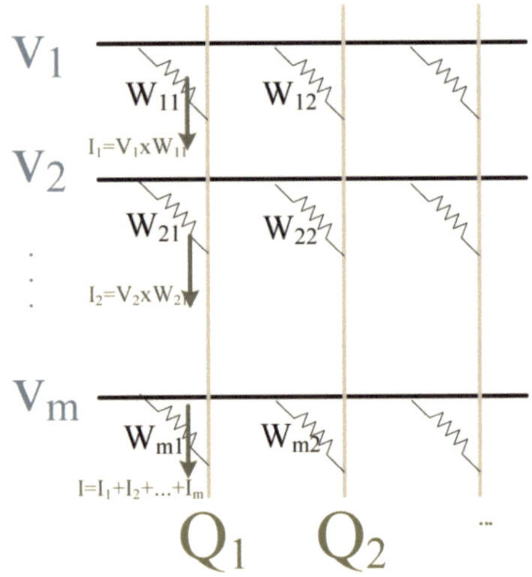

Figure 3.
RRAM crossbar structure.

Eq. (1) illustrates an example of VMM, where *W* represents a matrix of weights, *V* represents a vector of input, and *Q* represents a resulting vector of outputs. As shown in **Figure 3**, if inputs are applied as voltages and weights are represented in the form of conductances, the output can be easily obtained in O(1) time complexity by measuring the current flowing through the bitline, in accordance with Ohm's law, $I_n = \sum_{i=0}^{m} v_i G_{i,n}$.

$$\begin{bmatrix} Q_1 \\ \vdots \\ Q_n \end{bmatrix} = \begin{bmatrix} W_{11} \dots W_{m1} \\ \vdots \quad \dots \quad \vdots \\ W_{1n} \dots W_{mn} \end{bmatrix} \begin{bmatrix} V_1 \\ \vdots \\ V_m \end{bmatrix} \tag{1}$$

This in-memory VMM computation allows us to efficiently perform convolutional computations commonly used in deep neural networks (DNNs). **Figure 4** presents a weight mapping example, where (a) shows a W*W*C input feature map convolved

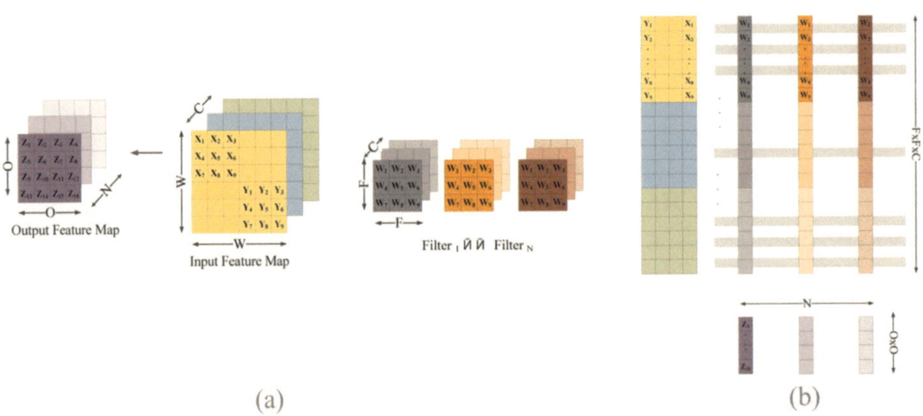

Figure 4.
Weight mapping method from (a) a convolutional computation to (b) RRAM XB with the corresponding IFM in each cycle.

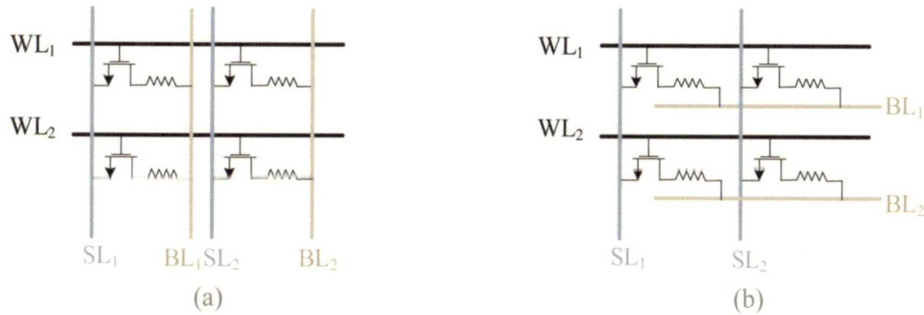

Figure 5.
Transformation from (a) conventional 1T1R array to (b) the suitable crossbar array.

with N kernels, each of size F*F*C, which results in an output feature map of size O*O*N. When unrolled into 1D, each kernel can be mapped on a column of the crossbar, and VMMs are performed as the corresponding inputs are fed in each cycle, which demonstrates the practicality and efficiency of the neuromorphic computation with RRAM.

A more advanced RRAM crossbar structure, such as the 1-Transistor-1-Rram (1T1R) configuration, can prevent the crosstalk between adjacent cells to build large-scale arrays. As depicted in **Figure 5(a)**, this configuration enables the meticulous control of each row of memristors with wordlines (WLs), which control the gates of the transistors. Input vector voltages are applied to the bitlines (BLs), with which the top electrodes of RRAM devices are connected. The weighted sum currents are read-out through selected lines (SLs) in parallel. However, this configuration does not support the execution of parallel weighted sum currents. This limitation can be tackled by rotating the BLs by 90°, illustrated in **Figure 5(b)**, thereby simulating the behavior of matrix multiplication shown in **Figure 4**.

4. RRAM multilevel characteristics

An essential characteristic allowing RRAM to perform neuromorphic computation is its capability to store multiple resistance states, which significantly enhances the memory storage density. The RRAM devices with multiple resistance states are called multilevel cells (MLC). There are two primary methods to achieve multilevel RRAMs:

First, achieving one HRS and multiple LRS states by altering the magnitude of Icc. As previously mentioned, Icc determines the strength of the conductive filament; a higher Icc results in a stronger filament and thus lower resistance. Therefore, several distinct LRS states can be achieved by controlling Icc through the gate voltage. Second, achieving one LRS and several HRS states by altering the magnitude of the reset voltage with a constant Icc. A stronger reset voltage leads to greater dissolution of the filament, increasing the gap between the filament and the electrode, which increases the resistance of HRS. Therefore, several HRS states can be obtained by varying the reset voltages.

The inherent variability within RRAM, caused by the stochastic nature of the filament formation during the RS procedure, presents as a reliability challenge for RRAM-based DNN accelerators. The variability in a resistance level can be modeled using normal or log-normal distribution. As illustrated in **Figure 6**, this variability leads to overlapping areas in the consecutive resistance levels, which can cause

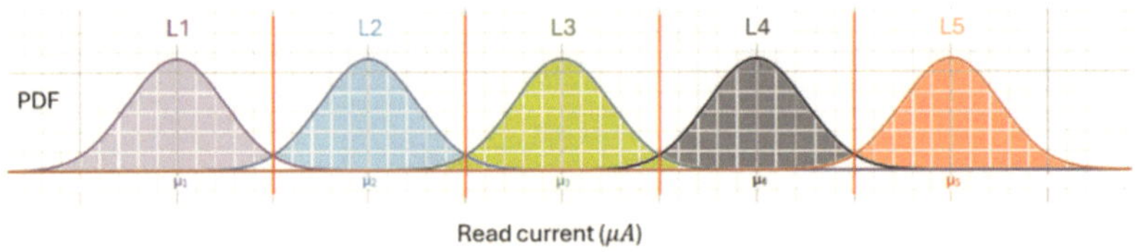

Figure 6.
Probability distribution of a RRAM device with five conductance values.

computational errors. MLC with more resistance levels is prone to higher variability issue. Therefore, precise control over different resistance states is crucial for achieving reliable operations with RRAM devices.

5. RRAM-based DNN accelerators

An RRAM-based DNN Accelerator, as illustrated in **Figure 7**, consists of numerous tiles, each containing multiple processing elements (PEs), functional units necessary for DNN computations and embedded DRAM (eDRAM) for storing input data. Within a PE, there are multiple RRAM crossbars (XBs) for performing VMMs, supported by digital-to-analog converters (DACs), analog-to-digital converters (ADCs), input/output registers, and shift-and-add (S&A) units. Due to the bit-level decomposition of inputs and weights, S&A units are responsible for assembling the outputs based on the bit positions of both inputs and weights.

VMM can be executed time-efficiently through RRAM-based crossbar structure thanks to its analog behavior. However, performing DNN computations necessitates converting the digital input data to analog voltage. Similarly, to obtain the output, the current measured in the bitline should also be converted back to digital data. Therefore, the inclusion of DACs and ADCs in an RRAM-based DNN Accelerator is essential. To better measure the currents for feeding into ADCs, sample-and-hold (S&H) circuits are usually utilized.

Although necessary, the presence of ADCs and DACs degrades the performance of the DNN accelerator due to their high energy consumption and area requirements. Previous studies have shown that ADCs and DACs account for over 60% of the energy consumption and 30% of the area. Furthermore, the energy consumption of DACs and ADCs scales exponentially with resolution.

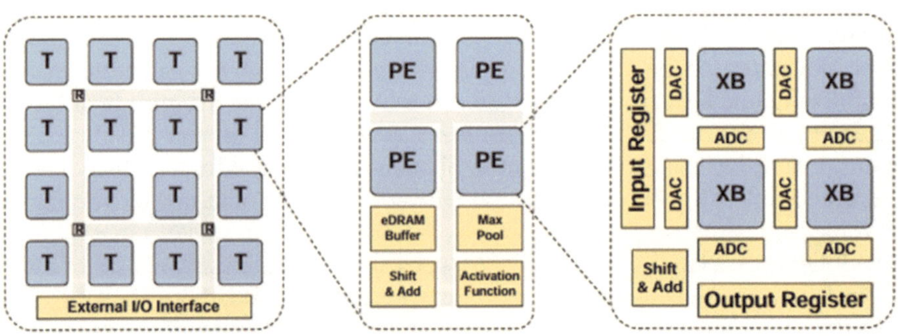

Figure 7.
Hierarchical architecture of an RRAM-based DNN accelerator.

DOI: http://dx.doi.org/10.5772/intechopen.1006094

To reduce the resolution of DACs, a common way is to perform *bit-slicing* of input, feeding it into the XBs bit-by-bit or two bits at a time, and then integrating the results with S&A operations. Bit-slicing can also contribute to the reduction of ADC resolution, while to further reduce its resolution, another way is to utilize lower-resolution RRAM devices. The ADC resolution (A) can be calculated with $A = \log_2(\mathrm{R} \times v \times w)$, where R represents number of rows in a XB, v represents input bit, and w represents RRAM cell resolution.

For example, assuming a 128×128 XB is used, and both weights and inputs are quantized to 8 bits with each RRAM device representing 2-bit weight, the output currents captured in this case require 8-bit resolution ADCs. If the input is sliced into 1-bit increments, 1-bit resolution DACs are used, but 8 cycles are required to perform a complete computation due to the bit-slicing of an 8-bit input data.

Besides the above-mentioned approaches, McDaniel et al. [2] proposed *term quantization (TQ)*, which imposes a limit on the maximum analog value for each BL to reduce the resolution requirement for ADCS. Specifically, TQ limits the number of nonzero power-of-two terms across a group of values. This approach leverages bit-level sparsity, allowing the replacement of 6-bit ADCs with six 3-bit ADCs, thereby significantly reducing both the area and power consumption.

$$\begin{bmatrix} Q_1 \\ Q_2 \end{bmatrix} = \begin{bmatrix} W_{11} W_{21} \\ W_{12} W_{22} \end{bmatrix} \begin{bmatrix} V_1 \\ V_2 \end{bmatrix} \tag{2}$$

To better comprehend the VMM operation on RRAM-based XB, let us consider an example with 2-bit input data, 4-bit weights, and 1-bit cell resolution, as shown in **Figure 8**. The XB size is 2 by 8, with 4 weights mapped onto it. We aim to perform a VMM operation presented in Eq. (2) using 1-bit input bit-sliding.

A key detail to note is that conductance is always a continuous positive value, whereas weights in neural networks can be both positive and negative. To address this, it is common to use two XBs: one to represent positive values and one to represent negative values. The final result is then obtained by subtracting the output of the negative XB from the output of the positive XB.

In the example in **Figure 8**, $W_{ij}[m]$ denotes the m-th bit of the weight, and $V_i[n]$ denotes the n-th bit of the input. It requires 2 cycles to process the entire input, typically starting from the most-significant bit (MSB) to the least-significant bit (LSB)

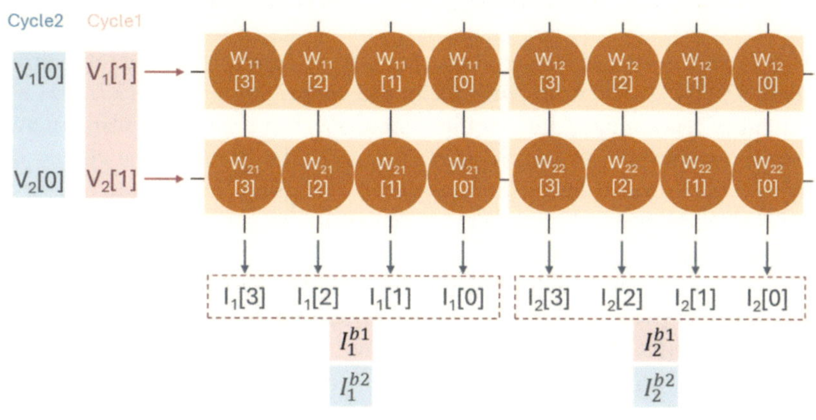

Figure 8.
Example of a VMM operation in RRAM XB.

in the input bit-slicing order. This way, when the partial result (I_j^{bn}) obtained in each cycle is accumulated and stored in the output buffer, it only needs to be shifted x bits per cycle, where x is the increment in input bit-slicing. In this case, x is 1.

To generalize, assume the input is quantized to $N \times x$ bits, and each cycle feeds an x-bit increment of the input into the XB. Over N cycles, partial results I_j^{bN} to I_j^{b1} are generated. The final result Q_j can be obtained using Eq. (3), which sums up the partial results after appropriate bit shifts.

$$Q_j = \sum_{n=1}^{N} (2^x)^n \times I_j^{bn} = \left(\left(\left(I_j^{bN} \ll x + I_j^{b(N-1)}\right) \ll x + I_j^{b(N-2)}\right) \ll x + \ldots\right) \ll x + I_j^{b1} \quad (3)$$

To understand how I_j^{bn} is generated, let us first consider the operations within a single cycle. In the first cycle, the 1st bit of the input is fed into the XB, and 8 outputs are generated. These outputs, $I_j[0]$ to $I_j[3]$ represent partial results, and they are passed to the S&A unit, where each is shifted to its bit significance: $I_j[1]$ is shifted by 1 bit ($\times 2$), $I_j[2]$ by 2 bits ($\times 2^2$), and $I_j[3]$ by 3 bits ($\times 2^3$), to obtain the I_j^{b1}.

To generalize, I_j^{bn} can be obtained with Eq. (4). Assume each weight is represented by $M \times c$ bits, where M is the number of cells, and c is the cell resolution in bits. Therefore, each bit of the weight is shifted by $c \times m$ bits, where m represents the m-th bit of the weight. The bitline current ($I_j[m]$) is accumulated across all enabled rows, say R rows, in accordance with Ohm's law.

$$I_j^{bn} = \sum_{m=0}^{M} (2^c)^m \times I_j[m] = \sum_{m=0}^{M} (2^c)^m \times \left(\sum_{i=1}^{R} V_i[n] \times W_{ij}[m]\right) \quad (4)$$

Increasing the resolution of the bit number of an input per cycle and the resolution of each RRAM device reduces the cycle numbers required for one computation and the number of computations, respectively, but exponentially increases the energy consumption due to the higher resolution requirement for DACs and ADCs. Furthermore, higher resolution of MLC RRAM devices is more susceptible to variability, leading to computational errors. This trade-off between resolution, energy consumption, and variability must be carefully considered in the design of RRAM-based DNN accelerators.

IR-drop or parasitic voltage drop is another critical concern for the reliability of RRAM-based DNN accelerators, with its impact increasing with the XB size. As the advancement of technology, the metallic wires in a chip shrink, resulting in an increase in the resistance per unit length. Because of the IR-drop, the voltage distribution within the crossbar becomes non-uniform, causing the input data sent to the RRAM cells on the same row to differ. Moreover, it also causes the current deviation of the output column in the crossbar.

The voltage of the top and bottom electrode of each RRAM device can be represented, respectively, as Eq. (5) and (6), where r is the wire resistance, which is assumed to be identical over the whole crossbar.

$$V_{i,j} = V_{i,j-1} - r \cdot \sum_{k=j}^{N} G_{i,k}\left(V_{i,k} - V'_{i,k}\right) \quad (5)$$

$$V'_{i,j} = V'_{i,j-1} - r \cdot \sum_{k=1}^{i-1} G_{k,j}\left(V_{k,j} - V'_{k,j}\right) \tag{6}$$

Eq. (5) and (6) can be easily derived by referring to **Figure 9**. According to Kirchhoff's current law, the current across row i can be represented by the sum of current split to the columns (Eq. (7)), each of which can be represented by voltage drop across the conductance times the conductance value.

$$I_i = I_{i,1} + I_{i,2} + I_{i,3} = \sum_{j=1}^{3} I_{i,j} = \sum_{j=1}^{3} \Delta V_{i,j} \cdot G_{i,j} = \sum_{j=1}^{3}\left(V_{i,j} - V'_{i,j}\right) \cdot G_{i,j} \tag{7}$$

Top electrode $V_{i,j}$ can be derived by removing the voltage drop of the wire resistance from the top electrode potential of the previous column. Similarly, bottom electrode $V'_{i,j}$ can be derived by removing the voltage drop of the wire resistance from the bottom electrode potential of the previous row. The followings are the examples for deriving the voltages of the top and bottom electrodes of $G_{3,2}$.

$$\begin{aligned} V_{3,2} &= V_{3,1} - \Delta V = V_{3,1} - r \cdot (I_3 - I_{3,1}) = V_{3,1} - r \cdot (I_{3,2} + I_{3,3}) \\ &= V_{3,1} - r \cdot \sum_{j=2}^{3}\left(V_{3,j} - V'_{3,j}\right) \cdot G_{3,j} \\ V'_{3,2} &= V'_{2,2} - r \cdot (I_{1,2} + I_{2,2}) = V'_{2,2} - r \cdot \sum_{i=1}^{2}(V_{i,2} - V'_{i,2}) \cdot G_{i,2} \end{aligned} \tag{8}$$

To mitigate the impact of IR-drop on the accuracy, Huang et al. [3] proposed to alleviate the current and voltage deviation by adding an additional tunable RRAM row. This approach adaptively compensates for current differences by tuning the input voltage and conductance of the RRAM cells in the additional row. The tunable

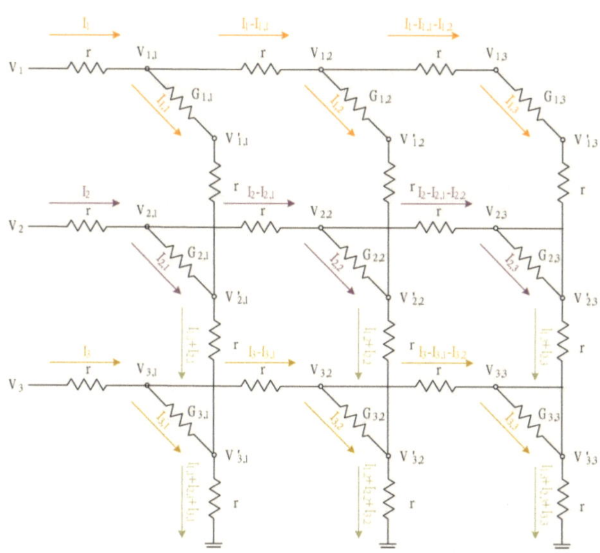

Figure 9.
Simplified 3x3 RRAM crossbar with IR-drop.

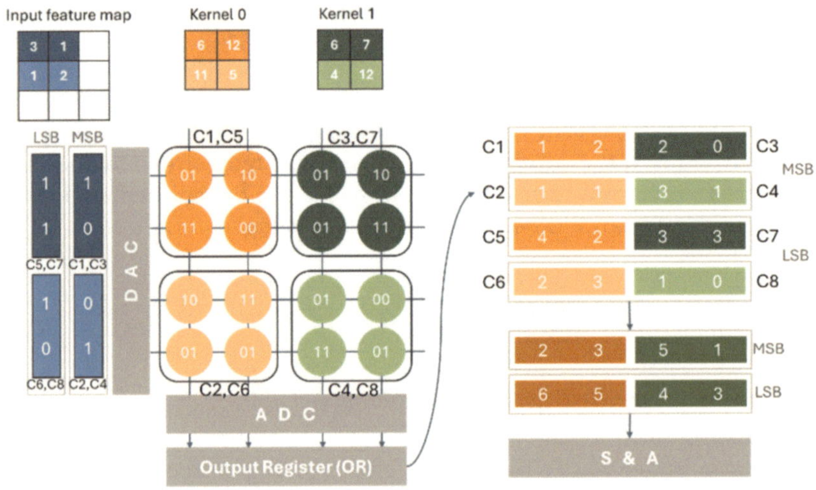

Figure 10.
OU-based RRAM architecture.

RRAM cells adjust their resistance to balance the current flow, thereby reducing the discrepancies caused by IR-drop and improving the overall accuracy of computations in the crossbar array.

Taking into account the limitations of the resolution of DAC and DAC as well as the impact of IR-drop in the design of the RRAM-based DNN accelerators, operation-unit (OU)-based or block-based computation, can be adopted [4]. An example of OU-based computation is shown in **Figure 10**. OU-based computation splits the XB into multiple OUs, each of which can be activated individually at a time with adjustable sizes. Even though this approach requires more cycles to complete one computation, it significantly reduces the resolution requirement and power consumption of ADCs and helps mitigate the voltage inconsistencies across the crossbar. To compensate for the potential performance degradation caused by the increased number of cycles, pipelining techniques can be employed in OU-based computation to enhance the overall efficiency and throughput of the RRAM-based DNN accelerators.

6. Real world AI applications with RRAM-based accelerators

In the previous sections, we detailed how RRAM-based accelerators efficiently perform VMM operations in O(1) time complexity. As mentioned in Section 3, VMM operations are fundamental to DNNs, which are mainly composed of convolutional (CONV) layers and fully connected (FC) layers. As illustrated in **Figure 4**, convolutional operations can be easily executed through RRAM XBs by sequentially providing the corresponding input across the sliding window in the input feature map (IFM). Similarly, FC layer operations follow the same procedure, with the primary difference being the size of the kernels, which match the IFM size, as shown in **Figure 11**.

Convolutional neural networks (CNNs), a prevalent form of DNNs, excel in object recognition tasks, including image classification [5], speech recognition [6], and self-play games [7, 8]. CNN typically consists of five [5] to a thousand [9] CONV layers, each performing high-dimensional convolution. One to three layers of FC layers

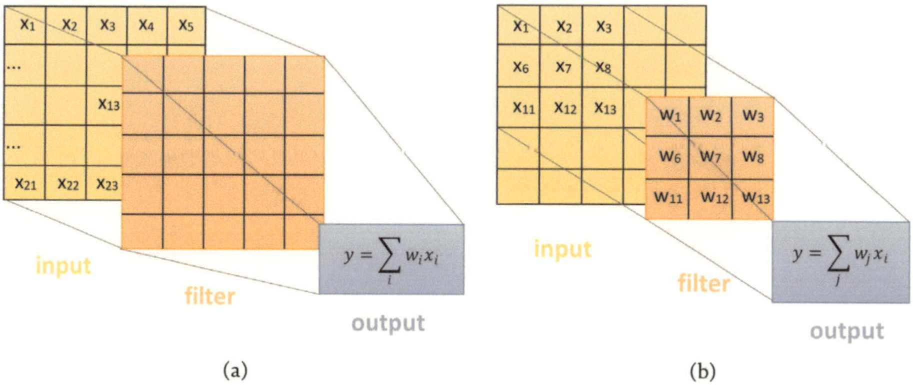

Figure 11.
(a) A fully connected layer (FC) and (b) a convolutional layer (CONV).

follow the CONV layers to learn the nonlinear combinations of high-level features for classification.

Aside from CONV layers and FC layers, various optional layers can be included in a CNN, such as nonlinearity, normalization, and pooling. These optional layers are usually carried out in nonlinear function units rather than in RRAM XBs in RRAM-based DNN accelerators [10].

6.1 Training and inference

We discussed performing VMM operations on RRAM-based DNN accelerators in previous sections, which are fundamental for the inference phase. Typically, these DNN models are trained in software before programmed onto the RRAM XBs allowing for immediate inference. However, there are scenarios where on-device learning is necessary to enhance performance. For instance, in environments with continuous data streams, incremental learning supports real-time inference more effectively. Additionally, classification performance can significantly degrade if a pre-trained model is directly programmed onto RRAM XBs due to defects in RRAM cells [11].

Small-scale RRAM XBs have been successful in simple pattern recognition tasks [11, 12]. However, in-situ training on RRAM XBs for larger-scale classification tasks faces challenges. The stochastic nature of the device introduces variability and abrupt switching during the set operation [12], while these challenges can be mitigated to a certain extent through material advancements such as utilizing HfAlyOx switching layer, which will be discussed in the next section. Another obstacle for larger-scale DNN application on RRAM XBs is the much higher power consumption of online learning compared to offline learning [13]. Inference typically uses low-resolution ADCs [14], while training requires high-resolution ADCs, ranging from 13-bit [15] to 16-bit [11] resolution. To address this, Yeo et al. [16] proposed replacing ADCs with 1-bit dynamic comparators, providing 1-bit A/D conversion by comparing the output voltage of the integrator, which converts the summed current of RRAM XBs to voltage, with a reference voltage.

Endurance is another critical reliability issue of RRAM, with cycles ranging from 10^5 to 10^7, potentially limiting its use for in-situ training. However, weight updates during training only require weak programming pulse to incrementally change

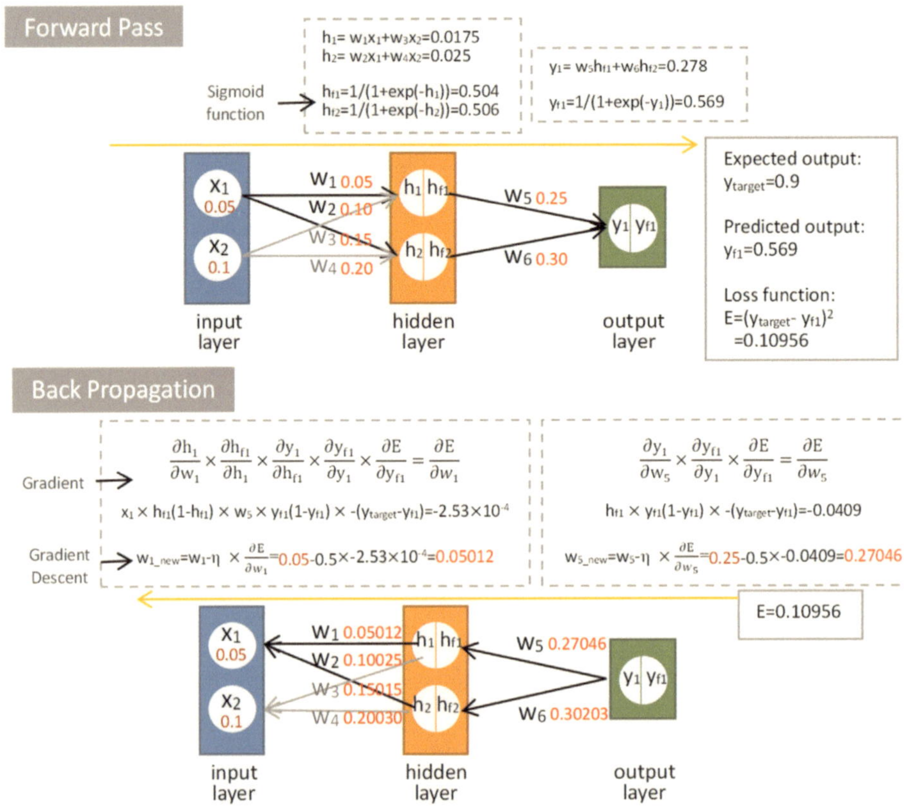

Figure 12.
Learning process of a simple 3-layer feedforward network.

conductance. Zhao et al. [17] demonstrated that RRAM cells remain operational even after applying over 10^{11} update programming pulses.

The training process of neural networks involves back propagation, which includes computing weight gradients and updates. This process is illustrated with a simplified 3-layer network example in **Figure 12**, where the nodes use a sigmoid function as the activation function (AF), as shown in Eq. (9), with the output presented as $node_{fi}$. The derivative of the sigmoid function, necessary for backpropagation, is shown in Eq. (10).

$$AF(x) = \frac{1}{1+\exp(-x)} \tag{9}$$

$$\begin{aligned}\frac{\partial}{\partial x}AF(x) &= \frac{\partial}{\partial x}(1+\exp(-x))^{-1} = -((1+\exp(-x))^{-2}\frac{\partial}{\partial x}(1+\exp(-x))\\ &= -((1+\exp(-x))^{-2}(-\exp(-x)) = \frac{\exp(-x)}{(1+\exp(-x))^2}\\ &= \frac{1}{1+\exp(-x)}\cdot\frac{\exp(-x)}{1+\exp(-x)}\\ &= \frac{1}{1+\exp(-x)}\cdot\left(1-\frac{1}{1+\exp(-x)}\right) = AF(x)\cdot(1-AF(x))\end{aligned} \tag{10}$$

To update w_1, the weight gradient is derived as in Eq. (11), where $\frac{\partial h_{f1}}{\partial h_1}$ and $\frac{\partial y_{f1}}{\partial y_1}$ are the derivatives of the sigmoid function shown (Eq. (10)), and $\frac{\partial E}{\partial y_{f1}}$ is the derivative of the mean squared error (MSE) loss function.

$$\frac{\partial E}{\partial w_1} = \frac{\partial h_1}{\partial w_1} \times \frac{\partial h_{f1}}{\partial h_1} \times \frac{\partial y_1}{\partial h_{f1}} \times \frac{\partial y_{f1}}{\partial y_1} \times \frac{\partial E}{\partial y_{f1}} = x_1 \times \frac{\partial h_{f1}}{\partial h_1} \times w_5 \times \frac{\partial y_{f1}}{\partial y_1} \times \frac{\partial E}{\partial y_{f1}}$$
$$= x_1 \times \left(h_{f1} \cdot (1 - h_{f1})\right) \times w_5 \times \left(y_{f1} \cdot (1 - y_{f1})\right) \times \left(y_{f1} - y_{target}\right) = -2.53 \times 10^{-4} \tag{11}$$

Similarly, the weight gradients of w_2 to w_4 are derived as follows, where the same parameters are marked as the same colors.

$$\frac{\partial E}{\partial w_2} = \frac{\partial h_2}{\partial w_2} \times \frac{\partial h_{f2}}{\partial h_2} \times \frac{\partial y_1}{\partial h_{f2}} \times \frac{\partial y_{f1}}{\partial y_1} \times \frac{\partial E}{\partial y_{f1}} = x_1 \times \frac{\partial h_{f2}}{\partial h_2} \times w_6 \times \frac{\partial y_{f1}}{\partial y_1} \times \frac{\partial E}{\partial y_{f1}}$$
$$= x_1 \times \left(h_{f2} \cdot (1 - h_{f2})\right) \times w_6 \times \left(y_{f1} \cdot (1 - y_{f1})\right) \times \left(y_{f1} - y_{target}\right) = -3.04 \times 10^{-4} \tag{12}$$

$$\frac{\partial E}{\partial w_3} = \frac{\partial h_1}{\partial w_3} \times \frac{\partial h_{f1}}{\partial h_1} \times \frac{\partial y_1}{\partial h_{f1}} \times \frac{\partial y_{f1}}{\partial y_1} \times \frac{\partial E}{\partial y_{f1}} = x_2 \times \frac{\partial h_{f1}}{\partial h_1} \times w_5 \times \frac{\partial y_{f1}}{\partial y_1} \times \frac{\partial E}{\partial y_{f1}}$$
$$= x_2 \times \left(h_{f1} \cdot (1 - h_{f1})\right) \times w_5 \times \left(y_{f1} \cdot (1 - y_{f1})\right) \times \left(y_{f1} - y_{target}\right) = -5.073 \times 10^{-4} \tag{13}$$

$$\frac{\partial E}{\partial w_4} = \frac{\partial h_2}{\partial w_4} \times \frac{\partial h_{f2}}{\partial h_2} \times \frac{\partial y_1}{\partial h_{f2}} \times \frac{\partial y_{f1}}{\partial y_1} \times \frac{\partial E}{\partial y_{f1}} = x_2 \times \frac{\partial h_{f2}}{\partial h_2} \times w_6 \times \frac{\partial y_{f1}}{\partial y_1} \times \frac{\partial E}{\partial y_{f1}}$$
$$= x_2 \times \left(h_{f2} \cdot (1 - h_{f2})\right) \times w_6 \times \left(y_{f1} \cdot (1 - y_{f1})\right) \times \left(y_{f1} - y_{target}\right) = -6.087 \times 10^{-4} \tag{14}$$

For the last layer weight w5 and w6, the derivatives are simpler, as shown in Eqs. (15) and (16).

$$\frac{\partial E}{\partial w_5} = \frac{\partial y_1}{\partial w_5} \times \frac{\partial y_{f1}}{\partial y_1} \times \frac{\partial E}{\partial y_{f1}} = h_{f1} \times \left(y_{f1} \cdot \left(1 - y_{f1}\right)\right) \times \left(y_{f1} - y_{target}\right) = -0.0409 \tag{15}$$

$$\frac{\partial E}{\partial w_6} = \frac{\partial y_1}{\partial w_6} \times \frac{\partial y_{f1}}{\partial y_1} \times \frac{\partial E}{\partial y_{f1}} = h_{f2} \times \left(y_{f1} \cdot \left(1 - y_{f1}\right)\right) \times \left(y_{f1} - y_{target}\right) = -0.04107 \tag{16}$$

Extending weight updates to conductance updates in RRAM XBs can be represented by Eqs. (17)-(20), where $P^L(n)$ is the output of the L -th layer for the n-th image in a batch size B, and η is the learning rate. P^{L-1} in Eq. (18) indicates the input of the L-th layer (output of the $(L-1)$-th layer), derived from $\frac{\partial P^L}{\partial G}$, corresponding to $\frac{\partial h_i}{\partial w_j}$ in Eqs. (11)-(14) and $\frac{\partial y_1}{\partial w_j}$ in Eqs. (15) and (16). Eqs. (19) and (20) represent the output error of the L-th layer and the last layer, respectively.

$$G^L_{new} = G^L_{old} - \Delta G^L \tag{17}$$

$$\Delta G^L = \eta \sum_{n=1}^{B} P^{L-1}(n)\delta^L(n) \tag{18}$$

$$\delta^L(n) = P^L(n)\big(1 - P^L(n)\big)G^L\delta^{L+1}(n) \tag{19}$$

$$\delta^L(n) = P^L(n)\big(1 - P^L(n)\big) \cdot \big(P^L(n) - T(n)\big) \tag{20}$$

In Yeo et al.'s implementation [13], ΔG^L is obtained through software and then converted into the number of programming pulses via FPGA. With these programming pulses, each RRAM conductance is updated.

By addressing these challenges and implementing innovative solutions, RRAM-based accelerators can potentially support both training and inference for large-scale DNN applications, making them a viable option for real-time, edge-based AI computations.

7. Challenges in RRAM-based computation

VMM computations can be executed in O(1) time complexity on an RRAM crossbar, but performing accurate computations poses several challenges. Some of these challenges and their corresponding solutions have been briefly discussed earlier, including the high energy and area requirements for DACs and ADCs, as well as the impacts of IR-drop. Variability and stuck-at-faults are also crucial problems affecting the reliability of RRAM-based computation.

Variability, or variation, can be categorized into temporal (cycle-to-cycle, C2C) and spatial (device-to-device, D2D) variations. As previously discussed, the stochastic nature of RRAM filaments is prone to variability, leading to different final states after each set and reset process within a single RRAM device, known as C2C variation. D2D variation, on the other hand, refers to the variability among different RRAM devices, where two devices may reach different final states even if the same programming pulse is applied. This is due to the imperfect fabrication, leading to non-uniform thickness of switching film, surface roughness of electrodes, etc.

Variations issues can be addressed at both the device level and algorithm level. At the device level, a wide variety of materials and material engineering methods are being investigated to enhance the uniformity of RRAM devices. For example, embedding a thin layer of Al buffer is found to stabilize the oxygen vacancies in HfO_2 films, which contributes to a more uniform set voltage and resistance distribution [18]. Programming techniques also significantly affect variability. For instance, the conductance spread can be reduced by increasing the gate voltage instead of top electrode voltage when programming a resistance state within an RRAM device [19].

While device-level techniques improve the variability of RRAM devices, leading to more consistent and mature memory, algorithm-level approaches are also essential for ensuring the reliability of RRAM-based computations. Unary-encoding has been proposed to mitigate the effects of variation on the most-significant bit (MSB) of a weight by equalizing the significance of each bit [20]. Leveraging the inherent redundancy within DNNs also proves to be effective against variation. Fritscher et al. [21] proposed three approaches: fault-aware training, the use of dropout layers, and the insertion of redundancy, to train DNNs that are less susceptible to variations.

Stuck-at-faults (SAFs) can occur due to immature fabrication. As reported by Chen et al. [22], SAFs frequently affect RRAM cells, with around 10% of RRAM cells exhibiting these faults, specifically, 9.04% of SA1 and 1.75% of SA0 in a fabricated 4-Mb HfO2-based RRAM test chip. When an RRAM cell is stuck at LRS, where a conductive filament cannot be dissolved through the reset voltage, it is referred to as *stuck-at-zero (SA0)*. SA0 can occur due to *over-forming*, which results in temporarily failed cells at excessively low resistance states, and require a stronger reset voltage for reset process, but their operation region may be mismatched with the capabilities of the write circuit [23]. However, 60% of these temporarily failed cells are capable of recovering from over-forming to normal cells, which makes the real physical mechanism that governs the phenomenon of SA0 unknown so far [22]. Conversely, *stuck-at-one (SA1)* occurs when an RRAM cell is stuck at a HRS. This fault is due to the broken WLs or permanently open switches in RRAM XBs, which results in no current flow, mimicking a HRS despite the actual state of the cell.

To address the over-forming issue, Shih et al. [23] proposed including an additional sequence of write operations after the initial forming process, which aims to concentrate reset state and set state of cells into a range approximate to the margin of normal HRS and LRS region. Although this technique can help repair some cells, there remain unrepairable cells. Several algorithm-level approaches have been proposed to tackle the SAF problem. These approaches generally fall into three categories: 1. (Re-)Training-based approaches, 2. Error-correction-based approaches, and 3. (Re-)-Mapping-based approaches.

(Re-)Training-based methods typically include modifying the objective functions, injecting the disturbance during training, or retraining the unmapped layers [24, 25]. The primary challenge with training-based approaches is the high runtime required and the potential difficulty in converging to high accuracy. Error-correction-based approaches involve measuring the defected output and performing the post-processing computation to compensate for the errors. This can include adding additional RRAM rows to compensate for the erroneous outputs or using alternative weight value to represent the original value [26–28]. However, these methods induce additional hardware overhead. (Re-)Mapping-based methods typically involve exchanging defected devices with normal devices through column/row-swapping or cell swapping [24, 25, 27]. While effective, these approaches also require additional peripheral hardware to manage the disordering input or output. Each of these strategies presents its own set of advantages and challenges, and often a combination of these methods is employed to ensure reliable operation in RRAM-based systems.

8. RRAM programming

To program an RRAM device, both set and reset processes are employed to modulate the resistance state. As illustrated in **Figure 13**, during the set operation, a set voltage is applied to the BL terminal of the cell, causing current to flow toward the SL terminal. While during the reset operation, a reset voltage is applied to the SL terminal of the cell, with current flowing toward the BL terminal.

Various programming techniques have been developed. L. Gao et al. [29] have suggested incremental step pulse programming (ISPP), where the amplitude or width of the V_{BL} or V_{SL} is incrementally increased with a fixed gate voltage (V_g), as illustrated in **Figure 14(a)**. Alternatively, Chen et al. [30] proposed incremental gate voltage programming (IGVP), which incrementally increases V_g while keeping the

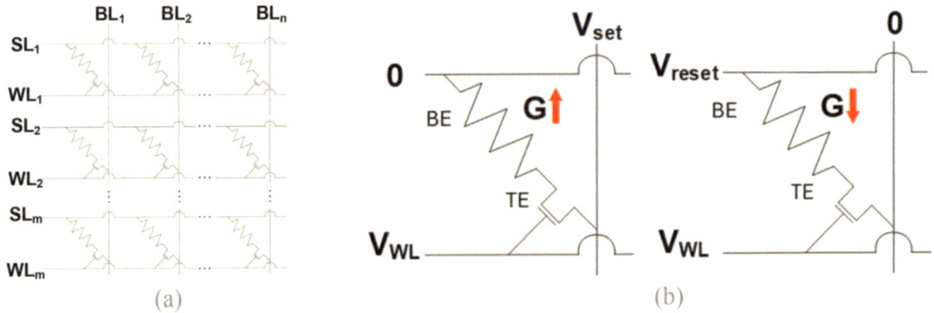

Figure 13.
(a) 1T1R RRAM crossbar (b) Set (left) and reset (right) operations.

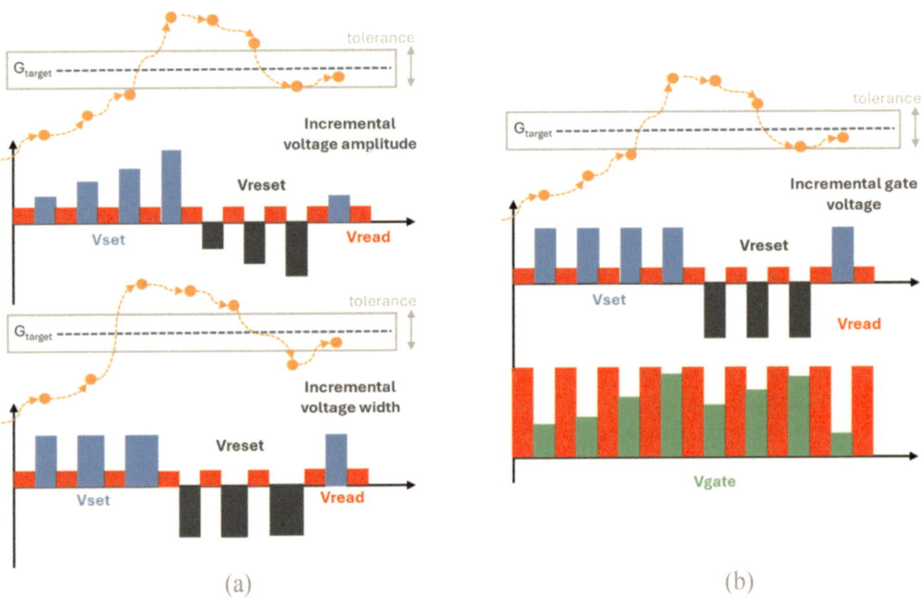

Figure 14.
(a) ISPP scheme and (b) IGVP scheme.

V_{BL} and V_{SL} constant, as illustrated in **Figure 14(b)**. To precisely tune the resistance to the target value, *write-and-verify* programming scheme has been adopted. Specifically, after each programming pulse, the device conductance is read out with a large V_g to minimize the voltage drop across the transistor, which allows us to monitor the programming state, ensuring that the resistance is adjusted to the desired target value. If the conductance has reached the target conductance with a defined tolerance margin, the programming procedure stops. Otherwise, an additional pulse with an incremental voltage step is applied.

8.1 RRAM programming model

The relationship between the applied voltages and the conductance change during programming is nonlinear [31], as illustrated in **Figure 15**. This programming

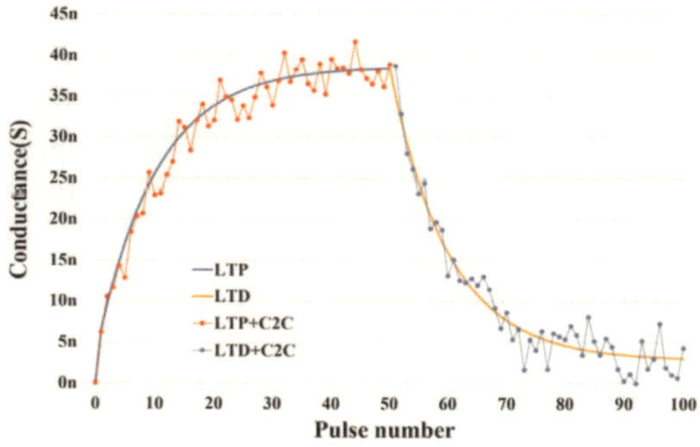

Figure 15.
Nonlinear programming curve.

nonlinearity can be modeled with Eqs. (21)-(24) where long-term potentiation (LTP) and long-term depression (LTD) indicate the continuous process of set and reset operations, respectively. The nonlinearity factor $\theta_{LTP/LTD}$ is used to adjust the nonlinear curve of conductance change during the set (LTP) and reset (LTD) operations. P_{max} denotes the maximum number of programming pulses, while G_{min}/G_{max} correspond to the maximum/minimum conductance of an RRAM device.

$$G_{LTP} = \beta_{LTP} \times \left(1 - e^{\frac{-P}{\alpha_{LTP}}}\right) + G_{min} \tag{21}$$

$$G_{LTD} = -\beta_{LTD} \times \left(1 - e^{\frac{P-P_{max}}{\alpha_{LTD}}}\right) + G_{max} \tag{22}$$

$$\beta_{LTP/LTD} = \frac{G_{max} - G_{min}}{1 - e^{\frac{-P_{max}}{\alpha_{LTP/LTD}}}} \tag{23}$$

$$\alpha_{LTP/LTD} = \theta_{LTP/LTD} \times P_{max} \tag{24}$$

As conductance changes over the pulse numbers, random variation occurs, depicted by the red and blue lines in **Figure 15**. These variations are due to C2C variation, which is induced by the stochastic nature of filament formation and dissolution, as previously discussed.

8.2 Row-by-row programming scheme

The most common programming scheme for RRAM devices is the cell-by-cell write-and-verify scheme [29]. However, as the model size increases, this approach becomes time-consuming. To improve programming efficiency, a row-by-row parallel-friendly IGVP scheme has been proposed [30]. By adjusting the conductance through controlling the Vg, programming multiple cells at a time becomes feasible. Although it is theoretically possible to program an entire row at once, practical limitations restrict the number of cells that can be simultaneously programmed. Therefore, the authors use the term 'parallel group' to describe the cells programmed at the same time.

Unlike the cell-by-cell programming scheme, which aims to minimize the average programming numbers (PN) for all cells across the entire crossbar, the parallel-friendly IGVP scheme focuses on minimizing the average critical path—the maximum PN within a parallel group—across all parallel groups. The presence of a critical cell can significantly reduce programming speed. Therefore, selecting an appropriate V_g step is crucial. A too small V_g step increases the number of pulses needed to fine-tune the conductance, while a too large Vg step leads to overshooting and oscillation around the tolerance margin, which also necessitates more pulses. It was shown that a V_g step of 0.2 V yields optimal results by minimizing the average critical path.

8.3 Multi-row programming scheme

To further enhance programming efficiency, the two-phase multi-row programming scheme has been proposed [32]. In the first phase, known as the predictive phase, the programming number for each RRAM device is initially estimated with the RRAM programming model at the largest voltage amplitude. A multi-row grouping method is then employed to determine which rows can be grouped together for simultaneous programming. An example of this method is shown in **Figure 16**. The estimated set and reset programming pulses are marked in the figure, and the cell with the highest pulse number in each row is encircled by a red block, referred to as the *dominant cell*. The BL voltage is applied based on the requirements of the dominant cell; if it requires set operations, a set voltage is applied, and if it requires reset operations, a reset voltage is applied.

The objective is to find as many rows as possible to be programmed simultaneously without affecting the dominant cell of each row. For example, the 0th and 1st rows cannot be programmed together because after one programming pulse, the dominant cell of the 1st row shifts from the leftmost to the rightmost cell, changing the pulse number from 3 to 4 reset pulses while the pulse number of the original dominant cell is changed from 4 to 3 set pulses. Therefore, in the example, 1st and 2nd rows are the only rows that can be selected as a group and programmed together in this programming pulse. The first phase continues until all the estimated programming numbers reach zeros. In the second phase, the fine-tuning phase, the actual conductances are read out and compared with the estimated conductance to calibrate the RRAM programming model. Subsequently, row-by-row and cell-by-cell programming are employed to fine-tune the resistance states.

The two-phase multi-row programming significantly enhances the programming efficiency compared to row-by-row programming. However, it faces challenges such as conflicts in voltage requirements for cells within the same column, forcing some programming to still be performed row-by-row. Additionally, even though it reduces the overall pulse numbers, it can increase the pulse number of certain cells, such as the

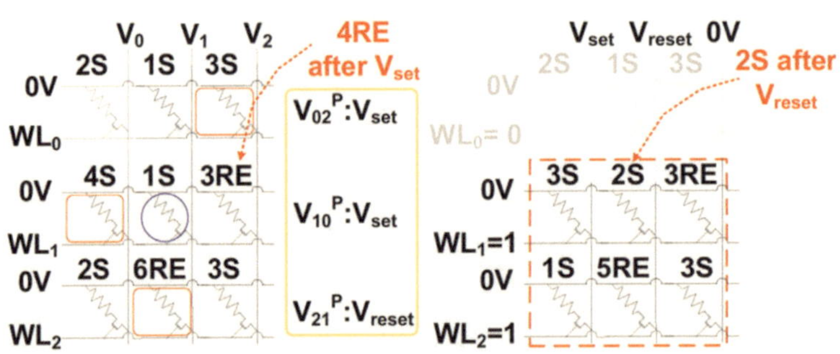

Figure 16.
Illustration of the multi-row grouping method.

middle cell on the 1st row whose pulse numbers increase from 1 to 2 set pulses. To address these problems, Chen et al. [31] have proposed a block-based programming scheme, which effectively manages the necessary pulse numbers and alleviates the potential IR-drop concerns. By confining the programming operations to smaller blocks, the scheme ensures more uniform voltage distribution and enhances the accuracy of the RRAM device states.

8.4 Block-based multi-line programming scheme

The block-based programming scheme is split into two phases: the approximation phase and the fine-tuning phase. The primary goal is to reach the target conductances as closely as possible with larger voltage steps during the approximation phase, thereby reducing the time and energy required in the fine-tuning phase, in which a finer voltage step is applied. Both phases utilize the block-based multi-line programming algorithm (BLMP), as depicted in **Figure 17(a)**.

In the BLMP, the strategy is to program only the necessary cells. Initially, two predictive programming maps are generated, each recording the number of pulses required for set and reset operations estimated by the RRAM programming model. **Figure 17(a)** exemplifies a set predictive programming map, where each value represents the required number of set pulses for a cell. To maximize the number of rows programmed simultaneously, the column with the highest total pulse count is selected for each iteration. In the example provided, during the first iteration, three columns have identical pulse numbers of 2; thus, the leftmost column is selected, in which 1st and 2nd rows require one programming pulse each, enabling the WLs of these two rows. Subsequently, the columns where the 1st and 2nd rows also require programming pulses are also selected, optimizing the number of cells programmed simultaneously. After each iteration, the predictive programming map is updated. During the second iteration, as shown in the figure, only the middle column is selected with its 0th and 2nd rows programmed. The BMLP algorithm ends when all values in the predictive map reach zeros.

To fully optimize the number of rows and columns simultaneously activated, it is desirable to have similar weight configurations, specifically, the same distribution of

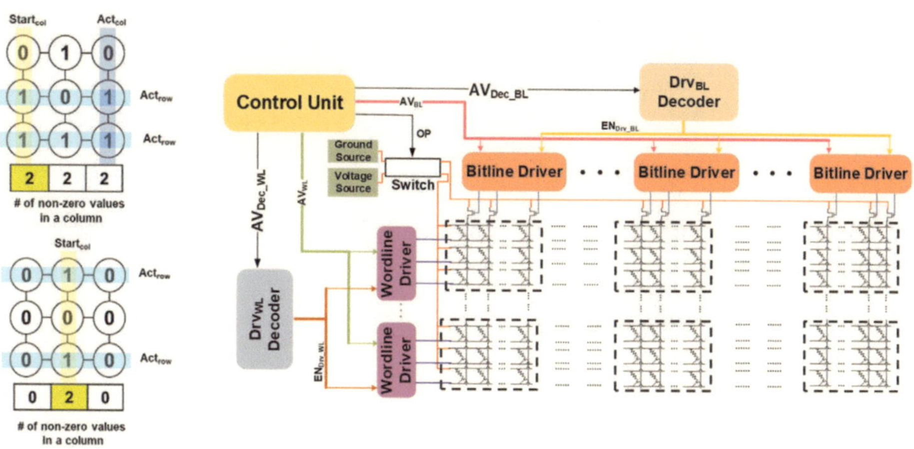

(a) (b)

Figure 17.
(a) An example of BLMP and (b) the block-based hierarchical architecture [31].

zeros and non-zeros in a column across different columns. This allows more columns to be chosen in a programming cycle. To achieve this, a programming-aware retraining method is proposed. In this method, the column with the fewest zero weights is selected, and all the rows where the zero weights are located are retrained to zeros across the columns. Meanwhile, the rest of the rows are ensured not to be zeros. This approach maximizes the number of rows and columns that can be programmed simultaneously, thereby improving the overall efficiency of the programming process.

To facilitate this multi-line programming, a hierarchical block-based architecture is designed, as illustrated in **Figure 17(b)**. Given the standard XB size of 128 by 128, reducing the hardware overhead for decoding such a large array necessitates a hierarchical design, which comprises decoders and drivers: the decoder selects the block to be programmed, and the driver enables the specific columns and rows.

9. Conclusion

In summary, resistive random-access memory (RRAM) has emerged as a focal point in research due to its ability to perform vector-matrix multiplication—an essential operation in deep neural networks—within O(1) time complexity using crossbar structures for in-memory computation. However, RRAM technology is not as mature as other memory types, and reliability remains a significant concern, including issues related to variation, stuck-at faults, and IR-drop. Additionally, the need for analog-to-digital converters (ADC) and digital-to-analog converters (DAC) hinders RRAM-based accelerators from achieving optimal energy efficiency. Programming weights onto RRAM crossbars is also a time-consuming process, emphasizing the importance of efficient programming and minimizing redundant energy consumption.

Researchers have proposed various approaches to address these challenges, as briefly summarized in this chapter. Furthermore, real-word AI applications on RRAM-based DNN accelerators have been discussed, illustrating how training and inference are realized through the analog switching behavior of RRAM.

Author details

Fang-Yi Gu
Department of Computer Science and Information Engineering, National Cheng Kung University, Tainan, Taiwan

*Address all correspondence to: p78101556@gs.ncku.edu.tw

References

[1] Hennessy JL, Patterson DA. Computer Architecture: A Quantitative Approach (The Morgan Kaufmann Series in Computer Architecture and Design). 5th ed. Morgan Kaufmann; 2011

[2] McDanel B et al. Saturation RRAM leveraging bit-level sparsity resulting from term quantization. In: Proc. International Symposium on Circuits and Systems. 2021 IEEE International Symposium on Circuits and Systems (ISCAS); 2021. pp. 1-5

[3] Huang C et al. Efficient and optimized methods for alleviating the impacts of IR-drop and fault in RRAM based neural computing systems. IEEE Journal of the Electron Devices Society. 2021;**9**:645-652

[4] Lin MY et al. DL-RSIM: A simulation framework to enable reliable ReRAM-based accelerators for deep learning. In: Proc. International Conference on Computer-Aided Design. 2018 IEEE/ACM International Conference on Computer-Aided Design (ICCAD); 2018. pp. 1-8

[5] Krizhevsky A, Sutskever I, Hinton GE. ImageNet classification with deep convolutional neural networks. In: Proceedings of the 25th International Conference on Neural Information Processing Systems. Vol. 1. Lake Tahoe, Nevada: Curran Associates Inc.; 2012. pp. 1097-1105

[6] Dahl GE et al. Improving deep neural networks for LVCSR using rectified linear units and dropout. In: 2013 IEEE International Conference on Acoustics, Speech and Signal Processing. IEEE; 2013. pp. 8609-8613

[7] Silver D et al. Mastering the game of go with deep neural networks and tree search. Nature. 2016;**529**(7587):484-489

[8] Silver D et al. A general reinforcement learning algorithm that masters chess, shogi, and go through self-play. Science. 2018;**362**(6419):1140

[9] He K et al. Deep residual learning for image recognition. In: 2016 IEEE Conference on Computer Vision and Pattern Recognition (CVPR). 2016. pp. 770-778

[10] Shafiee A et al. ISAAC: A convolutional neural network accelerator with in-situ analog arithmetic in crossbars. In: 2016 ACM/IEEE 43rd Annual International Symposium on Computer Architecture (ISCA). Vol. 44, No. 3. ACM SIGARCH Computer Architecture News; 2016. pp. 14-26

[11] Can L et al. Efficient and self-adaptive in-situ learning in multilayer memristor neural networks. Nature Communications. 2018;**9**(1):2385

[12] Yao P et al. Face classification using electronic synapses. Nature Communications. 2017;**8**(1):15199

[13] Injune Y et al. A hardware and energy-efficient online learning neural network with an RRAM crossbar array and stochastic neurons. IEEE Transactions on Industrial Electronics. 2020;**68**(11):11554-11564

[14] Chen W-H et al. A 65nm 1Mb nonvolatile computing-in-memory ReRAM macro with sub-16ns multiply-and-accumulate for binary DNN AI edge processors. In: 2018 IEEE International Solid-State Circuits Conference-(ISSCC). IEEE; 2018

[15] Cai F et al. A fully integrated reprogrammable memristor–CMOS

system for efficient multiply–accumulate operations. Nature Electronics. 2019;**2**(7):290-299

[16] Yeo I, Myonglae C, Byung GL. A power and area efficient CMOS stochastic neuron for neural networks employing resistive crossbar array. IEEE Transactions on Biomedical Circuits and System. 2019;**13**(6):1678-1689

[17] Zhao M et al. Characterizing endurance degradation of incremental switching in analog RRAM for neuromorphic systems. In: 2018 IEEE International Electron Devices Meeting (IEDM). IEEE; 2018

[18] Milo V et al. Multilevel HfO2-based RRAM devices for low-power neuromorphic networks. APL Materials. 2019;**7**(8)

[19] Milo V et al. Optimized programming algorithms for multilevel RRAM in hardware neural networks. In: 2021 IEEE International Reliability Physics Symposium (IRPS). 2021. pp. 1-6

[20] Sun Y et al. Unary coding and variation-aware optimal mapping scheme for reliable ReRAM-based neuromorphic computing. IEEE Transactions on Computer-Aided Design of Integrated Circuits and Systems. 2021; **40**(12):2495-2507

[21] Fritscher M et al. Mitigating the effects of RRAM process variation on the accuracy of artificial neural networks. In: International Conference on Embedded Computer Systems. Springer International Publishing; 2021

[22] Chen CY et al. RRAM defect modeling and failure analysis based on march test and a novel squeeze-search scheme. IEEE Transactions on Computers. 2015;**64**(1): 180-190

[23] Shih HC et al. Training-based forming process for RRAM yield improvement. In: 29th VLSI Test Symposium, Dana Point. 2011. pp. 146-151

[24] Xu Q et al. Reliability-driven neuromorphic computing systems design. In: 2021 Design, Automation & Test in Europe Conference & Exhibition (DATE). 2021. pp. 1586-1591

[25] Huang Y et al. Bit-aware fault-tolerant hybrid retraining and remapping schemes for RRAM-based computing-in-memory systems. IEEE Transactions on Circuits and Systems II: Express Briefs. 2022;**69**(7):3144-3148

[26] Shin H et al. Fault-free: A fault-resilient deep neural network accelerator based on realistic ReRAM devices. In: 2021 58th ACM/IEEE Design Automation Conference (DAC). 2021. pp. 1039-1044

[27] Zhang F, Hu M. Defects mitigation in resistive crossbars for Analog vector matrix multiplication. In: 2020 25th Asia and South Pacific Design Automation Conference (ASP-DAC). 2020. pp. 187-192

[28] He Z et al. Noise injection adaption: End-to-end ReRAM crossbar non-ideal effect adaption for neural network mapping. In: 2019 56th ACM/IEEE Design Automation Conference (DAC). 2019. pp. 1-6

[29] Gao L, Chen PY, Yu S. Programming protocol optimization for analog weight tuning in resistive memories. IEEE Electron Device Letters. 2015;**36**(11): 1157-1159

[30] Chen J et al. A parallel multibit programing scheme with high precision for RRAM-based neuromorphic systems. IEEE Transactions on Electron Devices. 2020;**67**(5):2213-2217

[31] Chen WL et al. A novel and efficient block-based programming for ReRAM-based neuromorphic computing. In: 2023 IEEE/ACM International Conference on Computer Aided Design (ICCAD). 2023. pp. 1-9

[32] Zhang GL et al. An efficient programming framework for memristor-based neuromorphic computing. In: 2021 Design, Automation & Test in Europe Conference & Exhibition. 2021. pp. 1068-1073

Chapter 2

Design and Optimization of Digital Neural Encoding for Neuromorphic Computing Systems

Ruizhe Li, Kang Jun Bai and Yang (Cindy) Yi

Abstract

The rapid growth of artificial intelligence and machine learning has brought neuromorphic computing as a key approach for achieving brain-like efficiency in handling complex data. Thus, the neural encoding algorithm plays a crucial role in transforming real-world information into discrete spikes for processing in neuromorphic systems. In this work, we examine the significance of refining these encoding algorithms to boost the efficiency and capabilities of neuromorphic computing in hardware. Field-Programmable Gate Arrays (FPGA) have emerged as a promising platform for implementing these algorithms due to their parallel processing capabilities and reconfigurability. This chapter aims to provide a comprehensive overview of the state-of-the-art neural encoding algorithms designed for FPGA implementation. It covers various encoding techniques and algorithmic strategies utilized to improve hardware efficiency, increase processing speed, and reduce latency. Recent research trends highlight a growing interest in hybrid encoding schemes that combine phase encoding with rate or temporal dynamics to balance computational complexity and accuracy. However, challenges remain in optimizing trade-offs between power efficiency, performance, and design scalability. This chapter will provide valuable insights into the current landscape of neural encoding algorithms in digital hardware implementation, identifying gaps and potential directions for future research.

Keywords: digital circuit design, neuromorphic computing, neural encoding algorithm, multiplexing temporal encoding, FPGA implementation, spiking neural networks

1. Introduction

Artificial neural networks (ANNs) have demonstrated impressive performance across diverse fields, including computer vision [1], speech processing [2], and robotics [3]. Nevertheless, these successes typically involve intensive computations, resulting in substantial energy demands [4]. Consequently, there is growing interest within both academia and industry in exploring Spiking Neural Networks (SNNs) as an energy-efficient alternative. Drawing inspiration from biological neural systems, SNNs encode and transmit data through discrete neuronal spikes, effectively mirroring natural neural communication. This approach enables parallel processing, event-driven computation, and decentralized memory, positioning these networks as highly promising candidates for enhancing computational efficiency and substantially reducing energy usage in various practical applications [5, 6].

The human brain stands out as an extraordinarily complex and efficient information processing system, uniquely capable of sophisticated cognition while consuming minimal energy. This efficiency arises from interactions between neurons, which are the basic processing elements that communicate through brief electrical signals known as spikes. These neurons transform sensory inputs into distinct patterns of spikes, forming neural codes. Understanding these neural coding patterns has become a significant research focus, as decoding them offers valuable insights into cognitive processes and reveals essential principles governing how information is effectively transmitted and processed in biological systems [7, 8].

Researchers have developed several neural encoding strategies based on attributes such as input intensity or timing to better understand how information is represented in the brain. One prevalent approach is rate encoding [9], which uses the frequency of neuronal spikes to indicate stimulus intensity. This method has long been favored due to its simplicity and robustness. Nevertheless, rate encoding can be inefficient due to relatively slow signal transmission, extended processing times, and low data capacity. To overcome these limitations, temporal encoding emerged, such as Time-To-First-Spike (TTFS), Inter-Spike-Interval (ISI), and phase encoding [10], emphasizing the precise timing of spikes to facilitate rapid and efficient neural responses. Each encoding scheme offers distinct advantages, making them suitable for different types of data and applications [11, 12], thereby enhancing the versatility and effectiveness of neuromorphic computing systems.

However, as the volume and complexity of data grow for specialized tasks [13], there is an escalating requirement for systems capable of managing higher data capacities effectively. Thus, to further enhance the data processing capability and robustness of the systems, a novel approach involving multiplexed encoding schemes has been proposed and explored within the neuromorphic computing paradigm [14]. These schemes combine multiple neural codes, particularly those operating on different time scales, to achieve higher data capacity. By integrating multiple independent encoding schemes, each capable of carrying a specific amount of information, multiplexing encoding significantly increases the overall information throughput. This approach holds promise for advancing neuromorphic computing by leveraging the diversity and efficiency inherent in biological neural processing.

Field-Programmable Gate Arrays (FPGAs) are highly valued in neuromorphic computing due to their parallel processing capabilities and adaptable architecture. These features make FPGAs particularly suitable for implementing and evaluating spike encoding algorithms and even accelerating artificial intelligence applications efficiently [15–17].

This paper provides an in-depth analysis and comparison of various spike encoding algorithms, emphasizing critical factors such as accuracy of signal reconstruction, hardware efficiency, processing speed, and energy consumption. It highlights recent developments in this area and identifies promising directions for future research in spike encoding methodologies.

2. Neural encoding algorithms

2.1 Rate encoding

Researchers have put much effort into finding practical encoding algorithms that are beneficial to the training of SNNs. Rate encoding is the most commonly used neural coding method in SNNs. This approach translates input stimuli into spike trains characterized by specific firing frequencies. The number of spikes can be either deterministic or probabilistic. A deterministic spike produces consistent outputs. On the other hand, probabilistic spike counts are often modeled using a Poisson distribution. To generate a Poisson spike train with different firing rates, the input has usually been compared with a random number, as shown in **Figure 1**. The spike frequency correlates with the intensity of the input signal within a defined sampling window. Higher input intensities generate more frequent spikes, whereas lower intensities result in fewer spikes. The sampling process ensures that the number of spikes produced reflects the strength of the input stimulus.

The simplicity of rate encoding is one of its key advantages. By relying on the average spike frequency, it abstracts away the need for precise timing information, making it easier to implement in neuromorphic systems. This simplicity can be beneficial for hardware development, as circuits designed for rate encoding are often less complex compared to those needed for temporal encoding.

2.2 Temporal encoding

While straightforward, the rate encoding algorithm has notable limitations, such as low data capacity and a lack of robustness against noise and errors [18]. Its reliance on comparison between input and random numbers for spike generation disregards the temporal structure of the input, making the process vulnerable to errors during encoding.

To overcome these challenges, an alternative solution is proposed to encode data into the relative timing of events, namely, temporal encoding [10]. Such an encoding scheme carries information through the number of spikes and their intrinsic temporal pattern, rather than the static values or rates of signals. A variety of temporal encoding algorithms are being widely used in both software and hardware, such as

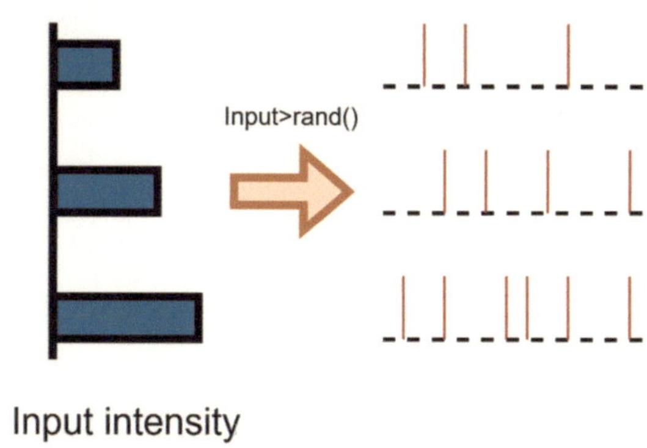

Figure 1.
Demonstration of rate encoding.

Time-To-First-Spike (TTFS), phase, Inter-Spike-Interval (ISI), and Temporal Contrast (TC) encoding.

2.2.1 Time-to-first-spike (TTFS) encoding

The TTFS algorithm is a widely recognized temporal encoding method that conveys information to target neurons through the timing of the first spike, enabling rapid signal transmission within a defined sampling period. For instance, a rapid and energy-efficient TTFS encoding algorithm was introduced, building a dynamically adjusting exponential-decay threshold to translate input intensities into first-spike patterns [19]. Input intensities are normalized by dividing them by their maximum value. Higher input intensities carry more informational weight and will trigger spikes earlier. A decay exponential function is used to compute the threshold V_{th}, which is defined as

$$V_{th}(t) = \theta \cdot e^{\left(-\frac{t}{\tau_{th}},\right)} \tag{1}$$

where the threshold constant θ is set to 1, and the time constant τ_{th} is a user-defined variable. A spike is generated when the input intensity surpasses the threshold; further firing of spikes is prohibited after firing the first spike. This encoding algorithm converts the input into the precise timing of the initial spikes, as shown in **Figure 2**.

2.2.2 Phase encoding

In phase encoding, information is encoded in the relative phase differences of oscillatory signals. This approach draws inspiration from observations of biological systems, where neurons synchronize with oscillatory rhythms to process information [20]. Thus, this approach requires an external periodic oscillation signal as a reference, and spike fires depending on the phase shift of the oscillation signal [21, 22]. In Ref. [23], a simple phase encoding method is proposed, where input intensities are converted into their binary representation and bit “1” means a spike as illustrated in **Figure 3**. The information is encoded by assigning distinct weights to each bit, with these weights varying periodically, which can be expressed as

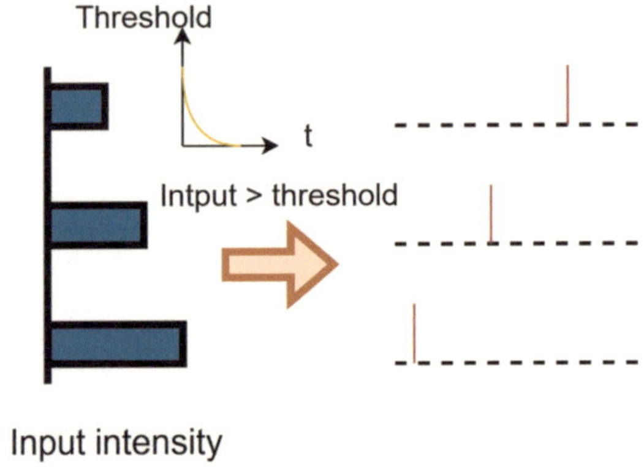

Figure 2.
Demonstration of TTFS encoding.

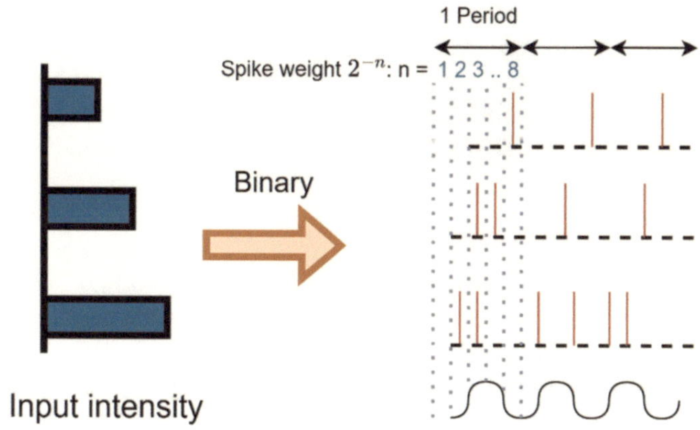

Figure 3.
Demonstration of phase encoding.

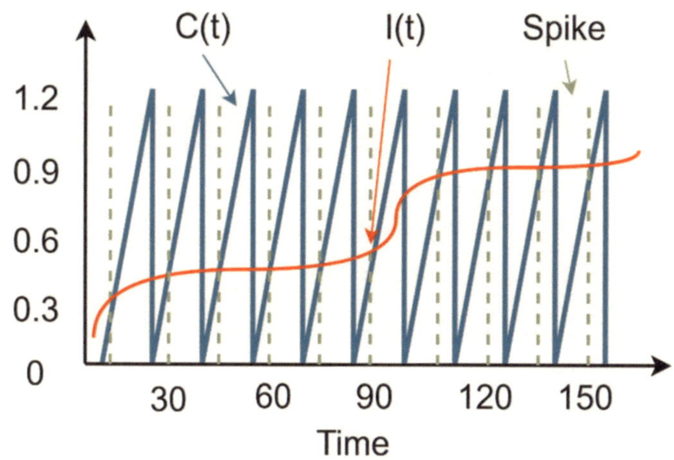

Figure 4.
Demonstration of PWM-based phase encoding.

$$W(t) = 2^{-(1 + mod(t-1, n))} \tag{2}$$

where t represents the number of time steps, and n denotes the number of phases within one period of the oscillation signal. The number of phases is determined by the maximum input intensity. The larger the input intensity, the more significant spikes it fires, and the more information it carries.

A robust and efficient phase encoding [24] was introduced afterward, which applies Pulse Width Modulation (PWM) principles to encode analog data into spikes due to its simplified hardware implementation, adaptability in parameters, and precise reconstruction of the analog signals. **Figure 4** demonstrates the resulting outcome of such an encoding algorithm, which triggers a spike when the carrier signal C(t) surpasses the input signal I(t). The effectiveness of this approach in conveying information mainly depends on the resolution of the carrier signal, defined as its ability to detect subtle variations in the input. Higher resolution enables more accurate signal reconstruction.

Phase encoding offers greater energy efficiency compared with rate encoding, as fewer spikes are needed to convey information. The emphasis on temporal relationships rather than prolonged spike trains reduces the computational burden. However, the overall efficiency and reliability of phase encoding would vary, as the firing activities rely heavily on the accuracy of the external periodic oscillation signal [25].

2.2.3 Inter-spike-interval (ISI) or burst encoding

ISI encoder [26] represents another form of temporal encoding, offering greater reliability compared with TTFS and phase encoding by generating bursts of multiple spikes, which enhances synaptic communication in neurons. In this encoding scheme, the burst conveys information through both the count of generated spikes (Ns) and the duration between successive spikes, known as the inter-spike interval (ISI). Higher input intensity typically results in more spikes and reduced intervals among spikes, while lower input intensity yields fewer spikes with longer intervals, as illustrated in **Figure 5**.

The following equations are used to generate the burst of encoded spikes from each discrete signal amplitude (A) value:

$$N_s(A) = \lceil N_{\max} \cdot A \rceil \tag{3}$$

where N_{max} is a constant value as a maximum number of spikes allowed for the encoder, and $\lceil \cdot \rceil$ is the ceiling function. The ISI value can then be calculated as

$$ISI(A) = \left\{ \begin{array}{l} \lceil -(T_{max} - T_{min}) \bullet A + T_{max} \rceil, N_s(A) > 1 \\ T_{max}, Otherwise \end{array} \right\} \tag{4}$$

where T_{max} and T_{min} are the maximum and minimum time intervals permitted for processing one input sample.

2.2.4 Temporal contrast (TC) encoding

Another subcategory of temporal encoding is TC encoding [27], which transforms an analog signal into a spike train by tracking changes in signal intensity, as shown in **Figure 6**. This approach is implemented through three primary algorithms: threshold-based representation, step-forward, and moving-window.

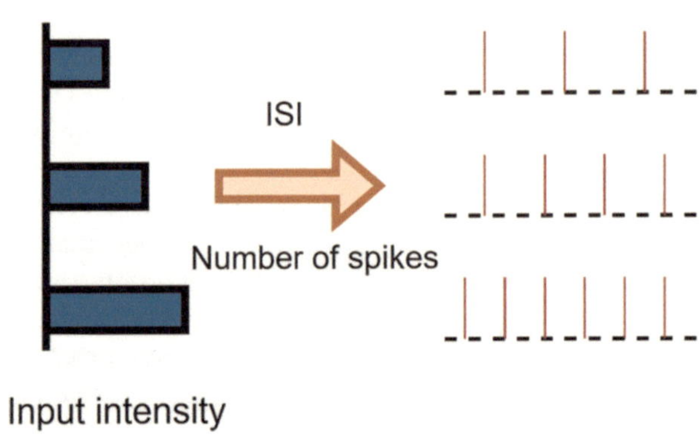

Figure 5.
Demonstration of ISI encoding.

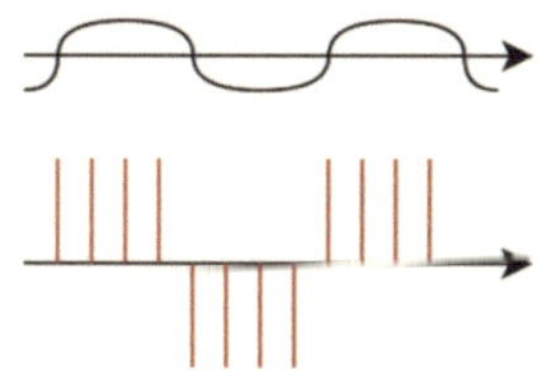

Figure 6.
Demonstration of TC encoding.

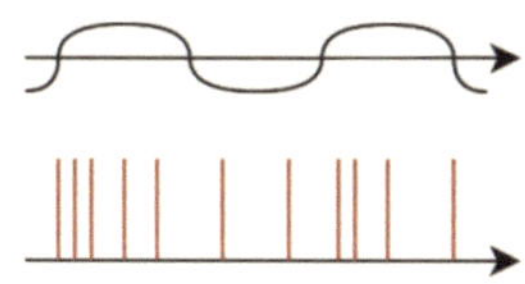

Figure 7.
Demonstration of BSA encoding.

In the threshold-based representation, the algorithm compares the absolute change in the input signal with a predefined threshold V_{th-TC}. Positive or negative spikes are generated based on whether the change exceeds or falls below V_{th-TC}. The threshold itself is determined by the sum of the mean derivative and the product of a scaling factor with the derivative's standard deviation.

The step-forward method operates differently by comparing the current signal value with a dynamic base value V_{base}, initially set to the first input sample. A positive spike is fired if the current signal exceeds $V_{base} + V_{th-TC}$ the base value is moved to the upper limit of the threshold. Conversely, if the current signal falls below $V_{base} - V_{th-TC}$., a negative spike is fired and the base value is updated to the lower limit of the threshold.

Lastly, the moving-window algorithm calculates the base value V_{base} as the mean of signal values within a specific window. The input signal is divided into two such windows, where the V_{base} is the mean of contained signal samples within a time window. Positive or negative spikes are triggered based on whether the current signal value exceeds the $V_{base} + V_{th-TC}$. or falls below the $V_{base} - V_{th-TC}$., respectively.

2.2.5 Ben's spiker algorithm (BSA) encoding

Another type of encoding scheme would encode an analog signal into a unipolar spike train (only positive spikes) by using a known filter like a Finite impulse response (FIR) filter, which is known as Ben's Spiker Algorithm (BSA) and its predecessor, Hough Spiker Algorithm (HSA) [28]. This encoding scheme utilizes a filter-based deconvolution approach, where spikes are generated based on error minimization criteria, for instance, when the convolution of signal and filter exceeds a certain threshold. Since this method can only process inputs of a specific range, the incoming signal must be normalized prior to conversion (**Figure** 7).

2.2.6 Multiplexing encoding

Recent advances in neuroscience have also revealed a unique encoding strategy within biological neural systems. In Ref. [29], it presents a novel strategy that blends encoding techniques functioning at distinct timescales to strengthen data processing

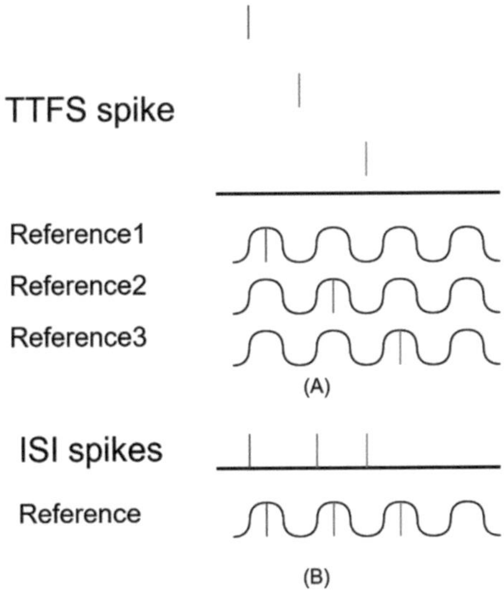

Figure 8.
Demonstration of multiplexing encoding. (A) TTFS-phase encoding. (B) ISI-phase encoding.

performance. This method, known as multiplexing encoding, leverages diverse schemes to represent complementary spatial and temporal aspects of the input, resulting in improved information density and greater robustness to noise. Building on this concept, additional studies have explored the application of multiplexing encoding within neuromorphic computing frameworks [14].

In Ref. [18], the evaluation of information density and noise resilience of various encoding schemes was discussed. Unquestionably, multiplexing encoding demonstrated the highest data capacity and robustness as compared to others. In general, multiplexing encoding consists of two primary steps [30]. The input signal is first converted into spikes with either rate or temporal encoding. Afterward, in the transformation phase, the generated spikes are aligned with the next local maximum of an external reference signal, as illustrated in **Figure 8**. For instance, in TTFS-phase encoding (**Figure 8a**), each spike is shifted to the subsequent local maximum of a sinusoidal reference signal. If multiple spikes coincide at the same local maximum, they are compressed into a single spike. Similarly, in ISI-phase encoding (**Figure 8b**), spikes are shifted to align with the next local maximum of the reference signal. In Ref. [18], hardware implementation of TTFS-phase and ISI-phase encoding techniques with analog integrated circuits was demonstrated.

3. Digital circuit implementation

Implementing spike encoding in hardware involves specialized circuits that convert real-world signals into spike trains. These circuits must ensure that the spikes accurately reflect the input's key characteristics and information-carrying ability while minimizing redundancy and noise. This section explores the digital hardware implementation of various encoding schemes across different platforms. While some encoding schemes are assessed within the framework of general digital systems, as utilized in advanced neuromorphic chips like Loihi [31] and TrueNorth [32], others are evaluated on Field-programmable gate array (FPGA) platforms [33].

In the state-of-the-art digital hardware architecture for rate encoding, as illustrated in **Figure 9a**, an n-bit linear feedback shift register (LFSR) with a specific configuration of XOR gate feedback is employed as a random number generator (RNG) to approximate a Poisson probability distribution [34]. The rate encoder includes several RNGs equal to the total timesteps, t, of the input signal. At each timestep, input signal values are compared in parallel against the corresponding generated random numbers, which serve as thresholds. These comparisons determine whether a spike event is generated at the output of each comparator. The architecture uses t comparators—one for each timestep—resulting in a spike train whose length matches the total number of timesteps, t, of the input signal. All LFSRs have a uniform bit width of n, enabling the input signal's maximum amplitude to 2^n - 1.

The advanced digital hardware design for phase encoding is both efficient and straightforward. It relies solely on multiplexers and n-bit registers to produce a periodic binary representation of the input signal, as illustrated in **Figure 9b**.

In contrast, the state-of-the-art hardware for TTFS encoding operates through a dual-component system [19]. The first component generates a time-decaying threshold and spike weights by utilizing memory tables (ROMs) to store pre-computed values from Eq. 2. The second component oversees the generation of the initial spike and manages the refractory period, during which subsequent spikes are inhibited.

The state-of-the-art digital hardware for ISI encoding, as illustrated in **Figure 9d**, is organized into four components. The first block tracks the total number of generated spikes, while the second and third blocks calculate the ISI and N_s, respectively. Lastly, the fourth block computes the time interval between consecutive spikes, ensuring a spike is generated only if the total number of spikes remains below N_s and the interval between spikes matches the ISI.

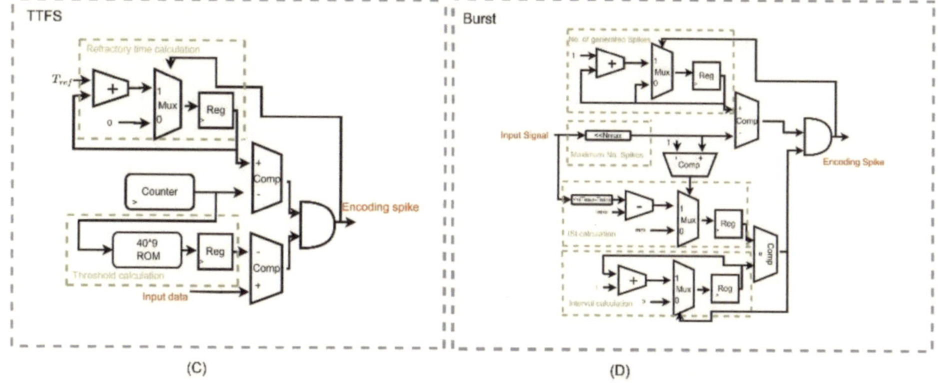

Figure 9.
Digital implementation of various neural coding algorithms [34]; (A) Rate encoding, (B) Phase encoding, (C) TTFS encoding, and (D) Burst encoding.

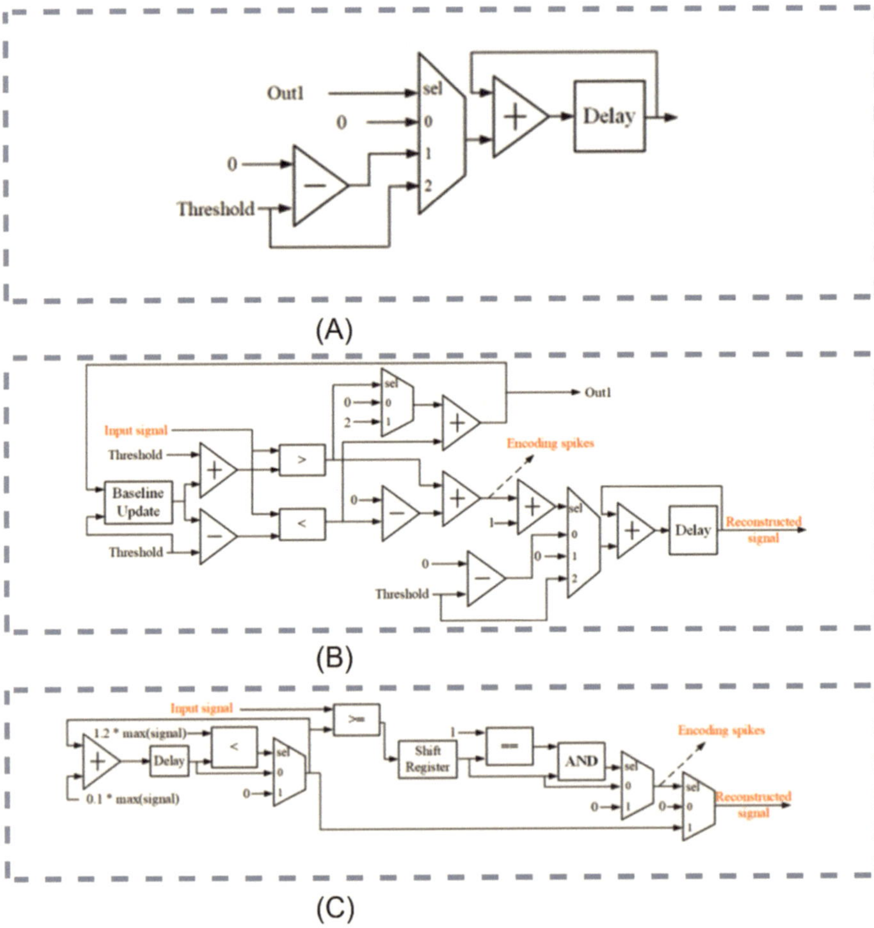

Figure 10.
The digital circuit implementation of SF and PWM-based (PWMB) encoding algorithms [33]. (A) The "baseline update" block used in SF encoding. (B) The implementation of SF encoding. (C) The implementation of PWMB phase encoding.

The optimization of these encoding algorithms is performed using a Genetic Algorithm (GA) in conjunction with parameter tuning for SNNs to achieve adequate classification accuracy [34].

In Ref. [33], hardware implementation of SF, BSA, and PWM-based phase encoding methods was demonstrated, highlighting their suitability for FPGA-based systems due to their ease of implementation. The practical designs are illustrated in **Figures 10** and **11**.

4. Performance analysis and its application

In Ref. [34], hardware resource utilization was analyzed for rate, TTFS, phase, and ISI encoding schemes by measuring the number of required logic gates. The variable N was used to represent the number of encoding modules involved in processing the input signal. When $N \leq 8$, TTFS encoding exhibited the highest logic utilization,

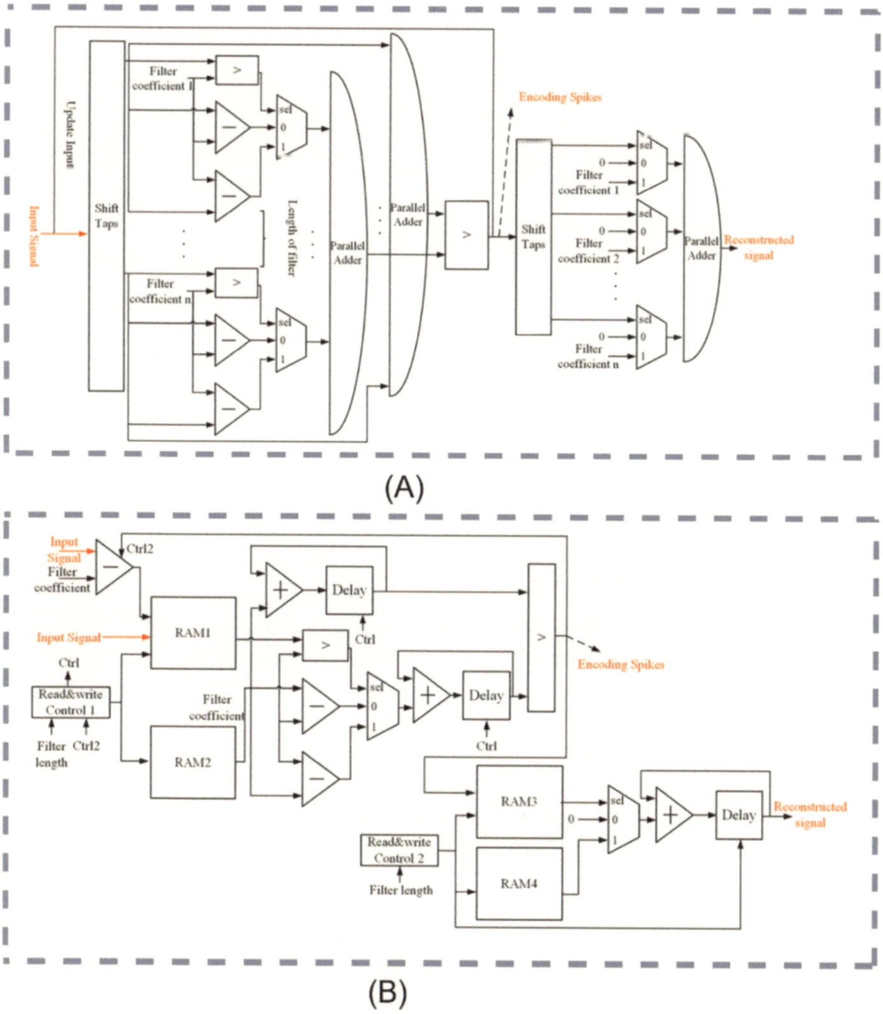

Figure 11.
The digital circuit implementation of the BSA encoding algorithm [33]. (A) The speed-priority implementation of the BSA encoding algorithm. (B) The area-priority implementation of the BSA encoding algorithm.

whereas for N > 8, ISI encoding required the most logic resources. Phase encoding consistently showed the lowest logic utilization across all cases.

Power consumption for each encoding scheme was estimated through an Xilinx VC709 FPGA board with a clock frequency of 100 MHz. TTFS encoding demonstrated a total power cost of 0.7 N + 0.93mW. Phase encoding, however, had the highest power consumption due to its elevated spiking activity. Interestingly, for $N \leq 2$, TTFS consumed more power than rate encoding, but for N > 2, TTFS proved to be the most power-efficient option.

In Ref. [35], the performance of spiking encoders was evaluated by comparing original input signals S(t) with reconstructed signals R(t), assessing their information processing capabilities and robustness. A variety of signal types was tested, including stepwise signals, sinusoidal signals, smooth signals, trended smooth signals, square signals, and event-like signals, as depicted in **Figure 12**. These signals were chosen to

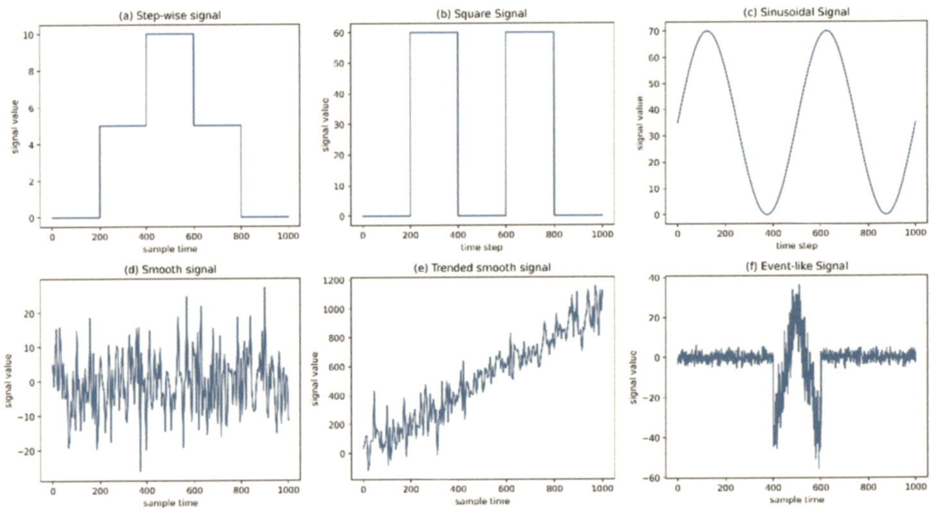

Figure 12.
Demonstration of different testing signals.

reflect the characteristics of Electroencephalography (EEG) data, which typically consist of sinusoidal waves mixed with multisource Gaussian noise. This diverse selection ensures that the findings are applicable to a wide range of real-world applications.

To thoroughly assess the encoders' performance, randomly generated signal parameters and the introduction of random white noise were applied to evaluate their resilience and accuracy under noisy conditions. Metrics, such as Root Mean Square Error (RMSE), Signal-to-Noise Ratio (SNR), average Absolute Error (aAE), and R-squared (R-Sq), were employed to quantify reconstruction accuracy, as depicted in Eq. 5. These measures provided a detailed evaluation of how closely the reconstructed signals matched the original inputs, highlighting the encoders' ability to minimize reconstruction error—a critical goal in signal processing. The analysis of these metrics also offered insights into the encoders' reliability and suitability for various SNN applications [36–38], contributing to a better understanding of their performance in real-world scenarios.

$$\begin{cases} RMSE = \sqrt{\dfrac{\sum_{t=1}^{N} (R(t) - S(t))^2}{N}} \\ SNR = 20 \times log \dfrac{Power(S(t))}{Power(S(t) - R(t))} [dB] \\ aAE = Average(|S(t) - R(t)|) \\ R - Sq = \dfrac{\sum_{t=1}^{N} (R(t) - S(t))^2}{\sum_{t=1}^{N} (S(t) - \bar{S}(t))^2} \end{cases} \tag{5}$$

When comparing TBR, SF, MW, and BSA encoding techniques using software implementations and optimized parameters, SF encoding consistently outperformed others in signal reconstruction across diverse test cases. From a software algorithmic perspective, SF encoding demonstrated effectiveness, especially in situations with limited prior knowledge about the input signal's nature, making it highly suitable for SNN applications. Similarly, recent work in [33] focused on hardware implementations of SF, BSA, and PWM-based (PWMB) phase encoding techniques. This study considered not only signal reconstruction accuracy but also processing speed, power consumption, and resource consumption through EP4CE115F29C7 FPGA development board, in which the power consumption was examined with a smooth signal, which represents the most complex testing scenario. Results demonstrated that the SF encoding algorithm consumes 397.68 mW, while BSA encoding consumes significantly more at 863.52 mW. In comparison, PWM-based phase encoding demonstrates the lowest power consumption at 262.43 mW.

While SF encoding outperformed other methods for most tested scenarios in terms of reconstruction accuracy, it produced larger errors when the input signal changed abruptly in amplitude, for example, square signals. Overall, the SF encoding algorithm offers simplicity and efficiency, requiring the adjustment of only one parameter—the threshold—to optimize its performance across various signal types. The threshold determines the magnitude of changes in the reconstructed signal at each time step. For signals with rapid fluctuations, such as high-frequency or abrupt changes in amplitude, a higher threshold is recommended to capture these dynamics effectively.

Another important aspect of SF encoding is its capability when handling signals with nonzero initial values, where the reconstructed signal could display an amplitude offset. To address this issue, the initial value of the reconstructed signal is aligned with that of the original input signal, effectively eliminating the offset and ensuring accurate reconstruction [33].

The digital circuit implementation of the SF algorithm is simple and resource-efficient. However, its architecture includes a signal and baseline block, which requires step-by-step updates. Such a sequential processing pipeline limits the parallel processing capability, resulting in relatively lower computing speed even with maximum operating frequency. As a result, the algorithm's suitability for SNN applications should be carefully evaluated, particularly for scenarios requiring high-speed processing [33].

The BSA encoding algorithm is specifically designed for positive signals, requiring a preprocessing operation to shift negative inputs into positive ones before the encoding takes place. This encoding algorithm encodes an analog signal into a spike train by convolution with an FIR filter. The effectiveness of the BSA algorithm relies on filter design, which has a direct impact on overall performance. Two critical parameters must be carefully considered for filter design: the filter amplitude and the filter order.

The filter amplitude is particularly important in the deconvolution process, as it determines the maximum value of the reconstructed signal. To ensure accurate reconstruction, the amplitude must be tailored to match the input signal's amplitude. The filter order directly influences how smooth the reconstructed signal appears—higher orders generally produce smoother results. However, this improvement comes at a cost. At the start of the signal, a higher-order filter causes a slower initial rise, as the system requires more time to respond. Toward the end, filtering constraints reduce the usable length of the signal, as part of it falls outside the effective encoding range. This leads to unavoidable information loss near the signal boundaries. The digital circuit implementation of BSA encoding is highly complex. This complexity encompasses both the encoding and reconstruction processes, posing significant challenges in practical hardware systems. Hence, a pair of application-specific hardware architectures was developed to realize BSA encoding, each tailored to address distinct application needs [33]. The first is an area-priority design, which significantly reduces resource consumption at the expense of longer computation times, as shown in **Figure 11a**. The second is a speed-priority design, as illustrated in **Figure 11b**, which prioritizes faster processing.

However, in general, BSA encoding is not recommended for SNN applications with limited hardware resources, except in cases where the input signals are square wave signals. Balancing the tradeoff between speed and resource efficiency remains a key challenge when adopting this encoding approach.

For the PWMB phase encoding, the signal reconstruction accuracy is primarily influenced by two parameters: the number of carrier signals (N_c) in the input signal and the number of points per carrier signal (N_{pc}). Generally, N_c determines the sampling rate, while N_{pc} affects the resolution of the encoding. Larger values for both parameters result in higher accuracy for the reconstructed signal.

However, when applying PWMB phase encoding to SNN applications that require synchronous real-time encoding, N_c and N_{pc} cannot be selected arbitrarily. If input signals for the SNN change dynamically during computation and synchronous encoding is required, the selection of $N_c$and N_{pc} must align with the discrete time steps of the system. This constraint ensures compatibility with the real-time processing demands of SNN applications while maintaining reasonable encoding accuracy.

The digital circuit implementation of PWMB phase encoding could be straightforward and requires minimal logical elements while supporting a high operating frequency. However, as its limitation, only discrete points can be obtained during signal reconstruction. As a result, interpolation algorithms are necessary to reconstruct the complete signal.

5. Conclusion

The rapid advancements in artificial intelligence and machine learning have positioned neuromorphic computing as a pivotal approach to achieving brain-like efficiency for processing complex data. Central to this process is neural encoding, which transforms real-world information into discrete spike patterns suitable for SNNs. This chapter emphasizes the importance of refining encoding algorithms to enhance the efficiency and functionality of neuromorphic hardware and provides an in-depth exploration and analysis of state-of-the-art encoding techniques tailored for digital circuit deployment. These include algorithmic strategies aimed at optimizing hardware efficiency, accelerating processing speeds, and minimizing signal reconstruction accuracy, thereby addressing key performance challenges in neuromorphic computing.

Recent research trends underscore the growing appeal of hybrid encoding schemes, multiplexing encoding, that integrate phase encoding with rate or temporal encoding. While progress has been made and advantages are showcased over other encoding schemes, continued exploration of efficient hardware designs, resilient decoding methods, and practical applications in SNNs will be essential to fully realizing the capabilities of this encoding approach.

By presenting a comprehensive overview of current neural encoding algorithms, as well as corresponding performance analysis and digital hardware implementations, this chapter highlights existing gaps and identifies promising directions for future research. These insights serve as a foundation for advancing the development of neuromorphic systems, paving the way for more efficient and adaptable solutions in this emerging field.

Acknowledgements

The views and conclusions contained herein are those of the authors and should not be interpreted as necessarily representing the official policies or endorsements, wither expressed or implied, of the Air Force Research Laboratory (AFRL) or the U.S. Government. This material has been cleared for public release, unlimited distribution (PA Case Number: AFRL-2025-1913, 14-Apr 2025).

Author details

Ruizhe Li[1], Kang Jun Bai[2] and Yang (Cindy) Yi[1*]

1 Virginia Tech, Blacksburg, United States

2 Air Force Research Laboratory Information Directorate, Rome, NY, United States

*Address all correspondence to: yangyi8@vt.edu

References

[1] Krizhevsky A, Sutskever I, Hinton G. ImageNet classification with deep convolutional neural networks. Communications of the ACM. 2017; **60**(6):84-90

[2] Han W, Zhang Z, Zhang Y, Yu J, Chiu CC, Qin J, et al. Contextnet: Improving convolutional neural networks for automatic speech recognition with global context. arXiv preprint arXiv:2005.03191. 7 May 2020

[3] Pierson HA, Gashler MS. Deep learning in robotics: A review of recent research. Advanced Robotics. 18 Aug 2017;**31**(16):821-835

[4] Han S, Pool J, Tran J, Dally W. Learning both weights and connections for efficient neural networks. Advances in Neural Information Processing Systems. 2015;**28**

[5] Sengupta A, Ye Y, Wang R, Liu C, Roy K. Going deeper in spiking neural networks: VGG and residual architectures. Frontiers in Neuroscience. 7 Mar 2019;**13**:95

[6] Zhou S, Chen Y, Li X, Sanyal A. Deep SCNN-based real-time object detection for self-driving vehicles using LiDAR temporal data. IEEE Access. 2020;**8**: 76903-76912

[7] Li M, Tsien JZ. Neural code—Neural self-information theory on how cell-assembly code rises from spike time and neuronal variability. Frontiers in Cellular Neuroscience. 30 Aug 2017;**11**:236

[8] Azarfar A, Calcini N, Huang C, Zeldenrust F, Celikel T. Neural coding: A single neuron's perspective. Neuroscience and Biobehavioral Reviews. 2018;**94**:238-247. DOI: 10.1016/j.neubiorev.2018.09.007

[9] Adrian ED, Zotterman Y. The impulses produced by sensory nerve-endings: Part II. The response of a single end-organ. The Journal of Physiology. 1926;**61**(2):151-171. DOI: 10.1113/jphysiol.1926.sp002281

[10] Dayan P, Abbott LF. Theoretical neuroscience: Computational and mathematical modeling of neural systems. Journal of Cognitive Neuroscience. Jan 2003;**15**(1):154-155

[11] Nuntalid N, Dhoble K, Kasabov N. EEG classification with BSA spike encoding algorithm and evolving probabilistic spiking neural network. In: Neural Information Processing: 18th International Conference, ICONIP 2011, Shanghai, China, November 13-17, 2011, Proceedings, Part I 18. Berlin, Heidelberg: Springer; 2011. pp. 451-460

[12] Kasabov N. Evolving spiking neural networks for spatio-and spectro-temporal pattern recognition. In: 2012 6th IEEE International Conference Intelligent Systems. IEEE; 6 Sep 2012. pp. 27-32

[13] Wu L, Yuan L, You J. Survey of large-scale data management systems for big data applications. Journal of Computer Science and Technology. 2015;**30**:163-183. DOI: 10.1007/s11390-015-1511-8

[14] Rezaei MR, Saadati Fard R, Popovic MR, Prescott SA, Lankarany M. Synchrony-division neural multiplexing: An encoding model. Entropy. 2023; **25**(4):589. DOI: 10.3390/e25040589

[15] Azmine MF, Li R, Sharma G, Yi Y. SpikeSpec: An on-chip learning neuromorphic accelerator for spectrum sensing with triplet-boosting and hardware friendly loss function. IEEE

Transactions on Computer-Aided Design of Integrated Circuits and Systems. 18 Feb 2025

[16] Lin C, Azmine MF, Liang Y, Yi Y. Leveraging neuro-inspired AI accelerator for high-speed computing in 6G networks. Frontiers in Computational Neuroscience. 21 Feb 2024;**18**:1345644

[17] Lin C, Azmine MF, Yi Y. Accelerating next-G wireless communications with FPGA-based AI accelerators. In: 2023 IEEE/ACM International Conference on Computer Aided Design (ICCAD). IEEE; 28 Oct 2023. pp. 1-8

[18] Zheng H, Bai K, Yi Y. Enabling a new methodology of neural coding: Multiplexing temporal encoding in neuromorphic computing. IEEE Transactions on Very Large Scale Integration (VLSI) Systems. 2023;**31**(3): 331-342

[19] Park S, Kim S, Na B, Yoon S. T2FSNN: Deep spiking neural networks with time-to-first-spike coding. In: 2020 57th ACM/IEEE Design Automation Conference (DAC), San Francisco, CA, USA. 2020. pp. 1-6. DOI: 10.1109/DAC18072.2020.9218689

[20] Montemurro MA, Rasch MJ, Murayama Y, Logothetis NK, Panzeri S. Phase-of-firing coding of natural visual stimuli in primary visual cortex. Current Biology. 2008;**18**(5):375-380

[21] Cattani A, Einevoll GT, Panzeri S. Phase-of-firing code. arXiv preprint arXiv:1504.03954. 15 Apr 2015

[22] Walter F, Röhrbein F, Knoll A. Computation by Time. Neural Process Letters. 2016;**44**:103-124. DOI: 10.1007/s11063-015-9478-6

[23] Kim J, Kim H, Huh S, Lee J, Choi K. Deep neural networks with weighted spikes. Neurocomputing. 2018;**311**: 373-386

[24] Arriandiaga A, Portillo E, Espinosa-Ramos JI, Kasabov NK. Pulsewidth modulation-based algorithm for spike phase encoding and decoding of time-dependent analog data. IEEE Transactions on Neural Networks and Learning Systems. 2020;**31**(10): 3920-3931. DOI: 10.1109/TNNLS.2019.2947380

[25] Park S, Kim S, Choe H, Yoon S. Fast and efficient information transmission with burst spikes in deep spiking neural networks. In: Proceedings of the 56th Annual Design Automation Conference 2019. 2 Jun 2019. pp. 1-6

[26] Eyherabide HG, Rokem A, Herz AV, Samengo I. Bursts generate a non-reducible spike-pattern code. Frontiers in Neuroscience. 2009;**3**(1):8-14. DOI: 10.3389/neuro.01.002.2009

[27] Kasabov N, Scott NM, Tu E, Marks S, Sengupta N, Capecci E, et al. Evolving spatio-temporal data machines based on the NeuCube neuromorphic framework: Design methodology and selected applications. Neural networks: the official journal of the International Neural Network Society. 2016;**78**:1-14. DOI: 10.1016/j.neunet.2015.09.011

[28] Auge D, Hille J, Mueller E, et al. A survey of encoding techniques for signal processing in spiking neural networks. Neural Processing Letters. 2021;**53**: 4693-4710. DOI: 10.1007/s11063-021-10562-2

[29] Panzeri S, Brunel N, Logothetis NK, Kayser C. Sensory neural codes using multiplexed temporal scales. Trends in Neurosciences. 2010;**33**(3):111-120

[30] Nadasdy Z. Information encoding and reconstruction from the phase of

action potentials. Frontiers in Systems Neuroscience. 28 Jul 2009;**3**:499

[31] Davies M, Srinivasa N, Lin TH, Chinya G, Cao Y, Choday S, et al. Loihi: A neuromorphic manycore processor with on-chip learning. IEEE Micro. 2018; **38**(1):82-99

[32] Merolla P, Arthur JV, Alvarez-Icaza R, Cassidy AS, Sawada J, Akopyan F, et al. A million spiking-neuron integrated circuit with a scalable communication network and interface. Science. 2014;**345**:668-673

[33] Wang K, Hao X, Wang J, Deng B. Comparison and selection of spike encoding algorithms for SNN on FPGA. IEEE Transactions on Biomedical Circuits and Systems. 2023;**17**(1):129-141

[34] Guo W, Fouda ME, Eltawil AM, Salama KN. Neural coding in spiking neural networks: A comparative study for robust neuromorphic systems. Frontiers in Neuroscience. 4 Mar 2021; **15**:638474

[35] Petro B, Kasabov N, Kiss RM. Selection and optimization of temporal spike encoding methods for spiking neural networks. IEEE Transactions on Neural Networks and Learning Systems. 2020;**31**(2):358-370. DOI: 10.1109/TNNLS.2019.2906158

[36] Nunez PL, Srinivasan R. Electric Fields of the Brain: The Neurophysics of EEG. Oxford University Press; 2006

[37] Virgilio GCD, Sossa AJH, Antelis JM, Falcón LE. Spiking neural networks applied to the classification of motor tasks in EEG signals. Neural Networks: The Official Journal of the International Neural Network Society. 2020;**122**: 130-143. DOI: 10.1016/j.neunet.2019.09.037

[38] Zhao S, Li Z, Cui R, Kang Y, Sun F, Song R. Brain–machine interfacing-based teleoperation of multiple coordinated mobile robots. IEEE Transactions on Industrial Electronics. 2017;**64**(6):5161-5170

Chapter 3

Neuromorphic Computing: Cutting-Edge Advances and Future Directions

Girish U. Kamble, Chandrashekhar S. Patil, Vidya V. Alman, Somnath S. Kundale and Jin Hyeok Kim

Abstract

Neuromorphic computing draws motivation from the human brain and presents a distinctive substitute for the traditional von Neumann architecture. Neuromorphic systems provide simultaneous data analysis, energy efficiency, and error resistance by simulating neural networks. They promote innovations in eHealth, science, education, transportation, smart city planning, and the metaverse, spurred on by deep learning and artificial intelligence. However, performance-focused thinking frequently ignores sustainability, emphasizing the need for harmony. Three primary domains comprise neuromorphic research: neuromorphic computing, which investigates biologically inspired data processing and alternative algorithms; neuromorphic devices, which utilize electronic and photonic advancements to fabricate novel nano-devices; and neuromorphic engineering, which replicates brain mechanisms using CMOS and post-CMOS technological advances. This chapter will discuss the current state of computing, the neuromorphic computing approach, established and upcoming technologies, material challenges, breakthrough computing concepts, and the advanced stage of emerging technologies. Along with software and algorithmic advancements in spike neural networks (SNNs) and neuromorphic learning algorithms, it will cover hardware improvements, such as memristors, synaptic devices, and neuromorphic processors. We will investigate applications in robotics, autonomous systems, edge computing, the Internet of Things (IoT), and sensory systems. In conclusion, the chapter will discuss future challenges and possibilities, emphasizing major findings and new research directions.

Keywords: neuromorphic computing, data processing, Internet of Things, memristors, and synaptic devices

1. Introduction

Neuromorphic computing is a novel paradigm that draws inspiration from the architecture and functionality of the human brain [1, 2]. Unlike von Neumann's architecture, which is used by traditional computers, neuromorphic systems mimic the neural networks found in the human brain. This allows machines to evaluate information concurrently and is also error- and energy-resistant [3]. Artificial intelligence (AI) has emerged as the frontier of human research in machine intelligence due to the exceptional achievement and widespread adoption of the technique of deep learning. The past few decades have witnessed accelerated growth in the computer industry and information technology (IT) [4]. Artificial intelligence (AI) and other data-driven apps are becoming more and more popular, and they are completely changing the way we engage with technology. These days, there's a lot of enthusiasm for more study, development, and application when AI and machine learning techniques are applied in novel and undiscovered domains [5]. These state-of-the-art applications often provide practical answers to complex, persistent issues that have remained for a long time [6]. Expanding the use of artificial intelligence and machine learning can lead to new opportunities and advancements in several fields, such as eHealth, scientific investigation, education, transportation, intelligent metropolitan planning, and the online universe. However, sometimes, our focus on performance solely leads us to overlook important details. For instance, we might be so dependent on quick access to information that we fail to consider the computing systems' environmental impact and energy usage that make it possible. Maintaining a balance between both performance and sustainability is crucial to the continued advancement of technologies [7, 8].

According to the literature that has been published thus far, in addition to Moore's law, significant advancements have been made by combining co-designing both software and hardware with intelligent architecture [9]. For instance, NVIDIA GPU performance increased 317 times between 2012 and 2021, surpassing Moore's law estimates [9]. Significant performance gains have been demonstrated by research and development initiatives, suggesting that more breakthroughs may be possible. Yet, considering the enormous costs associated with training the most sophisticated deep learning models, standard computing technologies are unlikely to be able to meet long-term requirements. Investigating different strategies is crucial to addressing these issues and guaranteeing the long-term viability of AI's quick advances [10–13].

Three primary categories can be used to group neuromorphic investigations. Firstly, "neuromorphic engineering" replicates the computing units and methods of the brain using either advanced post-CMOS innovations or CMOS technology (e.g., transistors working in a sub-threshold field). Secondly, "neuromorphic computing" studies novel techniques for processing data, which frequently take inspiration from biological processes and experiments with substitute algorithms such as spike-based computing. The third and last field is the creation of "neuromorphic devices." This field uses advances in photonic and electronic technology to design novel nanodevices that can perform desired functions, including in-memory computing, or replicate biological components like neurons and synapses [14]. Considering the recent trend so far this chapter deals with, the strategy is divided into multiple broad sections, including those that describe the state of the field of computing today, go over the neuromorphic computing approach, examine established and popular technologies, give an overview of emerging technologies, deal with material challenges, delve into novel concepts in computing, and evaluate the maturity of emerging technologies while outlining critical next steps for their advancement [15–18].

In this chapter, we will explore the most recent developments in neuromorphic computing, beginning with developing hardware technologies, neuromorphic processors, and hardware breakthroughs like memristors and synaptic devices. Next, we will explore software and algorithmic advancements, with a particular emphasis on neuromorphic learning algorithms and spiking neural networks (SNNs). We will communicate about applications and use cases, including edge computing and the Internet of Things (IoT), robotics with autonomous systems, and sensory systems.

DOI: http://dx.doi.org/10.5772/intechopen.1006712

We will now address upcoming issues and viewpoints before summarizing the most important discoveries and suggesting possible lines of inquiry for further study.

2. Cutting-edge advances in neuromorphic computing

Recently, there has been a growing trend in the optical community to incorporate machine learning and data science methods into photonics investigation, leading to successful applications in optical microscopy, ultrafast optics, and optical communication [19–21]. As the Internet grows, cloud computing becomes the backbone of these networked systems, allowing for automated decision-making, smart home automation, and real-time data transmission [22]. The overall architecture of a representative smart Home Energy Management System (HEMS) is depicted in **Figure 1**. The HEMS center features a centralized smart controller that offers homeowners monitoring modules and control functionalities via the home communication network [24]. The illustration provides information regarding how to facilitate the best possible demand dispatch. The main panel of a smart Home Energy Management System (HEMS) can gather real-time data on electricity use from both schedulable and non-schedulable in-home equipment. Furthermore, in a real-world deployment, a house gateway, like a smart meter, can function as an interactive communication interface between electricity utilities and the smart home. Power utilities often provide a demand responsiveness signal to the smart meter, which the smart HEMS uses as input to optimize home appliance scheduling for residential demand response.

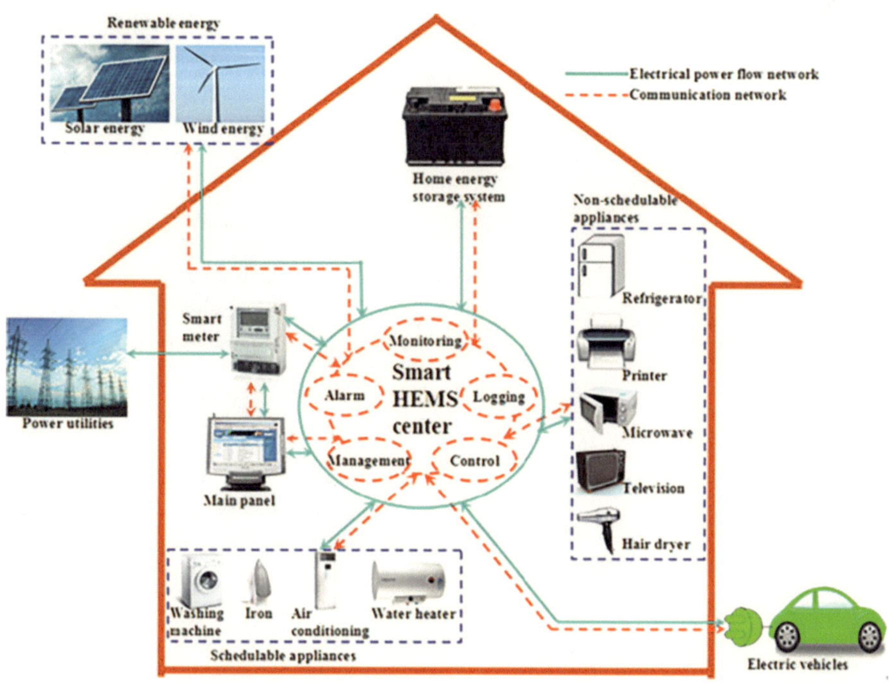

Figure 1.
Overall structure of an exemplary HEMS [23]. (Reproduced with permission from Bin Zhou et al., 2016, ELSEVIER).

Cloud-based robotics frameworks enable robots to gain computational capacity exceeding their onboard capacity through remote management and supervision [23].

Furthermore, many technological advancements in cloud computing and edge computing highlight critical advancements in nanosensors. **Figure 2** shows how enhanced edge computing, a feature essential for enabling effective, immediate, and localized AI processing right at the chip level, has evolved from cloud-based AI systems that rely on remote data processing to sophisticated AI sensors. This shift demonstrates the development of AI applications that are increasingly intelligent and self-sufficient. The capacity to run machine learning algorithms directly within nanoscale memory devices without requiring large-scale data transfers to cloud servers is demonstrated by memory computing.

This development is perfect for real-time applications because it drastically lowers latency and increases processing performance. Sustainability of energy is the goal of neuromorphic computing, which draws inspiration from the architecture and algorithms of the human brain [26]. Local processing can be revolutionized by incorporating neuromorphic units, also known as synaptic devices, into edge devices. By bringing intelligence closer to the data source, this combination facilitates quick, on-the-spot data processing and decision-making [27]. These advancements open the door to AI systems that are more energy-efficient and sensitive, which is especially advantageous for uses in industrial automation, smart homes, and driverless cars [26]. Neuromorphic computing is at the edge of revolutionary breakthroughs, with substantial improvements in hardware, software, and applications that have the potential to completely alter several industries [28, 29]. Hardware advancements that closely mimic brain neural networks, such as improved memristor technology and next-generation neuromorphic computers, will increase performance and energy efficiency. These systems can

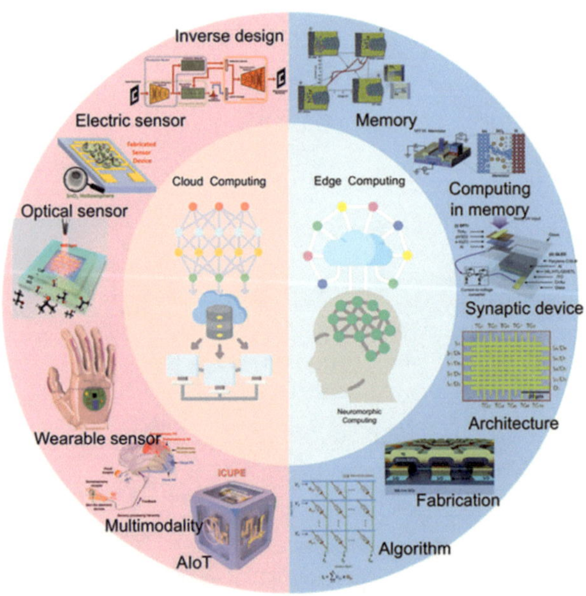

Figure 2.
A significant advancement in the field of nanosensors is highlighted by the development of cloud and edge computing technologies. This evolution demonstrates their shift from being tightly entwined with cloud computing to moving forward into the exciting field of chip-level edge computing [25]. (Reproduced with permission from Chengkuo Lee et al., 2023, Wiley-VCH GmbH).

become more compact and efficient through research into innovative nano-devices and three-dimensional integration. Developments in neuromorphic learning algorithms and spiking neural networks will improve learning capacities and create new pathways for problem-solving [30]. Enhancement of real-time behavior, low-latency processing, and more precise data interpretation will be advantageous for applications in robotics, autonomous systems, edge computing, the Internet of Things, and neurological systems. To reach its full potential, the discipline has to deal with scalability, integration, energy efficiency, ecological responsibility, as well as ethical and social aspects. By addressing these problems, neuromorphic computing can secure its long-term and ethical adoption into future technology landscapes [31].

2.1 Hardware innovations

Neuromorphic computing is seeing amazing gains in efficiency and performance because of hardware improvements [32]. At the cutting edge are memristors and synaptic devices; advancements in both fields allow for more accurate synaptic behavior replication, enhancing the functionality and energy economy of neuromorphic systems [33]. Technological breakthroughs are improving the scalability and integration of devices into neuromorphic systems in materials and manufacture [34]. The neuromorphic computers of the future will process information faster, more efficiently, and in parallel. Additionally, they will have better linkages and communication systems that more closely resemble the neuronal networks found in the human brain. Co-designing the entire stack—from software to hardware—can greatly improve these systems' efficiency and accessibility. Here, we investigate the possibilities of this strategy and its prospective uses (See **Figure 3**).

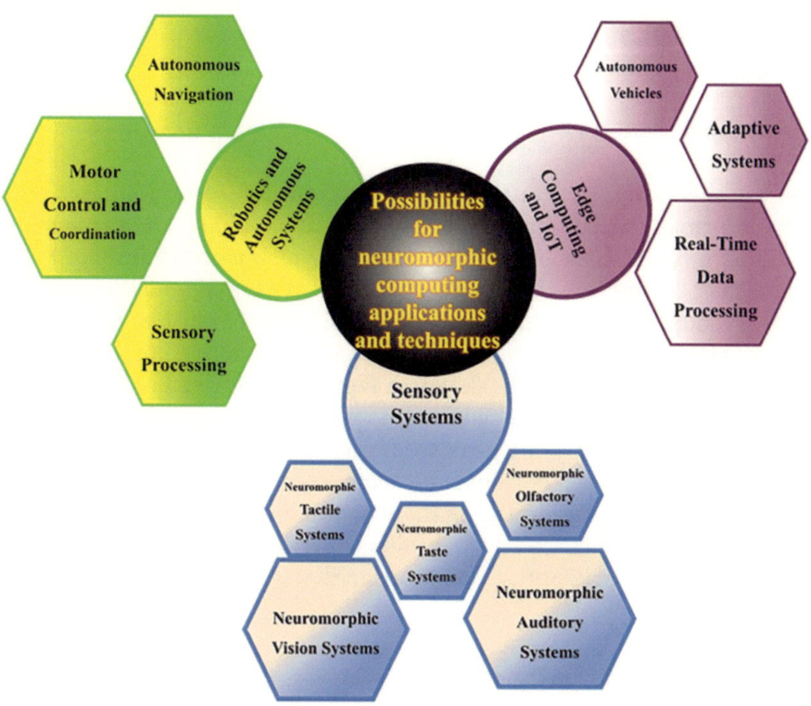

Figure 3.
Possibilities for neuromorphic computing applications and techniques.

Furthermore, studies into cutting-edge hardware technologies, such as innovative nano-devices and three-dimensional integration methods, hold the potential to produce neuromorphic systems that are more efficient and compact. Taken as a whole, these discoveries mark a substantial advancement and establish neuromorphic hardware as a key component in the advancement of computing technology [8]. In the coming section, we will discuss the advancements in the different sectors associated with cutting-edge neuromorphic advancements.

2.1.1 Memristors and synaptic devices

A memristor is an electrical device with two terminals that work similarly to a synapse in neurons, combining memory and resistor. A memristor's conductance can be progressively changed by controlling the charge or flux that passes through it, similar to a biological synapse [1, 2]. More specifically, we validate that a hybrid synapse/neuron circuit comprised of complementary metal-oxide semiconductor (CMOS) neurons and nanoscale memristor synapses is capable of spike-timing-dependent plasticity (STDP), an essential synaptic changes rule for competitive Hebbian learning (**Figure 4a**) and spike-time-dependent plasticity (SRDP). In a study by Wei Lu et al. [35], it was presented the experimental realization of synaptic functions in silicon-based memristors at the nanoscale. These investigations provide substantial experimental support for the neuromorphic systems based on recently proposed memristors. For example, in the crossbar hardware configuration schematically shown in **Figure 4a** CMOS-based pre- and postsynaptic neurons are linked at each cross point by a two-terminal memristor synapse [37]. Furthermore, memristors are suitable for in-sensor computing systems since they may display synaptic activities through multimodal signals like light, chemicals, or sound. Therefore, multimodal AI that runs with high efficiency and low power consumption can be constructed by integrating sensory functions into artificial synaptic devices.

2.1.2 Neuromorphic processors

Neuromorphic computing, another name for brain-like computing, is a system for processing information that mimics the resilience, adaptability, and productivity of the human brain [28]. On the other hand, information must constantly be transferred between the central processor unit (CPU) and memory unit due to their physical separation in modern computers (**Figure 4b**). The human brain's computational architecture is made up of neurons interacting with one another through connections known as synapses, which, as shown in **Figure 4b**, store memory as connection strength (synaptic weight) [36]. In addition to parallel distributed processing, this integrated storage and computing gives the human brain its resilience, energy efficiency, and self-adaptation. Neuromorphic technologies use memristors for synapses and transistors for neurons, mimicking the structure of the human brain. To store and process information simultaneously, they alter the conductance of synapses, allowing for effective, parallel, and adaptive computation that is akin to that of biological brain networks [38, 39].

2.1.3 Emerging hardware technologies

There are emerging technologies in neuromorphic computing, such as memristors, a type of emerging hardware for neuromorphic computing, that work by varying

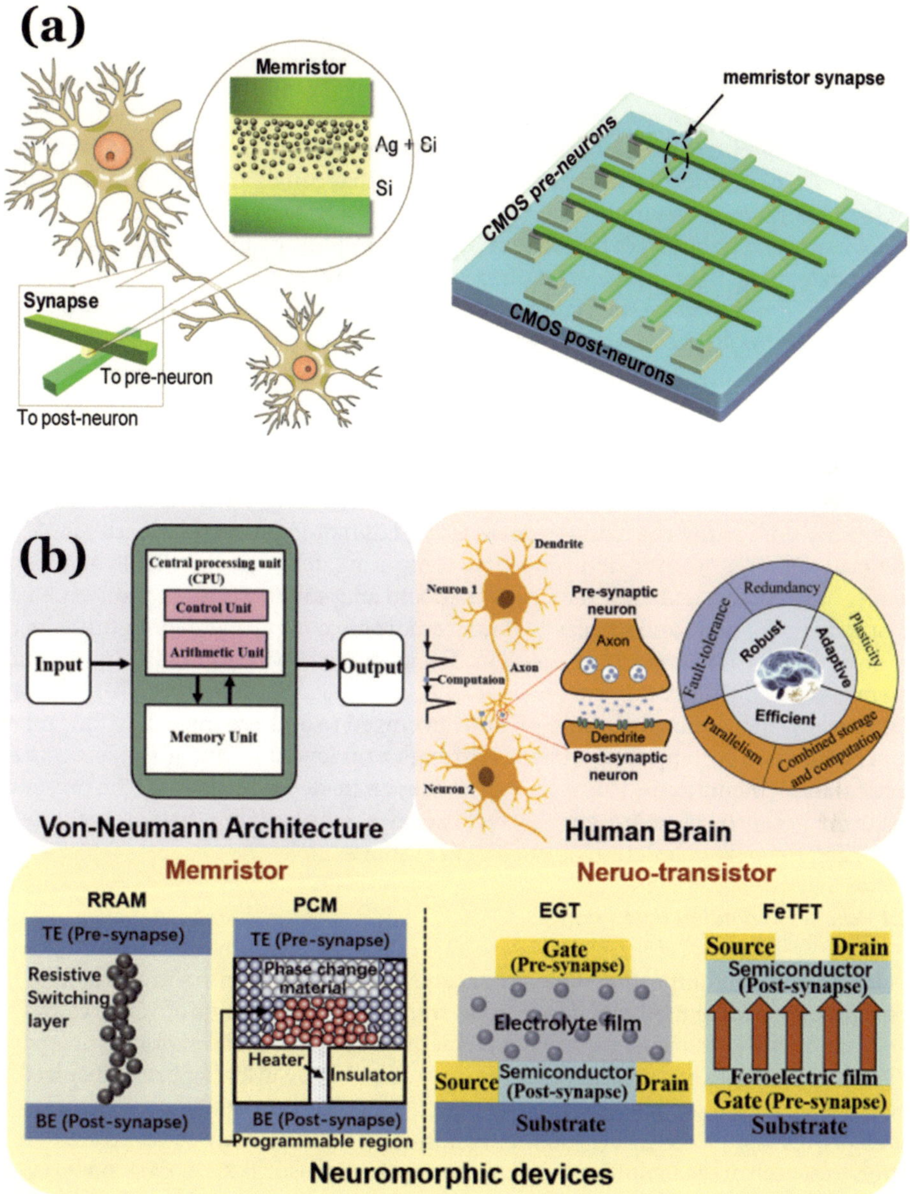

Figure 4.
(a) Features of nanoscale memristors and their use in synapses are shown, along with a conceptual diagram showing how memristors are used to connect neurons synaptically. The memristor's multilayer construction and two-terminal device geometry are explained in depth in the insets and diagrammatic depiction of a neuromorphic system with crossbar-arranged memristor synapses and CMOS neurons [35]. (Reproduced with permission from Wei Lu et al., 2010, ACS). (b) Depicts the computational architecture of the human brain (left) and the features of neural network information processing in the human brain (right), as well as the Von Neumann architecture with a separate central processor unit and memory unit. The functional mechanics and structural designs of neuromorphic devices [36]. (Reproduced with permission from Q. Wan et al., 2019, ELSEVIER).

resistance to store information in a way that mimics synaptic processes and allows for efficient and adaptive processing [40]. Furthermore, spintronic devices are low-power, high-speed data processing and storage devices that use electron spin instead of charge. Likewise, phase-change memory (PCM) is a nonvolatile, high-density memory technology that uses material phase transitions to store information, much like synapses [41]. Also, we have more progress in the field of, resistive switching is used in resistive RAM (ReRAM) to provide high-density, quick, and energy-efficient memory solutions. To boost processing power and connectivity, 3D integration builds several layers of circuitry, emulating the intricate network structure of the brain [42]. Additionally, neuromorphic circuits are emerging that can operate more quickly and efficiently because of the high-performance, energy-efficient transistors provided by carbon nanotube field-effect transistors (CNTFETs) [43]. By processing and transmitting data using light, optoelectronic devices improve system performance and enable high-speed, low-latency communication. These are a few of the emerging and developing technologies associated with neuromorphic computing [28].

2.2 Applications and use cases

Neuromorphic computing, inspired by the complexities of the human brain, marks a significant shift in the architecture and functionality of computational systems. By replicating the neural structures and dynamic processing methods of biological neural networks, neuromorphic computing delivers remarkable benefits in energy efficiency, real-time data handling, and adaptability. This section explores the broad applications and use cases of neuromorphic computing, highlighting its profound impact across multiple domains. Focusing on robotics [44, 45], autonomous systems [46, 47], edge computing IoT [48, 49], and sensory processing [50, 51], we illustrate how neuromorphic principles are leveraged to address the limitations inherent in conventional computing models. Through a review of recent advancements and practical implementations, this section provides an in-depth analysis of the present and future potential of neuromorphic technologies, emphasizing their crucial role in developing the next generation of intelligent systems.

2.2.1 Robotics and autonomous systems

Neuromorphic computing, which replicates the human brain's neural architectures and operational methods, is poised to transform the domains of robotics and autonomous systems. Neuromorphic systems achieve exceptional energy efficiency, real-time processing capabilities, and adaptive learning by utilizing brain-inspired mechanisms, such as spike-based communication, synaptic plasticity, and event-driven processing [52–54]. The robotics community has primarily concentrated on distinct research areas including sensing, perception, sensor fusion, data analysis, state estimation, localization, simultaneous localization and mapping (SLAM), and the application of AI to various image processing challenges. **Figure 5** presents data on these specific research targets, sourced from the Scopus abstract and citation databases. In this point, we explore the integration of neuromorphic computing in robotics and autonomous systems, referencing the latest scientific literature to showcase cutting-edge advancements and practical implementations. We analyze how these innovations are overcoming the limitations of traditional computing models, facilitating the development of more intelligent, efficient, and autonomous robotic systems that have the potential to revolutionize various industries.

Dynamic Vision Sensors (DVS), or event cameras, represent a major innovation in sensory processing for robotics. Unlike conventional frame-based cameras that capture images at regular intervals, DVS operates on an event-driven basis. They detect changes in the visual scene with microsecond precision, recording only the variations

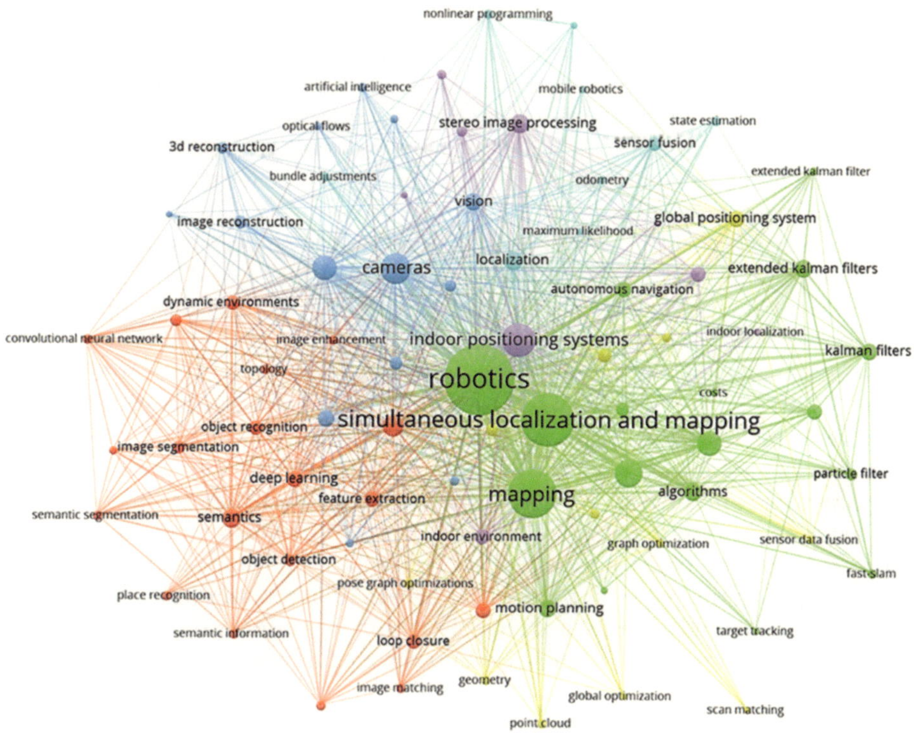

Figure 5.
Scopus database since 2015 covers research in robotics and SLAM. All the works focused on independent research areas that could be efficiently encompassed in one field of situational awareness for robots [55]. (Reproduced with permission from Hriday Bavle et al., 2023, Sensors).

in light intensity. This asynchronous data output offers several advantages, including high temporal resolution, minimal latency, and reduced data volume. The distinctive features of DVS make them highly suitable for applications that demand rapid response times and high temporal accuracy. One prominent application is high-speed object tracking. In dynamic settings, such as those faced by autonomous vehicles or drones, the capacity to swiftly detect and react to moving objects is vital. Traditional cameras often encounter challenges related to latency and data overload, but DVS excels in these conditions by efficiently tracking objects. Gallego et al. and their team demonstrated the superior performance of event-based cameras in dynamic environments. Their research illustrated how these cameras could greatly improve object tracking accuracy and responsiveness, which is critical for applications like autonomous driving and robotic surgery, where immediate reactions are necessary [56]. Integrating DVS with neuromorphic processors further enhances their efficiency. Neuromorphic processors, designed to emulate the brain's neural networks, process spiking data from DVS in an event-driven manner. This synergy allows robots to execute complex visual tasks more efficiently and effectively.

Neuromorphic auditory sensors are transforming how robots process sound by emulating the auditory processing capabilities of the human cochlea. These sensors capture and process sound in real time, replicating biological hearing mechanisms to interpret auditory signals better, more efficiently, and accurately. Sound localization is vital for robots operating in dynamic environments, such as autonomous vehicles or service robots in crowded areas. Traditional audio processing systems often face challenges in accurately pinpointing sound sources amidst background noise [57, 58]. In contrast, neuromorphic auditory sensors can swiftly and precisely determine the direction and distance of sound sources, enhancing the robot's situational awareness and interaction capabilities. Recent research has demonstrated the significant advantages of neuromorphic cochlea in real-time sound processing. These systems efficiently localize sounds and recognize speech patterns even in noisy environments, showcasing the practical potential of neuromorphic auditory sensors. Several studies highlighted how neuromorphic cochlea can improve real-time auditory processing, allowing robots to better understand and interact with their surroundings [59–61]. The integration of neuromorphic auditory sensors with neuromorphic processors further enhances their efficiency and functionality. Neuromorphic processors, designed to mimic the brain's neural networks, process spiking data from auditory sensors in an event-driven manner, which enhances overall system performance. This synergy between sensors and processors allows robots to perform complex auditory tasks more effectively. As research and development in neuromorphic computing continue, the integration of these technologies in auditory processing is expected to unlock new levels of autonomy and intelligence in robotic systems [62, 63]. This progress will pave the way for more capable and efficient robots, impacting various industries and applications.

Neuromorphic computing is particularly beneficial to robotics when it comes to reflexive actions and adaptive learning. By simulating the neural structures and processes of the brain, neuromorphic systems can enable robots to carry out complex motor tasks more efficiently and adaptability. In this point, we discuss recent advancements in these areas, delving into their scientific foundations and practical implications. Reflexive actions are quick, automatic responses to sensory stimuli, which are crucial for tasks requiring immediate reactions to changes in the environment. Implementing these reflexes in robotics is essential for ensuring safety and efficiency. For instance, it was demonstrated that neuromorphic controllers in robotic arms can adapt to environmental changes with minimal latency, enhancing performance in dynamic tasks such as object manipulation and obstacle avoidance [64–66]. Similarly, integrating neuromorphic chips into prosthetic limbs allows for reflexive movements, enabling quick adjustments in response to unexpected stimuli, thereby improving user safety and functionality.

On the other hand, adaptive learning in robotics involves systems adjusting their behavior based on experience, thus improving performance over time. Neuromorphic computing facilitates adaptive learning through synaptic plasticity, in which neuron connections strengthen or weaken based on activity. Researchers have shown that spike-timing-dependent plasticity (STDP) can be utilized in autonomous robotic navigation [67]. Robots equipped with STDP-based neuromorphic processors can learn to navigate complex environments by adjusting movements based on sensory feedback, leading to more efficient exploration and path planning. Additionally, adaptive control systems using neuromorphic principles enable robots to adjust grip strength when handling objects of varying textures and weights, in turn improving dexterity and precision in manipulation tasks [68, 69].

In particular, neuromorphic computing has advanced autonomous navigation, particularly in simultaneous localization and mapping (SLAM) and obstacle avoidance. The section "Limitations of Frame-Based Cameras in visual simultaneous localization and mapping (vSLAM)" provides a detailed discussion of the various types of VSLAM systems that have been developed using different camera technologies. Generally, the classical VSLAM framework consists of the following steps, illustrated in **Figure 6** sensor data acquisition, visual odometry (VO, also known as

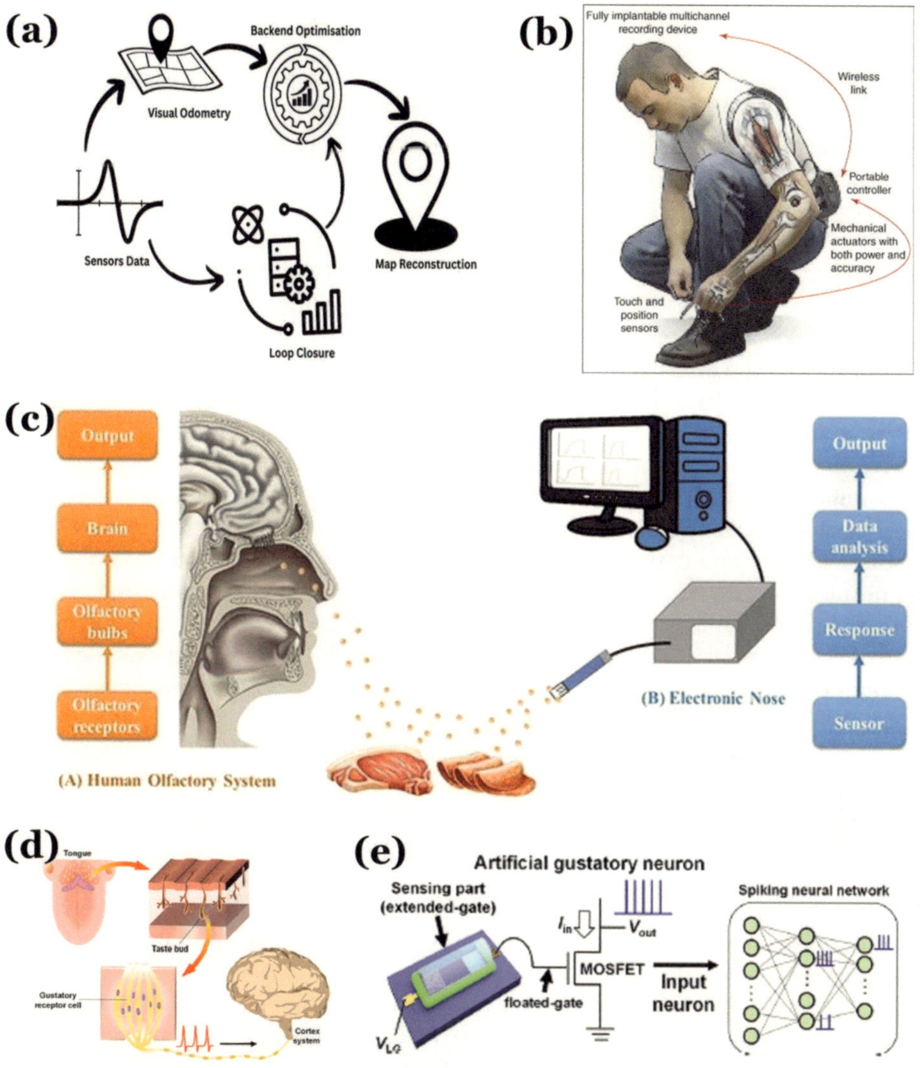

Figure 6.
(a) Classic visual SLAM framework. (Reproduced with permission from S. Tenzin et al., 2024, Biomimetics, MDPI) [70]. (b) Schematic of a fully implantable brain-machine interface (BMI) designed for wireless telemetry sensory system (Reproduced with permission from M.A. Lebedev et al., 2006, ELSEVIER) [71]. (c) Schematic illustration of the biological olfactory system and E-nose technology. (Reproduced with permission from Paulo E. S. Munekata et al., 2023, Sensors) [72]. (d) and (e) Comparison of the biological gustatory system and a proposed neuromorphic E-tongue system. (Reproduced with permission from Joon-Kyu Han et al., 2022, ACS) [73].

the front-end), back-end filtering and optimization, loop closure, and reconstruction. These systems mimic the brain's adaptability, enabling precise and reliable robot navigation in complex environments. Traditional SLAM uses intensive algorithms, while neuromorphic sensors offer a more efficient alternative, especially in dynamic and low-light conditions. Neuromorphic algorithms also enable rapid decision-making and real-time path adjustments, improving autonomous navigation in various applications [55, 70].

Overall, neuromorphic computing has the potential to transform robotics by offering efficient, adaptive, and real-time processing capabilities. Scientific reports support a wide range of applications, from sensory processing and motor control to autonomous navigation and edge computing. Future research is likely to focus on integrating neuromorphic computing with AI, scaling systems, and addressing ethical and societal challenges. These advancements underscore the significance of neuromorphic technologies in shaping the next generation of intelligent robotic systems.

2.2.2 Edge computing and IoT

Neuromorphic computing, inspired by the architecture and functionality of the human brain, uses specialized hardware to mimic the neural structure and operations of biological systems [74, 75]. This approach is particularly beneficial for edge computing and the Internet of Things (IoT), where efficiency, speed, and low power consumption are critical [76, 77]. Recent studies highlighted several cutting-edge advances and applications of neuromorphic computing in these areas. At the core of neuromorphic computing are spiking neural networks (SNNs), which emulate the communication method of biological neurons through discrete spikes. Unlike traditional artificial neural networks (ANNs) that rely on continuous values, SNNs use these discrete spikes to process information, closely mimicking the brain's neural communication [78, 79]. SNNs operate on an event-driven basis, processing information only when a spike is received. This leads to significant energy savings as computational resources are used sparingly. Additionally, SNNs naturally encode temporal information, making them particularly well-suited for processing time-series data, which is prevalent in IoT applications [4, 30, 53, 80].

The efficiency of SNNs significantly enhances edge computing capabilities by reducing latency and minimizing the need for data transfer to centralized servers. Neuromorphic chips like Intel's Loihi [81] and IBM's TrueNorth [82] are designed to support SNNs with features such as on-chip learning and real-time adaptation. Their architectures enable low power consumption and efficient processing, making them ideal for edge computing applications. A notable application of SNNs is in neuromorphic vision sensors used in surveillance systems. These sensors detect objects and anomalies directly on the sensor by processing visual information in real-time using SNNs. This event-driven approach not only minimizes energy consumption but also reduces latency, enabling more efficient and responsive surveillance.

Beyond real-time processing, SNNs also facilitate adaptive systems in edge devices, allowing them to learn from and adapt to dynamic environments and evolving user needs. For example, smart home devices integrated with SNNs can autonomously learn and predict user behaviors, adjusting settings such as lighting and heating in real time to enhance user comfort and energy efficiency. This on-device learning capability of SNNs supports the development of more intelligent and autonomous edge applications, contributing to the advancement of personalized and adaptive IoT solutions [83, 84].

In the rapidly advancing landscape of technology, spiking neural networks (SNNs) have emerged as pivotal tools for driving the progress of IoT. Their exceptional features, including low power consumption and real-time processing capabilities, make them indispensable for energy-efficient sensor networks. It has already been demonstrated that SNNs enable environmental monitoring sensors to effectively classify and detect sounds, ensuring prolonged deployment with minimal energy usage, thus contributing significantly to operational sustainability in remote and power-constrained environments [85–87]. Moreover, the utilization of SNNs in neuromorphic processors for autonomous vehicles and drones empowers these devices to perform essential real-time tasks such as object detection and autonomous navigation, thereby elevating flight safety and operational efficiency [88].

In addition to their role in IoT, SNNs play a critical role in advancing other technologies, such as AI and machine learning. By enabling efficient implementation of machine learning models at the edge, SNNs facilitate privacy-preserving and low-latency applications. Furthermore, SNNs are instrumental in Brain-Computer Interfaces (BCIs), allowing the interpretation of neural signals to control external devices and enhance the quality of life for individuals using prosthetics. Over the next 10 to 20 years, advancements in neuroprosthetic technology are envisioned to produce fully implantable systems capable of recording and wirelessly transmitting multiple electrical signals from thousands of neurons. These systems aim to interface with brain-machine interfaces (BMIs) that can decode both spatial and temporal aspects of movements, periods of immobility, and the cognitive characteristics associated with intended actions. As depicted in **Figure 6b**, such advanced neuroprosthetics will leverage cutting-edge developments in miniaturized electronics, wireless communication, and sophisticated decoding algorithms to provide seamless integration with neural circuits and enhance the functionality and autonomy of individuals with motor impairments [71].

Meanwhile, the integration of SNNs in various applications signifies a groundbreaking approach, offering substantial improvements in real-time data processing, adaptive system functionality, and energy efficiency. Ongoing research and development in neuromorphic systems are essential for overcoming existing challenges and unleashing the full potential of these technologies across diverse applications. By emulating the neural architecture and operations of biological systems, neuromorphic computing is poised to revolutionize the efficiency and responsiveness of edge devices and IoT networks, paving the way for a more connected and technologically advanced future.

2.2.3 Sensory systems

It is well known that neuromorphic computing is an innovative field that draws inspiration from the complex structure and operational principles of the human brain to create advanced computational systems [89, 90]. This biomimetic approach has led to significant progress in various areas, particularly in the development of artificial sensory systems that mimic human perceptual abilities. By incorporating concepts such as spiking neural networks (SNNs) and event-based processing, neuromorphic computing enables the creation of more efficient, adaptive, and resilient sensory information processing systems compared to traditional methods [28, 91]. This section comprehensively explores the latest advancements and diverse applications of neuromorphic computing in sensory systems. It includes an in-depth analysis of how these cutting-edge technologies revolutionize sensory modalities like vision, hearing, touch, smell, and taste [92, 93]. Additionally, it highlights the practical implications of these advancements through a variety of use cases, showcasing their transformative impact on industries, such as robotics, healthcare, and environmental monitoring [93–95]. This exploration aims to provide readers with a thorough understanding of the current state and potential future directions of neuromorphic sensory systems, emphasizing their essential role in the ongoing evolution of artificial intelligence and computational neuroscience. It shows how doctors, patients, and the entire network system are interconnected. All records are digitized and stored in databases, making them accessible to both doctors and clinical staff [96].

Neuromorphic computing is transforming the replication of sensory systems found in biological organisms, such as vision, hearing, touch, smell, and taste to enhance artificial sensory processing capabilities. A notable advancement in neuromorphic vision systems is the creation of event-based vision sensors, exemplified by Dynamic Vision Sensors (DVS). These sensors operate asynchronously by detecting changes in a scene, which results in high temporal resolution and significantly reduced data redundancy. For example, autonomous vehicles utilize DVS technology for real-time object detection and tracking, leading to quicker response times and lower energy consumption compared to traditional cameras [97]. Moreover, spiking neural networks (SNNs) are adept at processing data from event-based sensors, facilitating real-time visual pattern recognition. IBM's True North neuromorphic processor exemplifies this capability, having been employed for dynamic scene analysis and edge detection in robotics and surveillance applications [82]. These developments underscore the potential of neuromorphic computing to revolutionize artificial sensory systems by offering more efficient and adaptive solutions.

In the field of auditory systems, neuromorphic approaches are designed to emulate the function of the cochlea, transforming sound waves into neural signals. This principle is integral to advanced hearing aids and auditory prostheses that incorporate neuromorphic chips to enhance sound localization and speech recognition, particularly in noisy environments. These devices leverage neuromorphic cochlea models and spiking neural networks (SNNs) specifically optimized for auditory processing tasks. Recent research has validated the effectiveness of these systems, demonstrating that neuromorphic chips can enhance speech recognition accuracy in hearing aids by up to 30% compared to traditional digital signal processing methods [98–101]. Moreover, spiking auditory networks process auditory signals like the brain's auditory pathways, enabling real-time sound source localization and separation. This capability significantly improves the performance of voice-activated systems and acoustic monitoring devices. These advancements underscore the potential of neuromorphic computing to revolutionize auditory perception technologies, offering more accurate and efficient solutions for a range of applications [50, 102].

Neuromorphic tactile systems, such as Electronic Skin (E-skin), utilize advanced neuromorphic processors to accurately detect pressure, temperature, and texture, closely emulating the human sense of touch. These cutting-edge systems incorporate state-of-the-art materials and sensor arrays, enabling them to perceive a wide range of tactile stimuli with exceptional sensitivity and precision. For example, the integration of E-skin and neuromorphic tactile processing into robotic hands allows for delicate manipulations and object handling akin to human hands. This functionality is particularly vital for advanced prosthetics and industries requiring precise object manipulation [72, 103, 104].

A critical element of neuromorphic tactile systems is spiking tactile networks (STNs), which process tactile information with remarkable temporal resolution and adaptability, mimicking the dynamic and responsive nature of the human somatosensory system. In virtual reality (VR) and teleoperation applications, the incorporation of STNs into haptic feedback systems enhances the user experience, providing more immersive and realistic tactile feedback. In VR, these systems elevate the sense of presence and interaction with virtual objects, while in teleoperation, they enable remote operators to execute intricate tasks with enhanced accuracy and control. These advancements underscore the significant potential of neuromorphic tactile systems for enhancing tactile perception and manipulation across diverse applications [105, 106].

Neuromorphic olfactory systems leverage bioinspired olfactory circuits that replicate the olfactory bulb's functionality, enabling precise and efficient odor detection and discrimination. These systems find significant applications in environmental monitoring and quality control within the food and beverage industry. For example, electronic noses (e-noses) equipped with neuromorphic olfactory processors can analyze complex odor profiles in real-time, ensuring the quality and safety of products [107, 108]. An E-nose system comprises three main components: a sampling system, a sensor array, and a computer, as illustrated in **Figure 6c**. The sampling system is responsible for handling and storing samples during analysis. The sensor array collects signals resulting from the interaction between the sensing materials and various volatile compounds. Finally, the computer component manages data storage, preprocessing, and processing of the collected signals [72].

A key advancement in this field is the development of adaptive spiking neural networks (SNNs) for olfaction, which enhance the robustness and sensitivity of the system to changing environmental conditions. These adaptive SNNs emulate the neural processing pathways of the human olfactory system, allowing for rapid and accurate odor recognition even amid background noise or varying conditions. This technology has shown promise in the early detection of hazardous substances and diseases through breath analysis. For instance, recent studies demonstrated that neuromorphic olfactory systems could accurately identify specific biomarkers in human breath, facilitating early diagnosis of conditions such as lung cancer and diabetes. This exemplifies the transformative potential of neuromorphic olfactory systems in healthcare diagnostics and environmental safety, highlighting their ability to provide timely and accurate detection in various applications [109, 110].

Neuromorphic gustatory systems utilize artificial taste buds designed to replicate the chemical sensing capabilities of human taste buds. These systems integrate advanced neuromorphic processors to analyze complex taste profiles, playing a critical role in quality assessment within the food industry. By accurately detecting and interpreting a wide range of taste components, neuromorphic processors help ensure product consistency and safety. This capability is crucial for maintaining high standards in food production, as demonstrated by Baldwin et al. [111], where these systems identified subtle variations in flavor profiles, enabling manufacturers to detect deviations and maintain desired taste attributes.

In addition to quality control, spiking neural networks (SNNs) are essential in gustatory processing, providing efficient and precise recognition of taste signals. These networks mimic the neural pathways involved in human taste perception, which is key to developing advanced flavor detection systems. A study emphasized the potential of SNNs in supporting personalized nutrition and health monitoring. By analyzing individual taste responses and dietary needs, these systems can offer tailored dietary recommendations, promoting healthier eating habits and improving overall well-being. A neuromorphic gustatory system could analyze a person's unique taste profile and nutritional requirements, suggesting specific dietary adjustments to enhance health outcomes. For instance, Han and their team [73] developed an artificial gustatory neuron to perform sensing and neuronal functions, demonstrated in a neuromorphic-based E-tongue as an integrated sensory neuron. As shown in **Figure 6d**, the combined signals from gustatory receptor neurons are transmitted to the gustatory cortex in the brain, where distinct taste patterns are identified. The team mimicked gustatory neurons for sour and salty tastes using a metal-oxide-semiconductor field-effect transistor (MOSFET) with an extended gate functioning as a bioreceptor. This setup acts like an antenna to collect taste sources, achieving simultaneous sensing and spike encoding with the spiking frequency varying based on the concentrations of hydrogen and sodium ions. This artificial gustatory neuron serves as an input neuron for the spiking neural network (SNN), as illustrated in **Figure 6e** [73]. The neuromorphic architecture allows for a highly scalable and energy-efficient one-body type E-tongue suitable for mobile and IoT applications, as it transmits data using spikes and eliminates the need for bulky hardware components, such as ADCs, CPUs, and memory [112, 113].

Neuromorphic computing is transforming sensory systems by introducing more efficient, adaptable, and robust methods for processing sensory information. This significantly enhances the capabilities of artificial sensory systems. Advancements in neuromorphic vision have led to the creation of dynamic vision sensors that offer high temporal resolution for applications such as autonomous vehicles. In auditory systems, cochlea-inspired models and spiking neural networks (SNNs) improve sound localization and speech recognition in noisy environments, benefiting advanced hearing aids and voice-activated systems. Neuromorphic tactile systems, such as electronic skin (E-skin) and spiking tactile networks, provide precise and responsive touch perception, critical for advanced prosthetics and immersive virtual reality experiences. In olfactory systems, bioinspired circuits and adaptive SNNs enable efficient odor detection and disease diagnosis through breath analysis. In gustatory systems, artificial taste buds and SNNs ensure better product consistency and support personalized nutrition. As research continues to address current challenges, the integration of neuromorphic principles in sensory systems promises to yield even more sophisticated and capable artificial sensory processing technologies, with diverse applications in robotics, healthcare, environmental monitoring, and beyond.

2.3 Future directions

The future of neuromorphic computing is an exciting frontier filled with a wealth of possible developments and applications. The ongoing development of hardware designs consisting of memristors and transistors with verities of advanced nanoscale 2D materials capable of simulating the intricacy of human neural systems is one encouraging avenue. The creation of increasingly complex neuromorphic devices that have higher neuron densities and connectivity will make it possible to do increasingly complex tasks and mimic higher-order cognitive capabilities. Current investigations into innovative materials, like electromagnetic materials (for spintronics devices) and phase-change materials, have the potential to greatly enhance the scalability and energy efficiency of neuromorphic systems. This hardware has the potential to improve processor and memory function integration, leading to more potent and compact computing solutions. Additionally, improvements in deep learning and machine learning techniques for neuromorphic computing will facilitate the more successful integration of neuromorphic-based AI gadgets into daily life. Furthermore, to comprehend and replicate sophisticated brain functions, multidisciplinary partnerships involving computer science, neurology, and cognitive science are essential. Such cooperative efforts may result in advancements in neuromorphic systems' learning capacities and adaptability, which would open the door to the development of true artificial general intelligence. Another critical direction is the exploration of neuromorphic computing applications in real-world scenarios, such as autonomous vehicles and healthcare technologies. The integration of neuromorphic systems into these fields could revolutionize data processing techniques, enabling faster decision-making processes, real-time analysis, and enhanced sensory perception.

Finally, ethical considerations and societal implications will play a vital role in shaping the future of neuromorphic computing. As these systems become more integrated into everyday life, addressing issues related to privacy, transparency, and accountability will be essential to gain public trust and ensure societal benefits.

In summary, the future of neuromorphic computing is rich with possibilities, driven by advancements in hardware, materials science, interdisciplinary research, application discovery, and ethical considerations. It will be essential to follow these paths to fully realize the promise of neuromorphic systems and their revolutionary effects on technology and society.

3. Conclusion

In conclusion, neuromorphic computing represents a groundbreaking shift in the realm of computing paradigms, drawing inspiration from the intricate architecture and functionality of the human brain. By mimicking biological neural networks, neuromorphic systems possess the unique ability to process information concurrently, granting them enhanced efficiency, adaptability, and resilience against errors. As the field continues to evolve, significant advancements in hardware, algorithms, and interdisciplinary collaboration promise to unlock the full potential of these innovative systems. The quest for enhanced learning capacities and flexibility in neuromorphic computing creates new opportunities for applications in a range of sectors, including robotics, autonomous systems, and healthcare. As these technologies become more widely used in society, it will be critical to address ethical issues in order to build public confidence and promote responsible growth. As we look to the future, the ongoing research and innovations in neuromorphic computing hold the potential for transformative impacts on technology and society at large. By exploring the intersection of neuroscience, engineering, and computer science, we can harness the power of neuromorphic systems to create intelligent machines that not only think and learn but also adapt to the complexities of real-world environments. This exciting frontier invites researchers and practitioners alike to contribute to the next generation of artificial intelligence, redefining our understanding of computation and its role in augmenting human capabilities.

Author details

Girish U. Kamble[1], Chandrashekhar S. Patil[2], Vidya V. Alman[3], Somnath S. Kundale[4,5] and Jin Hyeok Kim[1]*

1 Optoelectronics Convergence Research Center and Department of Materials Science and Engineering, Chonnam National University, Gwangju, South Korea

2 Department of Ocean System Engineering, Jeju National University, Jeju, South Korea

3 Department of Materials Science and Metallurgical Engineering, Indian Institute of Technology, Hyderabad, Telangana, India

4 School of Materials Science and Engineering, Gyeongsang National University, Jinju, South Korea

5 Research Institute for Green Energy Convergence Technology, Gyeongsang National University, Jinju, Gyeongsangnam-do, Republic of Korea

*Address all correspondence to: jinhyeok@chonnam.ac.kr

References

[1] Mehonic A, Sebastian A, Rajendran B, Simeone O, Vasilaki E, Kenyon AJ. Memristors—From in-memory computing, deep learning acceleration, and spiking neural networks to the future of neuromorphic and bio-inspired computing. Advanced Intelligent Systems. 2020;**2**(11):022501

[2] Pereira ME, Martins R, Fortunato E, Barquinha P, Kiazadeh A. Recent progress in optoelectronic memristors for neuromorphic and in-memory computation. Neuromorphic Computing and Engineering. 2023;**3**(2):022002

[3] Walters B, Jacob MV, Amirsoleimani A, Rahimi Azghadi M. A review of graphene-based Memristive neuromorphic devices and circuits. Advanced Intelligent Systems. 2023;**5**(10):2300136

[4] Ning L, Dong J, Xiao R, Tan KC, Tang H. Event-driven spiking neural networks with spike-based learning. Memetic Computing. 2023;**15**(2):205-217

[5] Marković D, Mizrahi A, Querlioz D, Grollier J. Physics for neuromorphic computing. Nature Reviews Physics. 2020;**2**(9):499-510

[6] Chen Y, Li HH, Wu C, Song C, Li S, Min C, et al. Neuromorphic computing's yesterday, today, and tomorrow–an evolutional view. Integration. 2018;**61**:49-61

[7] Chen G, Cao H, Conradt J, Tang H, Rohrbein F, Knoll A. Event-based neuromorphic vision for autonomous driving: A paradigm shift for bio-inspired visual sensing and perception. IEEE Signal Processing Magazine. 2020;**37**(4):34-49

[8] Furber S. 2022 roadmap on neuromorphic computing and engineering. Neuromorphic Computing and Engineering. 2022;**2**(2):022501

[9] Shalf J. The future of computing beyond Moore's law. Philosophical Transactions of the Royal Society A. 2020;**378**(2166):20190061

[10] Mehonic A, Kenyon AJ. Brain-inspired computing needs a master plan. Nature. 2022;**604**(7905): 255-260

[11] Gokmen T, Vlasov Y. Acceleration of deep neural network training with resistive cross-point devices: Design considerations. Frontiers in Neuroscience. 2016;**10**:333

[12] Mehonic A. Energy-efficient AI systems based on Memristive technology. In: International Conference "New Technologies, Development and Applications". Sarajevo, Bosnia and Herzegovina: Springer; 2022. pp. 439-442

[13] Marinella MJ, Agarwal S, Hsia A, Richter I, Jacobs-Gedrim R, Niroula J, et al. Multiscale co-design analysis of energy, latency, area, and accuracy of a ReRAM analog neural training accelerator. IEEE Journal on Emerging and Selected Topics in Circuits and Systems. 2018;**8**(1):86-101

[14] Sebastian A, Le Gallo M, Khaddam-Aljameh R, Eleftheriou E. Memory devices and applications for in-memory computing. Nature nanotechnology. 2020;**15**(7):529-44

[15] Farmakidis N, Dong B, Bhaskaran H. Integrated photonic neuromorphic computing: Opportunities and challenges. Nature Reviews Electrical Engineering. 2024;**1**:358-373

[16] Yuan Y, Patel RK, Banik S, Reta TB, Bisht RS, Fong DD, et al. Proton conducting neuromorphic materials and devices. Chemical Reviews. 2024;**124**(16):9733-9784

[17] Kim K, Song MS, Hwang H, Hwang S, Kim H. A comprehensive review of advanced trends: From artificial synapses to neuromorphic systems with consideration of non-ideal effects. Frontiers in Neuroscience. 2024;**18**:1279708

[18] Sun Y, Wang H, Xie D. Recent advance in synaptic plasticity modulation techniques for neuromorphic applications. Nano-Micro Letters. 2024;**16**(1):1-32

[19] Shi Q, Dong B, He T, Sun Z, Zhu J, Zhang Z, et al. Progress in wearable electronics/photonics—Moving toward the era of artificial intelligence and internet of things. InfoMat. 2020;**2**(6):1131-1162

[20] Haroun A, Le X, Gao S, Dong B, He T, Zhang Z, et al. Progress in micro/nano sensors and nanoenergy for future AIoT-based smart home applications. Nano Express. 2021;**2**(2):022005

[21] Hui X, Yang C, Li D, He X, Huang H, Zhou H, et al. Infrared plasmonic biosensor with tetrahedral DNA nanostructure as carriers for label-free and ultrasensitive detection of miR-155. Advanced Science. 2021;**8**(16):2100583

[22] Manvi M, Swamy KM. Microelectronic materials, microfabrication processes, micromechanical structural configuration based stiffness evaluation in MEMS: A review. Microelectronic Engineering. 2022;**263**:111854

[23] Zhou B, Li W, Chan KW, Cao Y, Kuang Y, Liu X, et al. Smart home energy management systems: Concept, configurations, and scheduling strategies. Renewable and Sustainable Energy Reviews. 2016;**61**:30-40

[24] Kuzlu M, Pipattanasomporn M, Rahman S. Hardware demonstration of a home energy management system for demand response applications. IEEE Transactions on Smart Grid. 2012;**3**(4):1704-1711

[25] Zhang Z, Liu X, Zhou H, Xu S, Lee C. Advances in machine-learning enhanced nanosensors: From cloud artificial intelligence toward future edge computing at chip level. Small Structures. 2024;**5**(4):2300325

[26] Choi S, Yang J, Wang G. Emerging memristive artificial synapses and neurons for energy-efficient neuromorphic computing. Advanced Materials. 2020;**32**(51):2004659

[27] Aldoseri A, Al-Khalifa KN, Hamouda AM. Re-thinking data strategy and integration for artificial intelligence: Concepts, opportunities, and challenges. Applied Sciences. 2023;**13**(12):7082

[28] Prakash C, Gupta LR, Mehta A, Vasudev H, Tominov R, Korman E, et al. Computing of neuromorphic materials: An emerging approach for bioengineering solutions. Materials Advances. 2023;**4**(23):5882-5919

[29] Ahmed T. Bio-inspired artificial synapses: Neuromorphic computing chip engineering with soft biomaterials. Memories-Materials, Devices, Circuits and Systems. 2023;**6**:100088

[30] Javanshir A, Nguyen TT, Mahmud MP, Kouzani AZ. Advancements in algorithms and neuromorphic hardware for spiking

neural networks. Neural Computation. 2022;**34**(6):1289-1328

[31] Ahmed KS, Shereif FF. Neuromorphic Computing between Reality and Future Needs, Neuromorphic Computing. London, UK: IntechOpen; 2023. Submitted: 09 November 2022 Reviewed: 20 January 2023 Published: 01 April 2023

[32] Ajayan J, Nirmal D, Binola K Jebalin I.V, Sreejith S. Advances in neuromorphic devices for the hardware implementation of neuromorphic computing systems for future artificial intelligence applications: A critical review. Microelectronics Journal. 2022;**130**:105634

[33] Aguirre F, Sebastian A, Le Gallo M, Song W, Wang T, Yang JJ, et al. Hardware implementation of memristor-based artificial neural networks. Nature Communications. 2024;**15**(1):1974

[34] Najmaei S, Glasmann AL, Schroeder MA, Sarney WL, Chin ML, Potrepka DM. Advancements in materials, devices, and integration schemes for a new generation of neuromorphic computers. Materials Today. 2022;**59**:80-106

[35] Jo SH, Chang T, Ebong I, Bhadviya BB, Mazumder P, Lu W. Nanoscale memristor device as synapse in neuromorphic systems. Nano Letters. 2010;**10**(4):1297-1301

[36] Jiang S, Nie S, He Y, Liu R, Chen C, Wan Q. Emerging synaptic devices: From two-terminal memristors to multiterminal neuromorphic transistors. Materials Today Nano. 2019;**8**:100059

[37] Borghetti J, Li Z, Straznicky J, Li X, Ohlberg DAA, Wu W, et al. A hybrid nanomemristor/transistor logic circuit capable of self-programming. Proceedings of the National Academy of Sciences. 2009;**106**(6):1699-1703. DOI: 10.1073/pnas.0806642106

[38] Krizhevsky A, Sutskever I, Hinton GE. ImageNet classification with deep convolutional neural networks. Communications of the ACM. 2017;**60**(6):84-90. DOI: 10.1145/3065386

[39] Wang H, Zhao Q, Ni Z, Li Q, Liu H, Yang Y, et al. A ferroelectric/electrochemical modulated organic synapse for Ultraflexible, artificial visual-perception system. Advanced Materials. 2018;**30**(46):1803961. DOI: 10.1002/adma.201803961

[40] Sun B, Guo T, Zhou G, Ranjan S, Jiao Y, Wei L, et al. Synaptic devices based neuromorphic computing applications in artificial intelligence. Materials Today Physics. 2021;**18**:100393

[41] Nandakumar S, Le Gallo M, Boybat I, Rajendran B, Sebastian A, Eleftheriou E. A phase-change memory model for neuromorphic computing. Journal of Applied Physics. 2018;**124**(15):152135

[42] An H, Li J, Li Y, Fu X, Yi Y. Three dimensional memristor-based neuromorphic computing system and its application to cloud robotics. Computers & Electrical Engineering. 2017;**63**:99-113

[43] Kenarangi F, Hu X, Liu Y, Incorvia JAC, Friedman JS, Partin-Vaisband I. Exploiting dual-gate ambipolar CNFETs for scalable machine learning classification. Scientific Reports. 2020;**10**(1):5735

[44] Bhanja T, Nußbaum J, Abuibaid K, Legler T, Wagner A, Ruskowski M. The need for neuromorphic computing in industrial robotics. In: 2023 International Conference on Artificial Intelligence and Power Engineering (AIPE). Tokyo, Japan: IEEE; 2023. pp. 42-49

[45] Aitsam M, Davies S, Di Nuovo A. Neuromorphic computing for interactive robotics: A systematic review, Ieee. Access. 2022;**10**:122261-122279

[46] Chicca E, Stefanini F, Bartolozzi C, Indiveri G. Neuromorphic electronic circuits for building autonomous cognitive systems. Proceedings of the IEEE. 2014;**102**(9):1367-1388

[47] Vanarse A, Osseiran A, Rassau A. Neuromorphic engineering—A paradigm shift for future im technologies. IEEE Instrumentation & Measurement Magazine. 2019;**22**(2):4-9

[48] Covi E, Donati E, Liang X, Kappel D, Heidari H, Payvand M, et al. Adaptive extreme edge computing for wearable devices. Frontiers in Neuroscience. 2021;**15**:611300

[49] Fra V, Forno E, Pignari R, Stewart TC, Macii E, Urgese G. Human activity recognition: Suitability of a neuromorphic approach for on-edge AIoT applications. Neuromorphic Computing and Engineering. 2022;**2**(1):014006

[50] Liu S-C, Delbruck T. Neuromorphic sensory systems. Current Opinion in Neurobiology. 2010;**20**(3):288-295

[51] Dong Z, Ji X, Zhou G, Gao M, Qi D. Multimodal neuromorphic sensory-processing system with memristor circuits for smart home applications. IEEE Transactions on Industry Applications. 2022;**59**(1):47-58

[52] Khacef L, Klein P, Cartiglia M, Rubino A, Indiveri G, Chicca E. Spike-based local synaptic plasticity: A survey of computational models and neuromorphic circuits. Neuromorphic Computing and Engineering. 2023;**3**(4):042001. DOI: 10.1088/2634-4386/ad05da

[53] Shahsavari M, Thomas D, van Gerven M, Brown A, Luk W. Advancements in spiking neural network communication and synchronization techniques for event-driven neuromorphic systems. Array. 2023;**20**:100323

[54] Strukov D, Indiveri G, Grollier J, Fusi S. Building brain-inspired computing. Nature Communications. 2019;**10**:4838

[55] Bavle H, Sanchez-Lopez JL, Cimarelli C, Tourani A, Voos H. From SLAM to situational awareness: Challenges and survey. Sensors. 2023;**23**(10):4849

[56] Gallego G, Delbrück T, Orchard G, Bartolozzi C, Taba B, Censi A, et al. Event-based vision: A survey. IEEE Transactions on Pattern Analysis and Machine Intelligence. 2020;**44**(1):154-180

[57] Balamurali B, Lin KE, Lui S, Chen J-M, Herremans D. Toward robust audio spoofing detection: A detailed comparison of traditional and learned features. IEEE Access. 2019;**7**:84229-84241

[58] Aarabi P, Zaky S. Robust sound localization using multi-source audiovisual information fusion. Information Fusion. 2001;**2**(3):209-223

[59] Lenk C, Hövel P, Ved K, Durstewitz S, Meurer T, Fritsch T, et al. Neuromorphic acoustic sensing using an adaptive microelectromechanical cochlea with integrated feedback. Nature Electronics. 2023;**6**(5):370-380

[60] Schmid D, Oess T, Neumann H. Listen to the brain–auditory sound source localization in neuromorphic computing architectures. Sensors. 2023;**23**(9):4451

[61] James R. Spikes from Sound: A Model of the Human Auditory Periphery on SpiNNaker. United Kingdom: The University of Manchester. 2020;**56**(10):1-37

[62] Liu Y, Li E, Wang X, Chen Q, Zhou Y, Hu Y, et al. Self-powered artificial auditory pathway for intelligent neuromorphic computing and sound detection. Nano Energy. 2020;**78**:105403

[63] Galán DG. Neuromorphic Auditory Computing: Towards a Digital, Event-Based Implementation of the Hearing Sense for Robotics. Doctoral dissertation, Universidad de Sevilla; 2022

[64] Abdelrahman AF, Valdenegro-Toro M, Bennewitz M, Plöger PG, A neuromorphic approach to obstacle avoidance in robot manipulation. arXiv preprint arXiv:2404.05858. 2024

[65] Ayyad A, Halwani M, Swart D, Muthusamy R, Almaskari F, Zweiri Y. Neuromorphic vision based control for the precise positioning of robotic drilling systems. Robotics and Computer-Integrated Manufacturing. 2023;**79**:102419. DOI: 10.1016/j.rcim.2022.102419

[66] Hassan E, Zou Z, Chen H, Imani M, Zweiri Y, Saleh H, et al. Efficient event-based robotic grasping perception using hyperdimensional computing. Internet of Things. 2024;**26**:101207. DOI: 10.1016/j.iot.2024.101207

[67] Arena P, Danieli F, Fortuna L, Frasca M, Patané L. Spike-timing-dependent plasticity in spiking neuron networks for robot navigation control. SPIE Microtechnologies. 2005;**5839**:95-102

[68] Ramezanlou MT, Azimirad V, Sotubadi SV, Janabi-Sharifi F. Spiking neural controller for autonomous robot navigation in dynamic environments. In: 2020 10th International Conference on Computer and Knowledge Engineering (ICCKE). Mashhad, Iran: IEEE; 2020. pp. 544-548

[69] Novo A, Lobon F, Marina HGD, Romero S, Barranco F. Neuromorphic perception and navigation for Mobile robots: A review. ACM Computing Surveys. 2024;**56**(10):1-37. Article 246. DOI: 10.1145/3656469

[70] Tenzin S, Rassau A, Chai D. Application of event cameras and neuromorphic computing to VSLAM: A survey. Biomimetics. 2024;**9**:444

[71] Lebedev MA, Nicolelis MAL. Brain–machine interfaces: Past, present and future. Trends in Neurosciences. 2006;**29**(9):536-546. DOI: 10.1016/j.tins.2006.07.004

[72] Munekata PE, Finardi S, de Souza CK, Meinert C, Pateiro M, Hoffmann TG, et al. Applications of electronic nose, electronic eye and electronic tongue in quality, safety and shelf life of meat and meat products: A review. Sensors. 2023;**23**(2):672

[73] Han J-K, Park S-C, Yu J-M, Ahn J-H, Choi Y-K. A bioinspired artificial gustatory neuron for a neuromorphic based electronic tongue. Nano Letters. 2022;**22**(13):5244-5251

[74] Yang J-Q, Wang R, Ren Y, Mao J-Y, Wang Z-P, Zhou Y, et al. Neuromorphic engineering: From biological to spike-based hardware nervous systems. Advanced Materials. 2020;**32**(52):2003610. DOI: 10.1002/adma.202003610

[75] Olin-Ammentorp W, Cady N. Biologically-inspired neuromorphic computing. Science Progress. 2019;**102**(3):261-276

[76] Fayyazi A, Ansari M, Kamal M, Afzali-Kusha A, Pedram M. An ultra low-power memristive neuromorphic circuit for internet of things smart sensors. IEEE Internet of Things Journal. 2018;**5**(2):1011-1022

[77] Fu J, Liao Z, Liu J, Smith SC, Wang J. Memristor-based variation-enabled differentially private learning systems for edge computing in iot. IEEE Internet of Things Journal. 2020;**8**(12):9672-9682

[78] Wu J, Xu C, Han X, Zhou D, Zhang M, Li H, et al. Progressive tandem learning for pattern recognition with deep spiking neural networks. IEEE Transactions on Pattern Analysis and Machine Intelligence. 2021;**44**(11):7824-7840

[79] Wang H, Li Y-F, Gryllias K. Brain-inspired spiking neural networks for industrial fault diagnosis: A survey, challenges, and opportunities. arXiv preprint arXiv:2401.02429. 2023

[80] Pfeiffer M, Pfeil T. Deep learning with spiking neurons: Opportunities and challenges. Frontiers in Neuroscience. 2018;**12**:409662

[81] Davies M, Srinivasa N, Lin T-H, Chinya G, Cao Y, Choday SH, et al. Loihi: A neuromorphic manycore processor with on-chip learning. IEEE Micro. 2018;**38**(1):82-99

[82] Merolla PA, Arthur JV, Alvarez-Icaza R, Cassidy AS, Sawada J, Akopyan F, et al. A million spiking-neuron integrated circuit with a scalable communication network and interface. Science. 2014;**345**(6197):668-673

[83] Liu Q, Zhang Z. Ultralow power always-on intelligent and connected SNN-based system for multimedia IoT-enabled applications. IEEE Internet of Things Journal. 2022;**9**(17):15570-15577

[84] Tien PW, Wei S, Darkwa J, Wood C, Calautit JK. Machine learning and deep learning methods for enhancing building energy efficiency and indoor environmental quality–a review. Energy and AI. 2022;**10**:100198

[85] Vanarse A, Osseiran A, Rassau A. A review of current neuromorphic approaches for vision, auditory, and olfactory sensors. Frontiers in Neuroscience. 2016;**10**:115

[86] Putra RVW, Hanif MA, Shafique M. EnforceSNN: Enabling resilient and energy-efficient spiking neural network inference considering approximate DRAMs for embedded systems. Frontiers in Neuroscience. 2022;**16**:937782

[87] Pang L, Liu J, Harkin J, Martin G, McElholm M, Javed A, et al. Case study—Spiking neural network hardware system for structural health monitoring. Sensors. 2020;**20**(18):5126

[88] Spanne A, Jörntell H. Questioning the role of sparse coding in the brain. Trends in Neurosciences. 2015;**38**(7):417-427

[89] Jiang J, Gu L. Artificial synapses based on two-dimensional materials. 2023

[90] Schuman CD, Kulkarni SR, Parsa M, Mitchell JP, Kay B. Opportunities for neuromorphic computing algorithms and applications. Nature Computational Science. 2022;**2**(1):10-19

[91] Lobo JL, Del Ser J, Bifet A, Kasabov N. Spiking neural networks and online learning: An overview and perspectives. Neural Networks. 2020;**121**:88-100

[92] Zhao Z, Yang Q, Li R, Yang J, Liu Q, Zhu B, et al. A comprehensive review on the evolution of bio-inspired sensors

from aquatic creatures. Cell Reports Physical Science. 2024;**5**(7):102064

[93] Licardo JT, Domjan M, Orehovački T. Intelligent robotics—A systematic review of emerging technologies and trends. Electronics. 2024;**13**(3):542

[94] Pavithra N, Afza N. Harnessing the power of artificial intelligence and robotics impact on attaining competitive advantage for sustainable development in hospitals with conclusions for future research approaches. GMS Hygiene and Infection Control. 2024;**19**. ISSN 2196-5226

[95] Dwivedi YK, Sharma A, Rana NP, Giannakis M, Goel P, Dutot V. Evolution of artificial intelligence research in technological forecasting and social change: Research topics, trends, and future directions. Technological Forecasting and Social Change. 2023;**192**:122579

[96] Joyia GJ, Liaqat RM, Farooq A, Rehman S. Internet of medical things (IoMT): Applications, benefits and future challenges in healthcare domain. The Journal of Communication. 2017;**12**(4):240-247

[97] Lichesteiner P, Posch C, Delbruck T. A 128× 128 120 dB 15μsec latency asynchronous temporal contrast vision Sensro. IEEE Journal of Solid-State Circuits. 2008;**43**(2):566-576

[98] Juan Pedro Domínguez Morales, Domínguez Morales JP. Neuromorphic Audio Processing through Real-Time Embedded Spiking Neural Networks. Spain: Higher Technical School of Computer Engineering; Department of Computer Architecture and Technology; 2018

[99] Schoepe T, Gutierrez-Galan D, Dominguez-Morales JP, Greatorex H, Jimenez-Fernandez A, Linares-Barranco A, et al. Closed-loop sound source localization in neuromorphic systems. Neuromorphic Computing and Engineering. 2023;**3**(2):024009

[100] Chinnaraj G, Shetty HN, Palaniyappan V. Effect of digital noise reduction and directionality algorithms in hearing aids on temporal envelope distortion and speech recognition. The Journal of Health Science. 2021;**11**(4):19-29

[101] Deepu S, Kini R. Design and implementation of a signal processing ASIC for digital hearing aids. Microprocessors and Microsystems. 2022;**93**:104616

[102] Jiang C, Xu H, Yang L, Liu J, Li Y, Takei K, et al. Neuromorphic antennal sensory system. Nature Communications. 2024;**15**(1):2109

[103] Yamaguchi T, Kashiwagi T, Arie T, Akita S, Takei K. Human-like electronic skin-integrated soft robotic hand. Advanced Intelligent Systems. 2019;**1**(2):1900018

[104] Wang S, Fan X, Zhang Z, Su Z, Ding Y, Yang H, et al. A skin-inspired high-performance tactile sensor for accurate recognition of object softness. ACS Nano. 2024;**18**(26):17175-17184

[105] Potdar P, Hardman D, Almanzor E, Iida F. High-speed tactile braille Reading via biomimetic sliding interactions. IEEE Robotics and Automation Letters. 2024;**9**(3):2614-2621

[106] Ward-Cherrier B, Conradt J, Catalano MG, Bianchi M, Lepora NF. A miniaturised neuromorphic tactile sensor integrated with an anthropomorphic robot hand. In: 2020 IEEE/RSJ International Conference on Intelligent

Robots and Systems (IROS). Las Vegas, NV, USA: IEEE; 2020. pp. 9883-9889

[107] Kim C, Raja IS, Lee J-M, Lee JH, Kang MS, Lee SH, et al. Recent trends in exhaled breath diagnosis using an artificial olfactory system. Biosensors. 2021;**11**(9):337

[108] Kim C, Lee KK, Kang MS, Shin D-M, Oh J-W, Lee C-S, et al. Artificial olfactory sensor technology that mimics the olfactory mechanism: A comprehensive review. Biomaterials Research. 2022;**26**(1):40

[109] Imam N, Cleland TA. Rapid online learning and robust recall in a neuromorphic olfactory circuit. Nature Machine Intelligence. 2020;**2**(3):181-191

[110] Parnas M, McLane-Svoboda AK, Cox E, McLane-Svoboda SB, Sanchez SW, Farnum A, et al. Precision detection of select human lung cancer biomarkers and cell lines using honeybee olfactory neural circuitry as a novel gas sensor. Biosensors and Bioelectronics. 2024;**261**:116466

[111] Baldwin EA, Bai J, Plotto A, Dea S. Electronic noses and tongues: Applications for the food and pharmaceutical industries. Sensors. 2011;**11**:4744-4766

[112] Yang L, Wang Z, Zhang S, Li Y, Jiang C, Sun L, et al. Neuromorphic gustatory system with salt-taste perception, information processing, and excessive-intake warning capabilities. Nano Letters. 2022;**23**(1):8-16

[113] Soltic S, Wysoski SG, Kasabov NK. Evolving spiking neural networks for taste recognition. In: 2008 IEEE International Joint Conference on Neural Networks (IEEE World Congress on Computational Intelligence). Hong Kong, China: IEEE; 2008. pp. 2091-2097

Section 2

Neural Network Models

Chapter 4

Physics-Informed Neural Network: Principles and Applications

Seho Son, Jinho Jeong, Dayeon Jeong, Kyung ho Sun and Ki-Yong Oh

Abstract

This chapter delves into the fascinating characteristics of physics-informed neural networks (PINNs) by outlining their fundamental principles, including their mathematical foundations and structures. PINNs are designed by incorporating governing physical equations into the loss function as constraints, which helps to ensure precise output predictions even in areas with limited or no data. This chapter presents various strategies to apply PINNs to complex systems, thereby addressing the shortcomings of conventional PINNs. Additionally, multiphysics-informed neural networks (MPINNs) are introduced, with a special emphasis on complex mechatronic systems. The effectiveness of the MPINN framework is illustrated through examples such as an electric motor and a lithium-ion battery, demonstrating accurate and efficient multidimensional predictions for mechatronic systems despite limited data availability. These applications underscore the potential of MPINNs to mitigate data scarcity challenges in various industries.

Keywords: deep neural network, fundamental principles, governing equation, mechatronic system, physics-informed neural network, prognosis and health management, supervision of multiphysics

1. Introduction

Deep neural networks (DNNs) are widely used in various domains, including natural language processing [1–3] and image recognition [4–8]. For natural language processing, DNNs are employed in tasks like machine translation, sentiment analysis, and speech recognition, significantly enhancing the understanding and generation of human language. In the field of image recognition, DNNs are instrumental in object classification, feature detection, and image segmentation, finding applications in facial recognition systems and medical imaging diagnostics. The application of DNNs has surged in recent years across various scientific and engineering fields [9–13], including mechatronics, fluid dynamics, materials science, and biomedical engineering. The universal approximation theorem highlights the capability of DNNs to model any continuous function, enabling the effective estimation of complex and nonlinear behaviors in diverse systems [14]. Specifically, DNNs capture complex and nonlinear relationships between input and output through a training process that optimizes a loss function quantifying the discrepancy between predicted and actual output. Therefore, the performance of DNNs significantly depends on the volume of data available to account for system characteristics, suggesting that collecting sufficient high-quality data is crucial for ensuring robustness and generality in real-world applications. This extensive data requirement can be costly and resource-intensive, constraining the accurate prediction of system behaviors when relying on purely data-driven approaches [15]. Furthermore, DNNs are often considered "black boxes" because the decision-making processes are not easily interpretable. This lack of transparency in data-only training can be problematic in critical applications, where understanding the model's inferences is essential for trust and validation.

To overcome these limitations, research has shifted toward hybrid approaches that combine the robustness of physics-based models with the adaptability of data-driven methods [16–18]. One notable strategy in this area involves incorporating knowledge-based features derived through feature engineering. This approach addresses domain-specific knowledge to enhance model accuracy by integrating the strengths of both fundamental physics and data-driven predictions. However, these methods still struggle with managing noisy data and outliers effectively [19]. Data noise can obscure underlying relationships between input and output, complicating the learning process for models. Outliers, on the other hand, can distort model predictions, leading to unreliable results. Meanwhile, physics-informed neural networks (PINNs) have gained attention as a powerful hybrid approach in that this method could enhance the fidelity of model predictions by incorporating physics-based regularization directly into the learning process. Specifically, PINNs minimize a loss function that combines both data-derived and physical laws to ensure robust predictions even under data scarcity or noisy situation. These networks are versatile in handling both forward and inverse problems across various time and space scales [20]. For example, Raissi et al. [21] demonstrated the application of PINNs in solving forward and inverse problems for nonlinear PDEs, showcasing their potential in accurately modeling physical systems with limited data. Another study by Tartakovsky et al. [22] applied PINNs to subsurface flow problems, achieving high accuracy in predicting hydraulic conductivity fields.

Despite these advantages, PINNs face challenges such as addressing stiff partial differential equations (PDEs) and managing multi-physics in complex systems. Issues such as spectral bias, where neural networks struggle to accurately capture high-frequency components of solutions [23], and difficulties in applying PINNs to parametric PDEs, which involve varying parameters that change the behavior of the system [24], have further been identified. These challenges can impact the accuracy and robustness of PINNs, necessitating further research and development to enhance their performance in diverse applications. Therefore, various methods have been actively suggested to overcome these challenges, including adaptively weighting each loss term [25–28], domain decomposition [29, 30], improved architecture to manage interpolation and extrapolation [31, 32], and embedding input coordinate features [32–34]. These efforts extend the application of PINNs beyond solid mechanics [35], thermal dynamics [36, 37] fluid mechanics [38, 39], and electromagnetics [40], enabling practical use in multiphysics system. Furthermore, increasing insight of overcoming challenges with these hybrid approaches is driving active research to address challenges in new applications.

This chapter provides an overview of the main concepts and principles of PINNs and introduces various methods for their applications with practical examples in mechatronic systems. Specifically, the remainder of this chapter is organized as follows. Section 2 explains the fundamental principles and implementation of PINNs. Section 3 introduces the challenges and overcoming strategies in PINNs. In Section 4, the focus is on practical applications of PINNs in a complex mechatronic system. Finally, the chapter concludes with some remarks in Section 5.

2. Principles of physics-informed neural network

Physics-informed neural networks (PINNs) are designed to solve physical problems characterized by limited data availability, such as noisy measurements and time-consuming simulations [41]. These networks constrain the predicted solution to meet the laws of physics and fundamental principles to enhance predictive capabilities by overcoming a data scarcity problem. The physical laws are typically expressed through the governing equations, including parametrized and nonlinear partial differential equations (PDEs) in a generalized mathematical form [21] as

$$\frac{\partial u}{\partial t} + \mathcal{N}[u; \lambda] = 0, \quad x \in \Omega, t \in [0, T], \tag{1}$$

where u, $\mathcal{N}(u; \lambda)$, and Ω denote the hidden solution $u(t, x)$ depending on time t and spatial coordinates x, nonlinear differential operator parameterized by coefficient λ, and a subset of $\mathbb{R}^D$. This form can describe a variety of physics in nature and engineering system governed by dynamics, solid mechanics, thermodynamics, or fluid mechanics [21]. Some prominent examples include the Navier–Stokes equations elucidating fluid flows [36], the heat conduction equations for heat transfer [38], and Cauchy's equations of motion which depict solid deformation [42]. Therefore, this prior knowledge can be integrated into existing neural network models due to their mathematical representation, deriving the architecture of the PINNs.

The PINN architecture closely resembles a conventional MLP structure because the architecture comprises an input layer, several hidden layers, and an output layer (**Figure 1**). However, PINNs differ from conventional MLPs due to the placement of

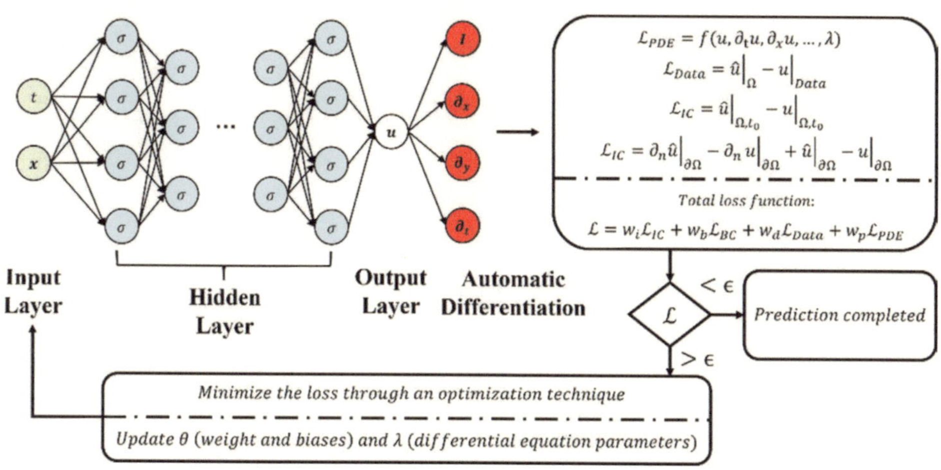

Figure 1.
A basic architecture of vanilla PINNs [43].

the differentiation layer (the red circles with differential symbols in **Figure 1**), right next to the output layer. Each of these layers plays a distinct and crucial role in the training process of PINNs. The spatiotemporal information, coordinates x and time t, are input to the neural network consisting of the hidden layers through the input layer. The neural network subsequently proceeds to predict the hidden solution u of the PDE through the output layers. The outputs u are directed into the subsequent differentiation layer. These layers perform automatic differentiation on neural networks with respect to both their input coordinates x and time t to construct each differential term of the PDE, resulting in the derivation of the loss function for network learning.

The loss function $\mathcal{L}$ of a PINN comprises the sum of two loss functions, $\mathcal{L}_{PDE}$ and $\mathcal{L}_u$ (as)

$$\mathcal{L} = \mathcal{L}_{PDE} + \mathcal{L}_u, \tag{2}$$

where $\mathcal{L}_{PDE}$ and $\mathcal{L}_u$ denote the loss function for penalization of the residual of the PDE, and loss function to satisfy the model predictions for data points [39]. Specifically, the first term $\mathcal{L}_{PDE}$ of $\mathcal{L}$ enforces the predicted solution $\hat{u}$ to obey the PDE at spatiotemporal points in a given computational domain [21] as

$$\mathcal{L}_{PDE} = \frac{1}{N_f}\sum_{i=1}^{N_f}\left|f\left(t_f^i, x_f^i\right)\right|^2, \tag{3}$$

where f denotes the residuals of the PDE expressed by the left-hand side of Eq. (1) at the collocation points t_f^i and x_f^i as

$$f\left(t_f^i, x_f^i\right) = \frac{\partial \hat{u}\left(t_f^i, x_f^i\right)}{\partial t} + \mathcal{N}\left[\hat{u}\left(t_f^i, x_f^i\right); \lambda\right]. \tag{4}$$

The second term $\mathcal{L}_u$ represents the sum of the loss functions aimed at ensuring the adherence of model predictions $\hat{u}$ to both initial and boundary conditions ($\mathcal{L}_{IC}$ and $\mathcal{L}_{BC}$), as well as labeled data ($\mathcal{L}_{data}$) as

$$\begin{aligned}\mathcal{L}_u &= \mathcal{L}_{IC} + \mathcal{L}_{BC} + \mathcal{L}_{data} \\ &= \frac{1}{N_{IC}}\sum_{i=1}^{N_{IC}}\left|\hat{u}\left(t_{IC}^i, x_{IC}^i\right) - u_{IC}^i\right|^2 \\ &+ \frac{1}{N_{BC_1}}\sum_{i=1}^{N_{BC_1}}\left|\hat{u}\left(t_{BC_1}^i, x_{BC_1}^i\right) - u_{BC_1}^i\right|^2 \\ &+ \frac{1}{N_{BC_2}}\sum_{i=1}^{N_{BC_2}}\left|\Gamma\left(\hat{u}_{BC_2}^i\right) - \Gamma_{BC_2}^i\right|^2 \\ &+ \frac{1}{N_{data}}\sum_{i=1}^{N_{data}}\left|\hat{u}\left(t_{data}^i, x_{data}^i\right) - u_{data}^i\right|^2,\end{aligned} \tag{5}$$

where BC_1, BC_2, and Γ denote Dirichlet, Neumann boundary conditions, and a function with derivatives of $\hat{u}$ at boundary points. N and the symbol ^ also denote the number of data points within each condition and the predicted solutions by the PINN.

$\{t_{IC}^i, x_{IC}^i, u_{IC}^i\}_{i=1}^{N_{IC}}$, $\left\{t_{BC_1}^i, x_{BC_1}^i, u_{BC_1}^i\right\}_{i=1}^{N_{BC_1}}$, $\left\{t_{BC_2}^i, x_{BC_2}^i, u_{BC_2}^i\right\}_{i=1}^{N_{BC_2}}$, and $\{t_{data}^i, x_{data}^i, u_{data}^i\}_{i=1}^{N_{data}}$ denote the initial training data, boundary training data of Dirichlet and Neumann conditions, and labeled data points. Note that the PINN's trainable parameters θ are updated via back propagation to minimize the loss function $\mathcal{L}$. During this optimization process, the ADAM optimizer [44] or L-BFGS optimizer [45] can be used.

To demonstrate the performance of PINN, the equation of motion of a 1-DOF mass-spring-damper system is used as a simple example. This equation is a linear ordinary differential equation (ODE) dependent on time t, describing the vibration of a mass. The governing equation is expressed as

$$\frac{d^2u}{dt^2} + 2\zeta\omega_n\frac{du}{dt} + \omega_n^2 u = 0, \quad t\in[0,1] \tag{6}$$

where u denotes the displacement, which is the ODE solution that PINN needs to predict. To this end, the PINN architecture uses temporal information, specifically time t, as network input and predicts the unknown solution u as output. The predicted solution u undergoes automatic differentiation within the differentiation layer to construct the loss function as Eqs. (3) and (4). Therefore, the total loss function for training PINN to solve the equation of motion is formulated as

$$\begin{aligned}\mathcal{L} = \mathcal{L}_{ODE} + \mathcal{L}_{Data} &= \frac{1}{N_f}\sum_{i=1}^{N_f}\left|\left(m\frac{d^2}{dt^2} + c\frac{d}{dt} + k\right)\hat{u}\left(t_f^i;\theta\right)\right|^2 \\ &+ \frac{1}{N_{data}}\sum_{i=1}^{N_{data}}\left|\hat{u}\left(t_{data}^i;\theta\right) - u_{data}^i\right|^2,\end{aligned} \tag{7}$$

where $\left\{t_f^i\right\}_{i=1}^{N_f}$ and $\{t_{data}^i, u_{data}^i\}_{i=1}^{N_{data}}$ denote the collocation points sampled within the range $t\in[0,1]$ and the training data points, including the initial conditions.

The PINN architecture for solving Eq. (6) consists of an input layer, multiple hidden layers, and an output layer as shown in **Figure 1**. The input layer has a single node, because it receives one-dimensional temporal information. The hidden layer consists of three layers, each containing 35 nodes and a hyperbolic tangent activation function. The output layer also comprises a single node to predict the displacement of a single DOF under free vibration conditions. To demonstrate the superiority of PINN, an artificial neural network (ANN) with identical architecture was constructed for comparison.

The training data points for both PINN and ANN were sampled from solutions of Eq. (6), with the damping ratio ζ set to 0.025 and the natural frequency ω_n to 20 rad/s. Specifically, the training dataset consisted of only five solutions, sampled at uniform time intervals. On the other hand, 30 collocation points were chosen for computing the physics loss in the PINN.

PINN and ANN were trained on the Colab environment with an Intel Xeon CPU and a Tesla T4. Both PINN and ANN were trained for 18,000 iterations, with identical hyper-parameters to ensure consistent comparisons except learning rates (**Table 1**).

Figure 2 shows the predicted solution by the trained PINN and ANN models, in comparison to the exact solution (the blue line in **Figure 2(a)** and **(b)**). Note that

	PINN	ANN
Number of input nodes	1	1
Number of hidden layers	3	3
Number of hidden nodes	35	35
Activation function	Tanh	Tanh
Number of output nodes	1	1
Learning rate	1e−4	1e−3
Epoch	18,000	18,000

Table 1.
Hyper-parameters of PINN and ANN.

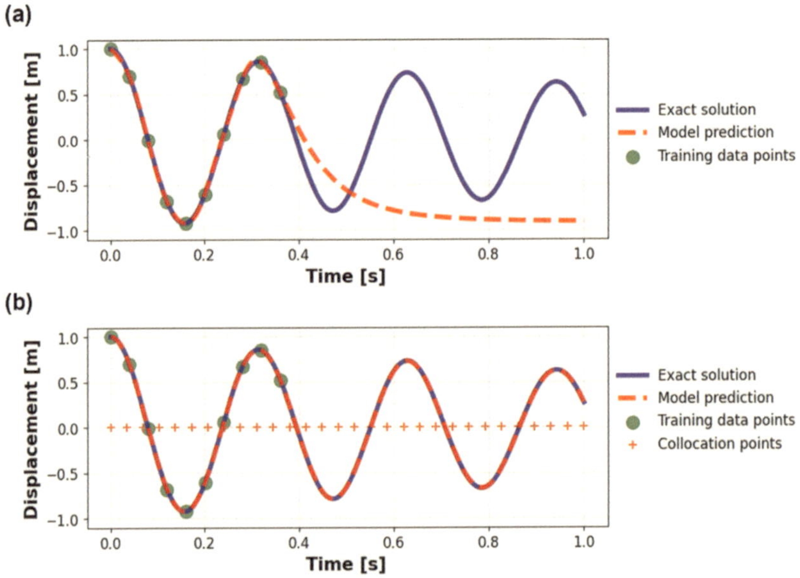

Figure 2.
Comparisons of the exact solution with the model prediction by ANN (a) and PINN (b).

ANN (the red dashed line in **Figure 2(a)**) accurately predicted only the data points on which it had been trained (the green circular marker in **Figure 2(a)**), failing to generalize to any other data. This result demonstrates the common issue of poor generalization performance in ANNs, where sparse training data limits the model's ability to learn the full spectrum of inherent physical properties, causing it to be biased toward only the observed data [43]. Therefore, the use of ANN in engineering and scientific field, where obtaining large amounts of training data is challenging [43], has significant limitations, suggesting the need for PINNs in scientific machine learning. **Figure 2(b)** confirms that the PINN accurately predicts the solution outside the training data region, outperforming the ANN with the same training data because the physical constraints embedded in the PINN guide the model predictions to conform to the underlying physical laws. This result suggests that PINN may exhibit superior generalization performance compared to ANN in real world applications where acquiring data is challenging.

3. Challenges and overcoming strategies in physics-informed neural networks

PINNs represent a significant advancement in the integration of scientific machine learning with physics, designed to model complex systems, where traditional data-driven approaches fall short. PINNs provide predictions that adhere to known physics and fundamental principles by embedding the governing equations of physical systems into neural networks. Hence, this architecture serves as an alternative to traditional data-driven methods for solving PDEs. However, a variety of challenges along with a series of promising results are being encountered as PINNs are actively researched. This section delves into these challenges and elucidates strategies to address them, thereby enhancing the robustness and versatility of PINNs across various scientific and engineering domains.

3.1 Mitigating complexity with domain decomposition

PINNs have shown remarkable abilities in addressing high-dimensional PDEs due to their superior approximation and generalization capabilities [46]. Despite this, PINNs can encounter difficulties when dealing with discontinuities in PDE solutions, often failing to accurately capture and predict sharp changes or discontinuities, which can lead to errors and reduce the accuracy of the solution [47]. To overcome these challenges, an innovative strategy known as extended PINN (XPINN) has been developed (**Figure 3**), which involves decomposing the computational domain into multiple subdomains [48]. This method employs localized, robust networks specifically in regions with high-gradient solutions, leveraging known prior knowledge about the solution characteristics. In particular, the computational domain can be partitioned into N_{sub} number of non-overlapping regular or irregular subdomains. Within the XPINN framework, the neural network's output for the kth subdomain is defined as

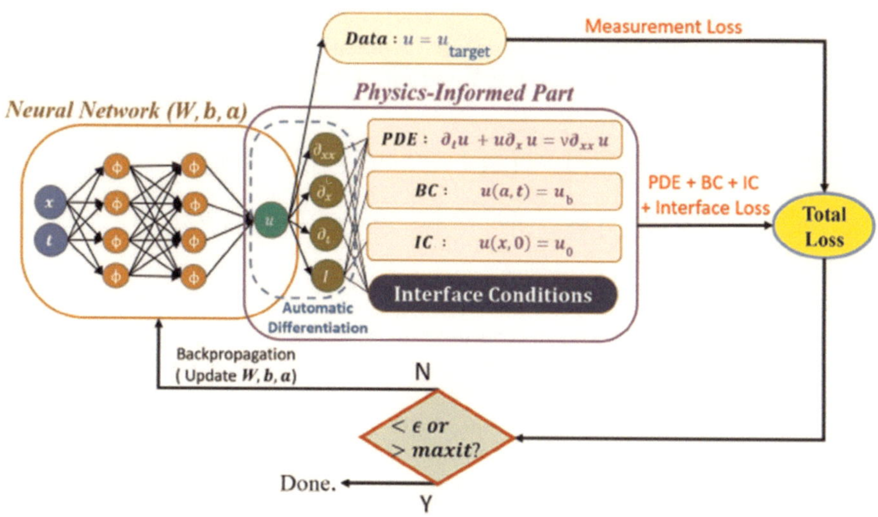

Figure 3.
The schematic of the XPINN sub-net employed in a subdomain, integrating neural network and physics-informed components [48].

$$u_{\tilde{\Theta}_k}(z) = N\left(z; \tilde{\Theta}_k\right) \in \Omega_k.\mathrm{k} = 1, 2, \ldots, N_{sub} \tag{8}$$

Then, the final solution is obtained as follows

$$u_{\tilde{\Theta}}(z) = \sum_{i=1}^{N_{u_k}} u_{\tilde{\Theta}_k}(z) \cdot \mathrm{I}_{\Omega_k}(\mathrm{z}), \tag{9}$$

where the indicator function $\mathrm{I}\Omega_k$ (z) is defined as

$$\mathrm{I}_{\Omega_k}(\mathrm{z}) = \begin{cases} 0, & \text{if } z \notin \Omega_k \\ 1, & \text{if } z \in \Omega_k \\ 1/S, & \text{if } z \text{ is on the interface within } \Omega_k \end{cases}, \tag{10}$$

where S denotes the number of subdomains intersecting along the interface. Each individual PINN operates independently within its assigned subdomain, thereby improving the network's capability to accurately capture and represent complex behaviors.

The XPINN framework leverages the deployment of multiple neural networks across smaller subdomains [49]. A key advantage of XPINNs is their enhanced representation and parallelization capacity, which is essential for accurately predicting complex PDE solutions. By enabling both spatial and temporal parallelization, XPINNs can significantly reduce training costs. In each subdomain, the networks can be optimally designed with specific hyperparameters such as network depth and width of hidden layers, the number and placement of residual points, nonlinear activation functions, and optimization strategies. For subdomains with complex solution characteristics, deeper networks may be employed, whereas shallower networks can be utilized in regions with simpler, smoother solutions.

The XPINN is designed to minimize a comprehensive loss function that considers both individual subdomain losses and interface losses, effectively balancing data accuracy and adherence to physical laws across the entire system. The XPINN loss function is defined at the subdomain level, while also incorporating interface conditions to ensure continuity and coherence between subdomains. Training an XPINN involves minimizing this complete loss function, which is defined as:

$$\begin{aligned} \mathcal{L}\left(\tilde{\Theta}_k\right) = {} & W_{u_k}\mathcal{L}_{u_k}\left(\tilde{\Theta}_k; \left\{x_{u_k}^{(i)}\right\}_{i=1}^{N_{u_k}}\right) + W_{\mathcal{F}_k}\mathcal{L}_{\mathcal{F}_k}\left(\tilde{\Theta}_k; \left\{x_{\mathcal{F}_k}^{(i)}\right\}_{i=1}^{N_{\mathcal{F}_k}}\right) \\ & + W_{I_k}\mathcal{L}_{u_{avg}}\left(\tilde{\Theta}_k; \left\{x_{I_k}^{(i)}\right\}_{i=1}^{N_{I_k}}\right) + W_{I_{\mathcal{F}_k}}\mathcal{L}_{\mathcal{R}}\left(\tilde{\Theta}_k; \left\{x_{I_k}^{(i)}\right\}_{i=1}^{N_{I_k}}\right) \end{aligned} \tag{11}$$

where $k = 1, 2, \ldots, N_{sub}$. The weight W_{u_k}, $W_{\mathcal{F}_k}$, W_{I_k} and $W_{I_{\mathcal{F}_k}}$ correspond to the loss term for discrepancies in data, residual errors, and interface conditions, including both residual and average solution continuity at the interface, respectively. Each loss function is defined as:

$$\mathcal{L}_{u_k}\left(\tilde{\Theta}_k; \left\{x_{u_k}^{(i)}\right\}_{i=1}^{N_{u_k}}\right) = \frac{1}{N_{u_k}}\sum_{i=1}^{N_{u_k}}\left|u^i - u_{\Theta_k}\left(x_{u_k}^i\right)\right|^2 \tag{12}$$

$$\mathcal{L}_{\mathcal{F}_k}\left(\tilde{\Theta}_k; \left\{x_{\mathcal{F}_k}^{(i)}\right\}_{i=1}^{N_{\mathcal{F}_k}}\right) = \frac{1}{N_{\mathcal{F}_k}}\sum_{i=1}^{N_{\mathcal{F}_k}}\left|\mathcal{F}_{\tilde{\Theta}_k}\left(x_{\mathcal{F}_k}^i\right)\right|^2 \tag{13}$$

$$\mathcal{L}_{u_{avg}}\left(\tilde{\Theta}_k; \left\{x_{I_k}^{(i)}\right\}_{i=1}^{N_{I_k}}\right) = \sum_{\forall k^+}\left(\frac{1}{N_{I_q}}\sum_{i=1}^{N_{I_k}}\left|u_{\tilde{\Theta}_k}\left(x_{I_k}^i\right) - \left\{\left\{u\left(x_{I_k}^i\right)\right\}\right\}\right|^2\right) \tag{14}$$

$$\mathcal{L}_{\mathcal{R}}\left(\tilde{\Theta}_k; \left\{x_{I_k}^{(i)}\right\}_{i=1}^{N_{I_k}}\right) = \sum_{\forall k^+}\frac{1}{N_{I_k}}\sum_{i=1}^{N_{I_k}}\left|\mathcal{F}_{\tilde{\Theta}_k}\left(x_{I_k}^i\right) - \mathcal{F}_{\tilde{\Theta}_{k^+}}\left(x_{I_k}^i\right)\right|^2 \tag{15}$$

where terms $\mathcal{L}_{u_k}$ and $\mathcal{L}_{\mathcal{F}_k}$ represent the data mismatch and residual losses, respectively, and $\mathcal{F}_{\tilde{\Theta}_k}$ denotes the PDEs residual terms of each subdomain. The residual loss term $\mathcal{L}_{\mathcal{R}}$ ensures residual continuity at the interface region between separate networks in subdomains k and k^+, where the superscript $^+$ indicates neighboring subdomain(s). Both $\mathcal{L}_{\mathcal{R}}$ and $\mathcal{L}_{u_{avg}}$ are defined for all neighboring subdomain k^+, as indicated by the summation over all k^+ in their respective expressions. These interface conditions enable the transfer of information between neighboring subdomains, playing a vital role in the convergence and overall accuracy of the subdomain solutions.

The XPINN architecture simplifies complex PDE solutions by decomposing them into multiple simpler components, thereby reducing the complexity required to learn each part and enhancing generalization. XPINNs also provide flexibility through time-domain decomposition for all differential equations and the ability to manage arbitrarily shaped complex sub-regions. This methodology ensures robust and accurate estimation of responses and other complex phenomena in systems modeled by PINNs.

3.2 Loss balancing with adaptive weighting

Most PINNs encounter a common convergence issue due to loss function imbalance, which arises from different optimization rates of multiple loss functions. Specifically, each of these functions contributes to the overall training objective but may have vastly different scales and sensitivities. For example, one loss function might represent the governing equation in thermodynamics, while another could enforce an initial condition. The different complexity in training these loss functions can lead to discrepancies in the magnitudes of optimizing gradients during training. This discrepancy often results in a situation where optimizing one loss function significantly overshadows the others, thereby stalling the overall convergence of the network.

To overcome this challenge, adaptive weighting methods are being actively researched, including self-adaptive [26] and learning rate annealing [28]. These methods achieve convergence by adjusting the gradient differences derived from each loss function. In particular, adaptive weighting using the neural tangent kernel (NTK) [50], a widely used method, addresses the optimization imbalance caused by multiple loss functions. This strategy uses NTK to dynamically adjust adaptive weights during training, guaranteeing that all loss terms converge equitably and thereby preserving overall balance. The standard loss function of PINNs with adaptive weights is as follows:

$$L(\theta, \lambda_D, \lambda_P, \lambda_B, \lambda_I) = \lambda_D L_D(\theta) + \lambda_P L_P(\theta) + \lambda_I L_I(\theta) + \lambda_B L_B(\theta) \tag{16}$$

where θ, L_D, L_P, L_B, L_I, and λ_* represent the trainable parameters, data fitting loss, physics loss, boundary condition loss, initial condition loss, and adaptive weights for each loss function, respectively. Note that the vanilla loss function of PINNs is the same as when λ_* is 1. Note also that there may not be a specific loss function depending on the problem being solved using PINN. To determine the adaptive weights for each loss in Eq. (16), the NTK of PINN $H^{NTK}(\theta)$ is defined as follows:

$$H_{ij}^{NTK}(\theta_n) = \left\langle \frac{dT^i(\theta_n)}{d\theta_n}, \frac{dT^j(\theta_n)}{d\theta_n} \right\rangle, \quad i,j = 1,2,\cdots,N,$$
$$T^k(\theta_n) = \begin{cases} X^k - \hat{X}^k, 1 \le k \le N_D \\ \widehat{Res_P}^k, N_D < k \le N_D + N_P \\ \widehat{Res_{BC}}^k, N_D + N_P < k \le N_D + N_P + N_B \\ {X_0}^k - \widehat{X_0}^k, N_D + N_P + N_B < k \le N \end{cases}, \tag{17}$$

where θ_n denotes parameters of the PINN at the n-th iteration, and $N = N_D + N_P + N_I + N_B$ represents the total collocation points considering data fitting, physics, initial condition, and boundary condition. Then, λ^k, representing the adaptive weights of the k-th collocation point, is obtained as follows:

$$\lambda_\psi = \frac{\sum_{k=1}^{N} H_{kk}^{NTK}(\theta_n)}{\sum_{k=1}^{N_\psi} H_{kk}^{NTK}(\theta_n)}, \psi \in \{D,P,B,I\} \tag{18}$$

where H_{kk}^{NTK} represents the k-th diagonal entry of the NTK matrix, which indicates the backpropagation gradient of the loss function. This balancing strategy is crucial because unbalanced gradients can significantly hinder the optimization process, preventing the network from finding a solution that satisfies the imposed physical constraints.

3.3 Extending capabilities through deep neural operator

In real-world applications, engineers often face the challenge of predicting outcomes under diverse operating conditions that differ from the specific conditions in which the neural network was trained. However, conventional PINNs that use DNNs are typically designed to train and predict based on specific initial, boundary, or geometric conditions. These inherent characteristics necessitate independent training processes, such as retraining or transfer learning [51], to adapt to new operating conditions. This additional training is not only time-consuming but also computationally expensive, limiting its use as a surrogate model. Therefore, significant research efforts have been directed toward developing more capable neural network to address these challenges.

Deep Operator Network (DON) has become a state-of-the-art surrogate model due to its ability to approximate nonlinear operators through function-to-function mapping [31]. Hence, once DON is trained, it can predict results for new operational conditions, effectively addressing both interpolation and extrapolation tasks without additional retraining. Specifically, DON integrates two distinct neural networks (**Figure 4**): the branch and trunk networks. The branch network handles discretized inputs from the input functions, such as initial conditions, boundary conditions, or external forcing terms, represented as $\boldsymbol{u} = [u(t_1), u(t_2), u(t_3), \cdots, u(t_{N-1}), u(t_N)]$, whereas the trunk network uses spatiotemporal coordinates $\boldsymbol{y} \in \mathbb{R}^d$ as inputs. The branch network is responsible for encoding

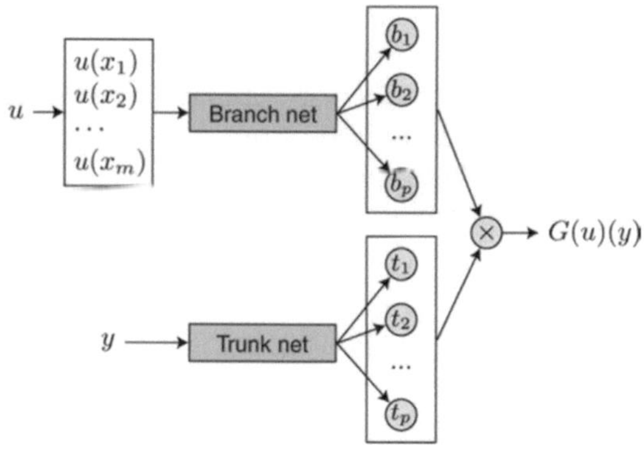

Figure 4.
Graphical illustration of DON [31].

the input function at specific points within the domain. This process is crucial for enabling the network to serve as a surrogate model under varying specific initial or boundary conditions. Simultaneously, the trunk network is designed to handle the spatial temporal coordinates for values of interest. Then, the outputs of both networks are integrated through a dot product operation, such that $G(\boldsymbol{u})(\boldsymbol{y})$ becomes a function of $\boldsymbol{y}$ on $\boldsymbol{u}$. Specifically, the outputs from both networks are obtained by forward propagation through an L-hidden layer DON based on a multilayer perceptron, as detailed below. The hidden layer outputs $\boldsymbol{H}_u$ and $\boldsymbol{H}_y$ for the branch network and the trunk network are obtained as follows:

$$\boldsymbol{H}_u^{(1)} = \varnothing\left(\boldsymbol{W}_u^{(1)}\boldsymbol{u} + \boldsymbol{b}_u^{(1)}\right), \boldsymbol{H}_y^{(1)} = \varnothing\left(\boldsymbol{W}_y^{(1)}\boldsymbol{y} + \boldsymbol{b}_y^{(1)}\right), \tag{19}$$

$$\boldsymbol{H}_u^{(l)} = \varnothing\left(\boldsymbol{W}_u^{(l)}\boldsymbol{H}_u^{(l-1)} + \boldsymbol{b}_u^{(l)}\right), \boldsymbol{H}_y^{(l)} = \varnothing\left(\boldsymbol{W}_y^{(l)}H_y^{(l-1)} + \boldsymbol{b}_y^{(l)}\right), \quad l = 2, \cdots, L-1, \tag{20}$$

$$\boldsymbol{O}_u = \boldsymbol{H}_u^{(L)} = \varnothing\left(\boldsymbol{W}_u^{(L)}\boldsymbol{H}_u^{(L-1)} + \boldsymbol{b}_u^{(L)}\right), \boldsymbol{O}_y = \boldsymbol{H}_y^{(L)} = \varnothing\left(\boldsymbol{W}_y^{(L)}H_y^{(L-1)} + \boldsymbol{b}_y^{(L)}\right), \tag{21}$$

where $\varnothing$ represents an activation function and $\left\{\boldsymbol{W}_u^{(l)}, \boldsymbol{b}_u^{(l)}\right\}_{l=1}^{L}$ and $\left\{\boldsymbol{W}_y^{(l)}, \boldsymbol{b}_y^{(l)}\right\}_{l=1}^{L}$ refer to the weights and biases of the hidden layers for the branch network and the trunk network, respectively. In both networks, the initial hidden layers take $\boldsymbol{u}$ and $\boldsymbol{y}$ as inputs, whereas following hidden layers utilize the outputs of the previous hidden layer $\boldsymbol{H}_u^{(l-1)}$ and $\boldsymbol{H}_y^{(l-1)}$. The inputs $\boldsymbol{u}$ and $\boldsymbol{y}$ are converted to output vectors $\left[O_u^1, O_u^2, O_u^3, \cdots, O_u^{q-1}, O_u^q\right]^T \in \mathbb{R}^q$ and $\left[O_y^1, O_y^2, O_y^3, \cdots, O_y^{q-1}, O_y^q\right]^T \in \mathbb{R}^q$ through the branch and trunk networks, respectively. Finally, the neural network predictions are derived by integrating the output vectors from the branch and trunk networks as follows:

$$G(\boldsymbol{u})(\boldsymbol{y}) \approx \hat{G}(\boldsymbol{u})(\boldsymbol{y}) = \sum_{k=1}^{q} \underbrace{O_u^k(u(t_1), u(t_2), \cdots, u(t_N))}_{branch} \underbrace{O_y^k(\boldsymbol{y})}_{trunk} \tag{22}$$

where $\hat{G}(\boldsymbol{u})(\boldsymbol{y})$ denotes a predicted DON value, while $G(\boldsymbol{u})(\boldsymbol{y})$ corresponds to the ground truth value.

The capability of DON to capture operators can be leveraged as a powerful surrogate model for multiphysics systems governed by a range of ODEs and PDEs. Therefore, active research has been directed toward predicting responses under a variety of conditions within the fields of elastic-plastic stress [52], heat conduction [53], and fracture mechanics [54]. Furthermore, numerous studies are dedicated to improving the capabilities of DON through architectural advancements, integrating neural networks such as encoders [55], LSTM [56], or ResUNet [52].

3.4 Improving architecture through Fourier feature embedding

PINNs often face challenges when addressing multi-scale problems. PINNs operate with a relatively limited number of data points within the computational domain. One significant challenge is spectral bias, a phenomenon where multi-layer perceptron tends to train solutions and their PDE residuals starting with the lowest frequency components. Spectral bias is an intriguing characteristic observed in the neural networks training, where these networks tend to learn simpler or lower-frequency components before capturing more complex or higher-frequency components of the target function [57]. This phenomenon can significantly influence the training dynamics and generalization abilities of neural networks.

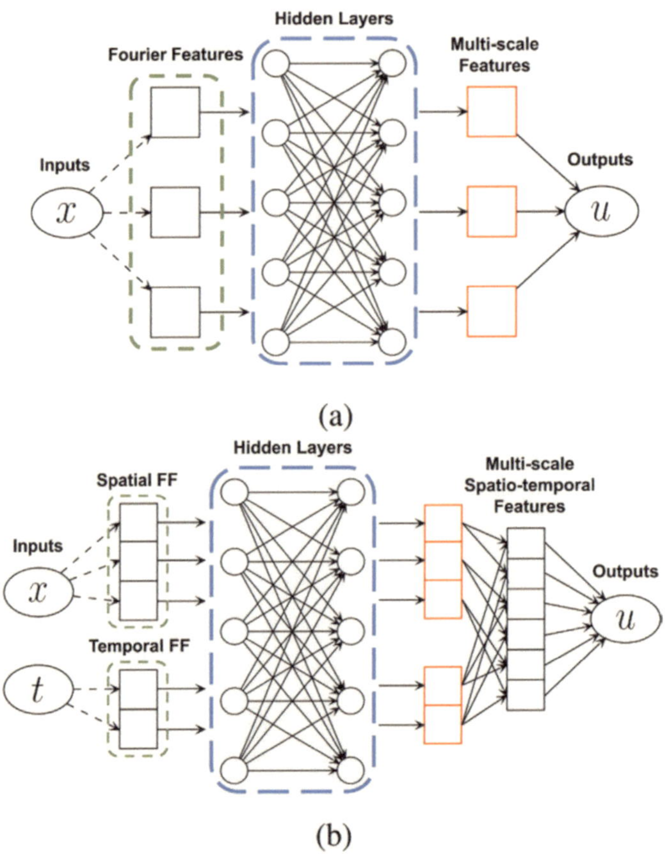

Figure 5.
(a) Multi-scale Fourier feature network, and (b) Spatio-temporal multi-scale Fourier feature network [57].

To address the multi-scale problem challenges in PINNs, particularly spectral bias, an innovative network architecture incorporating Fourier feature embeddings has been developed [33]. This approach involves enhancing the input space using Fourier features, which helps the network represent and learn higher frequency components more effectively.

As illustrated in **Figure 5(a)**, the methodology involves applying Fourier feature embeddings. The inputs are embedded with the Fourier feature and then fed into a conventional multi-layer perceptron. The final outputs are concatenated using a linear function. The forward pass of Fourier feature embedding is detailed as follows:

$$\boldsymbol{\alpha}^i(\boldsymbol{x}) = \begin{bmatrix} \cos\left(2\pi \boldsymbol{F}^i \boldsymbol{x}\right) \\ \sin\left(2\pi \boldsymbol{F}^i \boldsymbol{x}\right) \end{bmatrix}, \quad \textit{for } i = 1, 2, \dots, M, \tag{23}$$

$$\boldsymbol{H}_1^i = \phi\left(\boldsymbol{W}_1 \cdot \boldsymbol{\alpha}^j(\boldsymbol{x}) + \boldsymbol{b}_1\right), \quad \textit{for } i = 1, 2, \dots, M, \tag{24}$$

$$\boldsymbol{H}_l^i = \phi\left(\boldsymbol{W}_l \cdot \boldsymbol{H}_{l-1}^j(\boldsymbol{x}) + \boldsymbol{b}_l\right), \quad \textit{for } l = 2, \dots, i = 1, 2, \dots, M, \tag{25}$$

$$f_\theta(\boldsymbol{x}) = \boldsymbol{W}_{L+1}\left[\boldsymbol{H}_L^1, \dots, \boldsymbol{H}_L^M\right] + \boldsymbol{b}_{L+1} \tag{26}$$

where ϕ and $\boldsymbol{\alpha}^i$ represent nonlinear activation functions and Fourier feature mappings, respectively. Each $\boldsymbol{F}^i$ is sampled from the normal distribution $\mathcal{N}\left(0, \sigma^i\right)$, and remains fixed during model training, meaning that $\boldsymbol{F}^i$ are not trainable parameters [33]. The inputs are embedded with different frequencies, and after forward propagation, all frequency components are combined through a linear layer to ensure they are learned at the same convergence rate [58].

Time-dependent problems exhibit multi-scale behavior not only across spatial dimensions but also over temporal scales. To address these multi-scale challenges in spatial-temporal domains, an innovative multi-scale Fourier feature architecture has been proposed [59]. Specifically, the neural network's feed-forward pass is defined as follows

$$\boldsymbol{\alpha}_s^i(\boldsymbol{x}) = \begin{bmatrix} \cos\left(2\pi \boldsymbol{F}_s^i \boldsymbol{x}\right) \\ \sin\left(2\pi \boldsymbol{F}_s^i \boldsymbol{x}\right) \end{bmatrix}, \boldsymbol{H}_{t,1}^i = \phi\left(\boldsymbol{W}_1 \cdot \boldsymbol{\alpha}_t^i(t) + \boldsymbol{b}_1\right), \quad \textit{for } i = 1, 2, \dots, M_s, \tag{27}$$

$$\boldsymbol{\alpha}_t^j(t) = \begin{bmatrix} \cos\left(2\pi \boldsymbol{F}_t^j t\right) \\ \sin\left(2\pi \boldsymbol{F}_t^j t\right) \end{bmatrix}, \boldsymbol{H}_{s,1}^i = \phi\left(\boldsymbol{W}_1 \cdot \boldsymbol{\alpha}_t^i(\boldsymbol{x}) + \boldsymbol{b}_1\right), \quad \textit{for } j = 1, 2, \dots, M_t, \tag{28}$$

$$\boldsymbol{H}_{s,l}^i = \phi\left(\boldsymbol{W}_l \cdot \boldsymbol{H}_{s,l-1}^i + \boldsymbol{b}_l\right), \quad \textit{for } i = 1, 2, \dots, M_x \textit{ and } l = 2, \dots, L, \tag{29}$$

$$\boldsymbol{H}_{t,l}^j = \phi\left(\boldsymbol{W}_l \cdot \boldsymbol{H}_{t,l-1}^j + \boldsymbol{b}_l\right), \quad \textit{for } i = 1, 2, \dots, M_t \textit{ and } l = 2, \dots, L. \tag{30}$$

$$\boldsymbol{H}_L^{i,j} = \boldsymbol{H}_{s,L}^i \odot \boldsymbol{H}_{t,L}^i, \tag{31}$$

$$f_\theta(\boldsymbol{x}, t) = \boldsymbol{W}_{L+1}\left[\boldsymbol{H}_L^{1,1}, \dots, \boldsymbol{H}_L^{M_t, M_x}\right] + \boldsymbol{b}_{L+1}. \tag{32}$$

where $\boldsymbol{\alpha}_x{}^i$ and $\boldsymbol{\alpha}_t{}^i$ represent spatial and temporal Fourier feature mappings, respectively, with $\odot$ denoting the point-wise multiplication. Each entry of $\boldsymbol{F}_x^i$ and $\boldsymbol{F}_t^j$

is sampled from $\mathcal{N}(0, \sigma_x^i)$ and $\mathcal{N}\left(0, \sigma_y^j\right)$, respectively, and these values are kept constant during the training of the model.

This structured approach ensures that the PINN can manage the natural low-frequency bias of neural networks and is capable of effectively learning and predicting high-frequency phenomena within the PDEs solutions. By embedding Fourier features directly into the input layer and merging them before producing the final output, the network utilizes the rich frequency information to achieve more precise and robust solutions for PDE. This architecture significantly improves the ability of PINNs to solve complex, multi-scale problems that are typically challenging for conventional machine learning models and some numerical methods. Note that the proposed models maintain computational efficiency by avoiding the introduction of additional trainable parameters and not requiring significantly more operations for their forward or backward pass compared to conventional PINN models.

4. Case studies in engineering applications

The potential of PINNs is actively being explored for real-world engineering applications. To address the inherent multiphysics nature of most real-world systems, PINNs should be extended to account for multiphysics in the system of interest [35]. However, incorporating multiphysics into a neural network increases the complexity, leading to convergence issues due to the more challenging training process. Additionally, having a comprehensive understanding of the target system and employing suitable strategies are crucial to ensuring optimal performance. This section presents two examples, where PINNs are applied to complex mechatronics systems, specifically involving a motor and a battery, by utilizing appropriate training strategies.

4.1 Application on an electric motor for virtual sensing and PHM

This subsection introduces the novel MPINN framework for virtual sensing and prognostics and health management (PHM) of electric motors [40]. The proposed framework is designed to accurately estimate electromagnetic responses in electric motors under various operational conditions. This MPINN utilizes novel strategies to manage complexities associated with rotational dynamics, improving both the accuracy and efficiency of network's predictions. The MPINN specifically estimates various electromagnetic fields, including magnetic vector potentials (A_z), electric fields (E_z), magnetic flux densities (B_x and B_y), and magnetic fields (H_z).

The proposed MPINN architecture integrates three crucial features to overcome the challenges of conventional networks. First, the MPINN utilizes various PDEs to describe the electromagnetic properties of motors [60], ensuring precise and reliable predictions even with limited data availability. These PDEs guide the neural network, providing supervision for accuracy. A notable innovation is the conversion of the motor's rotor coordinates from rotational (based on angular speed) to Cartesian coordinates. This transformation overcomes the limitations of conventional PINNs, which have difficulty with rotational machinery due to their fixed coordinate systems. By aligning the rotor and stator coordinates into a unified Cartesian framework, the MPINN effectively resolves component representation mismatches and accurately depicts the electromagnetic fields influenced by rotor movement. Second, the architecture incorporates distinct networks for each domain, integrating estimation results by considering the interface loss between the two sperate domains [49]. This approach allows for more targeted training on specific components, significantly enhancing the accuracy of electromagnetic response estimations. Additionally, an interface loss function merges the outputs from these separate networks, reducing discrepancies and errors at the interface between two domains. Third, the MPINN guarantee convergence of neural networks during training by implementing a learning rate annealing method. This method adjusts adaptive weights to balance the gradient stiffness across different loss types, thereby minimizing the overall loss [25]. This enhancement not only improves the accuracy and reliability of predictions but also makes the neural network more robust in managing the complexities associated with different loss functions.

The proposed MPINN was validated under five conditions, as detailed in **Table 2**. These conditions include four typical operating scenarios of the PMSM and one fault condition involving rotor axis eccentricity, which is the most common mechanical defect [61]. The MPINN was trained using data generated from a Finite Element Model (FEM) that covers the entire domain of the PMSM. The performance of MPINN was verified by comparing torques measured from an experimental PMSM testbed. Additionally, comparisons with the FEM confirmed the accuracy of electromagnetic characteristics across the entire domain [62, 63].

The accuracy of the MPINN for the electric motor was validated by comparing the experimental measurements from the those estimated by the FEM and MPINN. The torque measurements are only compared because measuring electromagnetic fields directly through the experiments is difficult, and only torque can be obtained. As illustrated in **Figure 6**, the torques predicted by the FEM (red line) and MPINN (blue line) are compared with those obtained from the experiments (black line) across the five different operational scenarios. Both models predicted the dynamic PMSM's torques accurately when controlling the motor driver's three-phase currents and rotor rotational speed. The average RMSEs for the FEM and MPINN were 0.0105 Nm and 0.0166 Nm, respectively, demonstrating the accurate estimation of the PMSM's electromagnetic responses by both models. Furthermore, these results highlight the potential of MPINN in effectively managing complex and nonlinear behaviors in data, showcasing its applicability in various scenarios.

The effectiveness of the proposed MPINN in predicting electromagnetic fields across the entire domain was demonstrated by comparing its results with those obtained from FEM. The prediction of electromagnetic fields from the FEM and MPINN is shown in **Figure 7**, along with the error of the proposed MPINN compared to the FEM under eccentricity fault conditions. Specifically, the RMSEs are 8.78e−5

Case	Description	Condition	Load	Speed [RPM]
1	Starting,no load	Normal	—	$0 \rightarrow 60$
2	Variational speed, no load	Normal	—	$60 \rightarrow 600 \rightarrow 60$
3	Constant speed, linearly increasing load	Normal	0 to 0.4 Nm (linear increase)	60
4	Breaking	Normal	Brake	$60 \rightarrow 0$
5	Starting, no load, eccentricity	Eccentricity	—	$0 \rightarrow 60$

Table 2.
Experimental datasets under various operational conditions [40].

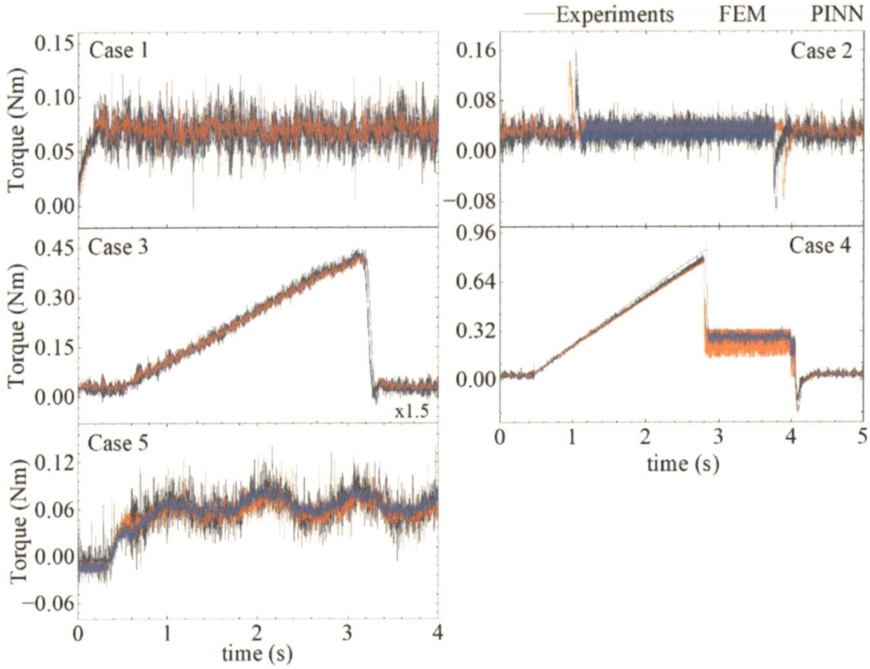

Figure 6.
Comparison of experimentally torque measurements with estimation results of FEM and MPINN across five different conditions [40].

for the magnetic vector potential, 4.86e−2 for the electric field, 5.64e−2 and 1.29e−1 for the magnetic flux density in the x and y directions, respectively, and 3.56e4 and 3.95e4 for the magnetic field in the x and y directions, respectively. These results show that the MPINN accurately estimates electromagnetic fields for the entire PMSM domain. Notably, errors in the electric field were observed across the entire domain due to a higher number of spatial training points compared to temporal ones, while errors in the magnetic flux density were confined to specific areas. This difference can be explained by the neural networks' tendency to provide more accurate estimates where training data points are more abundant.

This study highlights the superior performance of MPINN, which integrates physical constraints, compared to a conventional ANN lacking such constraints. As illustrated in **Figure 8**, the comparison of RMSEs for the electromagnetic responses predicted by the MPINN and the conventional ANN against the values derived from FEM. These results indicate that the RMSEs for the MPINN are consistently lower than those for the ANN in tested scenarios. Compared to the ANN, the MPINN achieves notable reductions in average RMSEs for the estimated values: 21.64% for the magnetic vector potential, 80.09% for the electric field, 70.91% and 39.44% for the magnetic flux densities in the x and y directions, respectively, and 58.39% and 53.83% for the magnetic fields in the x and y directions, respectively. These comparisons highlight the advantages of incorporating physical regularizations into the neural networks, enhancing the accuracy and robustness of estimation results compared to purely data-driven methods.

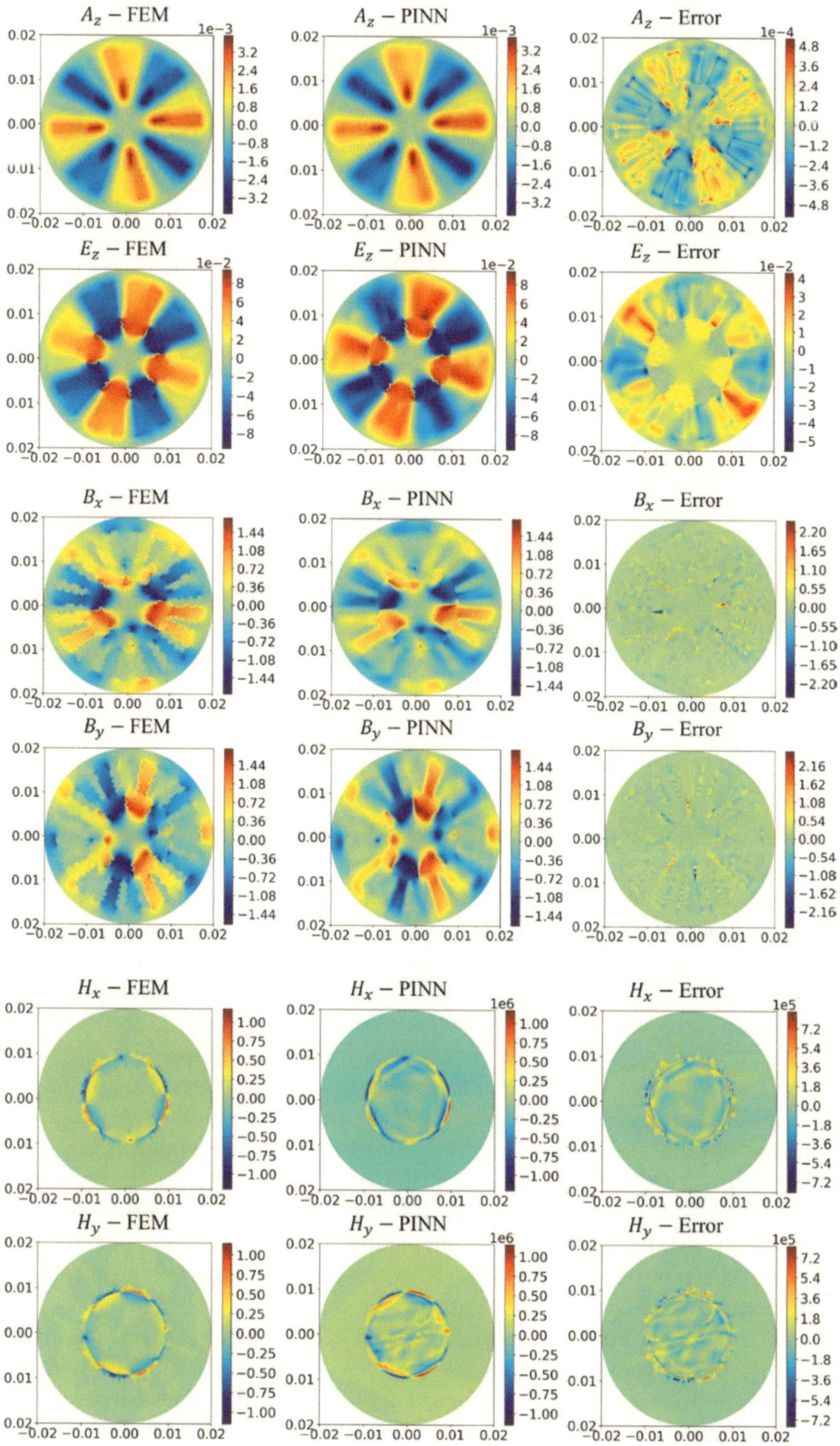

Figure 7.
Comparison of reference and estimated electromagnetic fields across eccentricity fault condition [40].

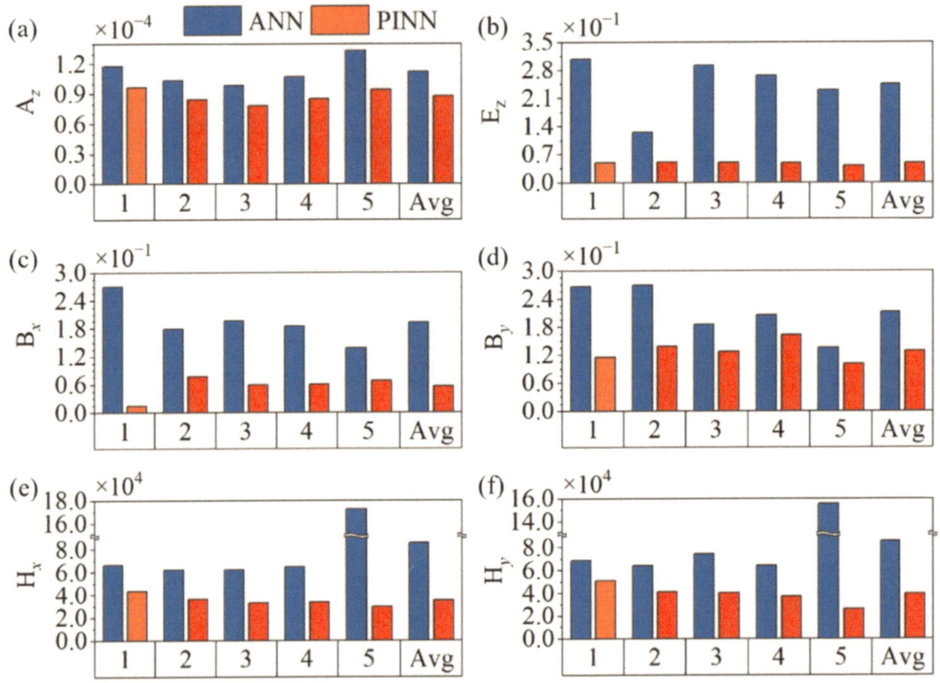

Figure 8.
RMSE comparison between ANN and MPINN estimation: (a) magnetic vector potential A_z, magnetic flux densities (b) B_x and (c) B_y, (d) electric field E_z, and magnetic fields (e) H_x, and (f) H_y [40].

Notably, as shown in **Figure 8(b)**, the MPINN could accurately estimate electromagnetic responses even when operational conditions changed significantly over time. In contrast, the purely data-driven approach faced difficulties in accurately capturing these variations. This highlights the effectiveness of incorporating physical principles, such as the temporal differentiation of the electric field and the magnetic vector potential via the PDE. This sharply contrasts with the ANN, which frequently violates physical laws due to having less data available compared to the network's capacity. Additionally, the distorted magnetic fields from asymmetric rotation pose significant challenges for the ANN when estimating electromagnetic responses under eccentric conditions. Consequently, the ANN is constrained in its ability to account for all intricate phenomena occurring in the PMSM under these operational conditions. Conversely, the MPINN, guided by the governing equation that defines the relationship between inputs and outputs, achieves robustness of estimation results. These analyses indicate that incorporating prior knowledge is crucial for PINN estimation. With the same dataset size, MPINNs enhance accuracy and ensure high reliability compared to conventional data-driven methods.

This research highlights that the proposed MPINN is a powerful and reliable solution for analyzing electromagnetic responses of PMSMs. While conventional FEM are accurate, they require substantial computational resources, and physical experiments typically yield data only for partial domains. In contrast, MPINNs offer a cost-effective alternative with rapid and accurate electromagnetic characterization capabilities. The MPINN not only addresses the limitations of conventional numerical methods by offering a mesh-free solver approach but also proves more efficient and cost-effective for characterizing electromagnetic properties in both normal and fault conditions.

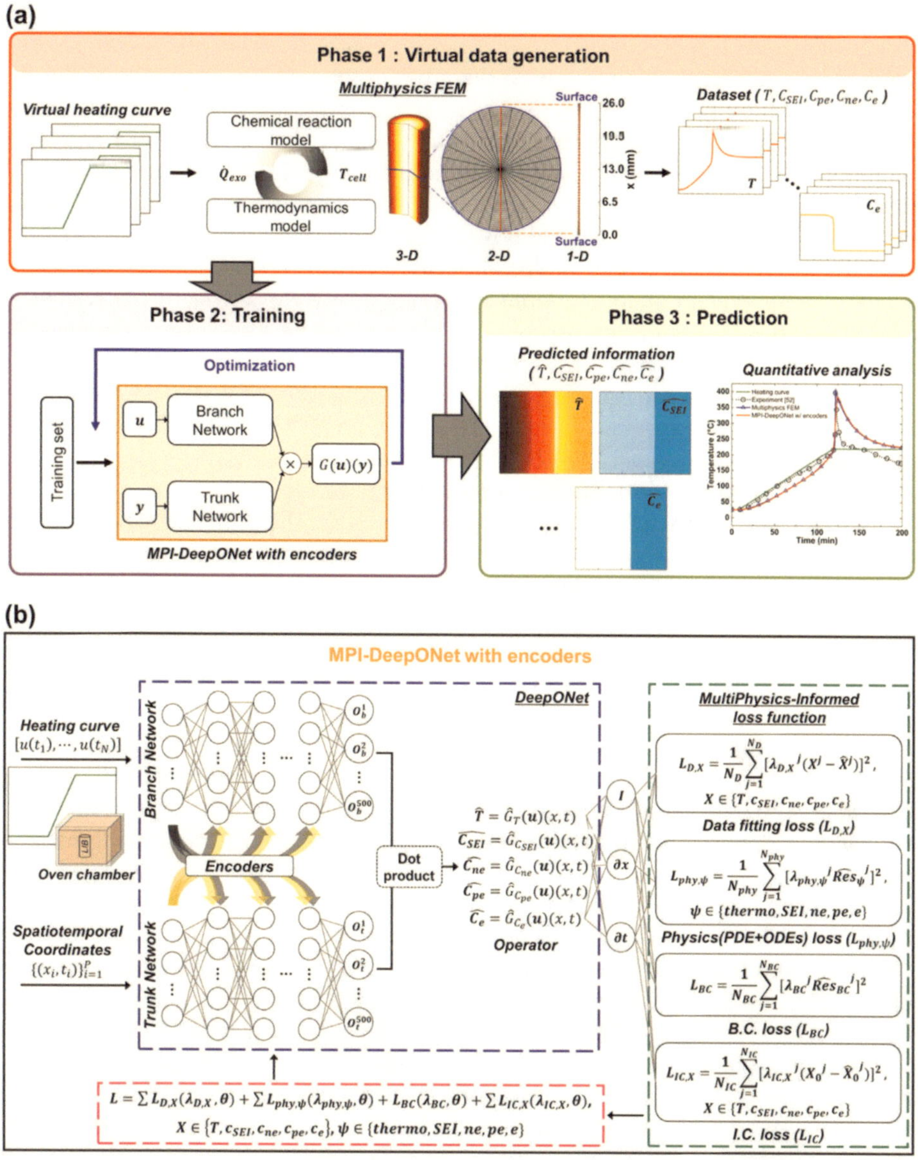

Figure 9.
(a) Flowchart for TR prediction, and (b) in-depth illustration of the MPI-DON incorporating encoders [37].

This makes MPINNs particularly suitable for PHM applications in electric vehicles and cyber-physical systems in production facilities, where control-oriented objectives are crucial.

4.2 Application for predicting thermal runaway of a lithium-ion battery

The integration of PINN and DON, called multiphysics-informed deep operator network (MPI-DON or MPI-DeepONet) incorporating encoders, is proposed for predicting thermal runaway (TR) under a range of heating conditions, providing a rapid and accurate surrogate model for TR prediction. This neural network uses the heating curve, representing thermal abuse conditions, as input to output the chemical concentrations of the positive electrode, negative electrode, solid electrolyte interphase (SEI), and electrolyte along with the internal temperature response of the lithium-ion battery (LIB).

MPI-DON incorporating encoders have three main features that play a crucial role in attaining accurate final stage TR predictions, organized into three phases (**Figure 9(a)**). First, phase 1 generates virtual data by employing FEA [64] at various heating conditions (**Figure 9(a)**, red box). Specifically, virtual data is generated to reflect the mechanism of chemical decomposition of LIB components due to temperature-dependent chain reactions involving positive electrode, negative electrode, SEI, and electrolyte. This mechanism is governed by the energy balance equation [65], Arrhenius equation [66], and heat transfer equations. MPI-DON incorporating encoders are trained with virtual data because it is challenging and expensive to conduct experiments for all operating conditions. This strategy also facilitates MPI-DON incorporating encoders in capturing hidden physics, such as four main chemical concentrations and the internal temperature response of the LIB during the training phase (**Figure 9(a)**, purple box). Therefore, the proposed neural network can function as a virtual sensor in practical uses by acquiring this key information through FEA. Note that virtual data generated under various heating conditions are separated into a training set and a test set, with the test set validating the capability of interpolation and extrapolation. Second, DON serves as a surrogate model for predicting TR in untrained conditions, utilizing the branch network and the trunk network for operator regression (**Figure 9(b)**, blue dashed box). As explained in Subsection 3.3, this strategy uses the branch and trunk networks to map one function (i.e., the heating condition) to another function (i.e., the responses of the cell) to approximate the solution of a nonlinear system of equations, which outperforms traditional neural networks that have to be retrained for every unseen condition. Furthermore, encoders [55] are added to the architecture of DON to resolve the issue of restricted information exchange, where branch network and trunk network interact only in the last layer. These encoders improve the ability of the DON to capture the complex response of the TR phenomenon by smoothing the input information flow to each hidden layer. Third, incorporating a novel training strategy that supervises multiple equations governing the TR of LIBs (**Figure 9(b)**, green dashed box), along with adaptive weights allocation based on the NTK method (**Figure 9(b)**, pink dashed box), can enhance the robustness and accuracy of the DON with encoders during the training phase. Thus, MPI-DON incorporating encoders can achieve convergence to the global minimum, thanks to the governing equations regulating the training process. Note that the input values and output values are normalized to convert the dimensionless values, addressing the mismatch between the neural network values and the physical quantities represented by the governing equations. After completing phase 2, phase 3 predicts the hidden states of a LIB, encompassing chemical concentrations and internal temperature distribution at diverse heating conditions (**Figure 9(a)**, green box).

The effectiveness of physics constraints is demonstrated by comparing MPI-DON incorporating encoders supervised by physics constraints to DON that relies solely on data during training. **Figure 10** shows an example of predicting an interpolation task in a test set, confirming the effectiveness of physics constraints for improving accuracy. Specifically, MPI-DON, achieving an RMSE of 7.6°C in temperature predictions (**Figure 10(a)**, red line), accurately predicts temperature evolutions over all time domains, even in regions without labeled data points. In contrast, DON, achieving an RMSE of 30.5°C in temperature predictions (**Figure 10(a)**, blue line), shows large

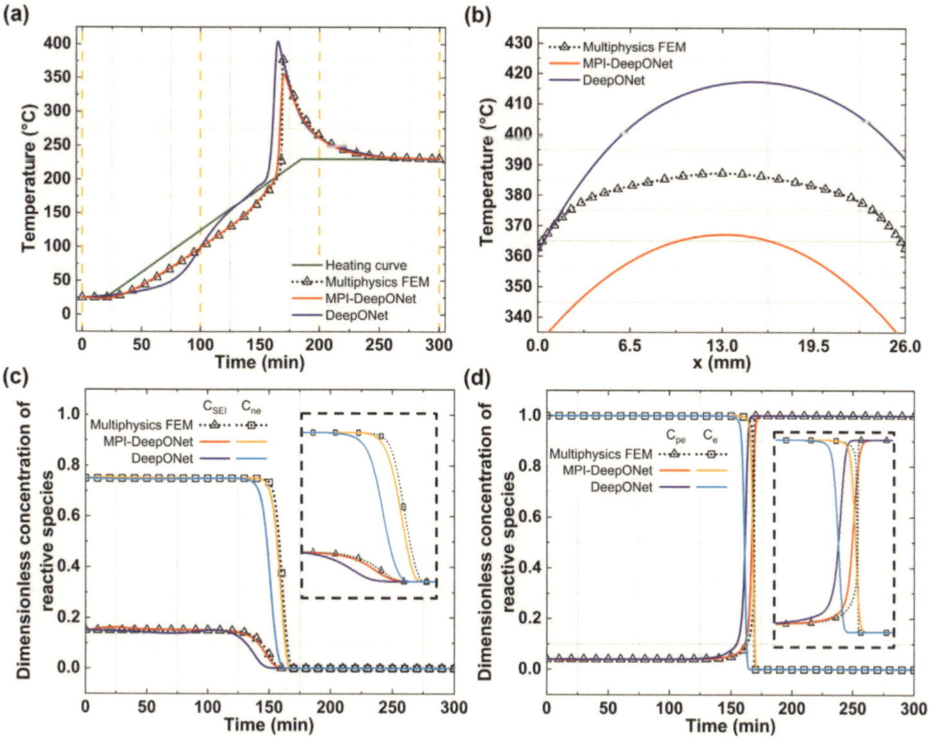

Figure 10.
Comparison of MPI-DON and DON with multiphysics FEMs for TR in test set 1: (a) predicted mean temperature evolution, (b) internal LIB temperature distribution at TR peak, (c) predicted mean c_{SEI} and c_{ne} evolution, and (d) predicted mean c_{pe} and c_e evolution [37].

errors in the time domain without labeled data points when TR occurs. Remarkably, DON shows little error on the trained data points labeled 0, 100, 200, and 300 min (**Figure 10(a)**, yellow dashed line), but significant error on the untrained data points. MPI-DON predicts responses accurately across all time domains due to physics constraints. This result suggests that purely data-driven methods may be incapable of predicting the multiphysics response of LIBs, resulting in convergence to a local minimum due to insufficient training data. **Figure 10(b)** compares the internal temperature distribution along the center cross-section line of the LIB at the peak point, illustrating results from multiphysics FEM (black dotted line with triangles), MPI-DON (red line), and DON (blue line). This result reveals the role of physics constraints in ensuring predictions match the multiphysics characteristics of LIBs. Specifically, the symmetrical internal temperature distributions within the LIB shown by multiphysics FEM and MPI-DON, centered around the midpoint due to isotropic conduction, contrast with the asymmetric temperature distribution produced by DON, confirming the effectiveness of physics constraints. In **Figure 10(c)** and **(d)**, the chemical concentrations are compared among multiphysics FEM (black dotted lines with triangles and squares), MPI-DON (red and orange lines), and DON (blue and light blue lines). The inset figure shows that MPI-DON accurately predicts the sharp variations in chemical concentration during TR, in contrast to DON, which shows significant inaccuracies. This result confirms that MPI-DON accurately predicts TR occurrence from heating conditions, predicting key chemical concentrations and temperature accurately.

The contribution of supervision from multiphysics is highlighted by comparing predictions from MPI-DON and DON based on varying numbers of data collocation points. Data collocation intervals of 15, 20, 30, 50, 60, and 100 minutes correspond to 14,364, 10,944, 7524, 4788, 4104, and 2736 points, respectively, for training the neural networks. All other training conditions, including physics, initial, and boundary condition collocation points, remain constant. The mean and 95% confidence interval of RMSE for temperature prediction are determined for the test sets with five random initial parameters (**Figure 11**). Results show that MPI-DON consistently predicts TR phenomena more accurately than DON, regardless of data collocation point density, due to supervision by multiphysics characteristics. Conversely, RMSE of DON increases significantly as data become sparse, indicating a high dependence on data. The confidence interval for MPI-DON is narrower, especially with 100-minute intervals, indicating better stability even with sparse data. This observation suggests robustness of MPI-DON in industrial applications where data is often limited. While DON is cost-effective with ample data (intervals less than 30 minutes), physics constraints are generally advantageous for real-world applications.

MPI-DON incorporating encoders offers a significantly faster inference time compared to multiphysics FEM. Specifically, MPI-DON takes just 0.5 ms for TR prediction, while multiphysics FEM takes about 7 seconds, making MPI-DON 10,000 times faster. After a 720-minute training phase, MPI-DON continues to provide instant predictions, unlike multiphysics FEM, whose prediction time increases linearly with the number of heating cases. This efficiency makes MPI-DON more versatile and effective for testing LIB reliability under various conditions through Monte Carlo analysis, a task that would be time-consuming and costly with FEM. The speed of MPI-DON also suits real-time applications, such as TR management in thermal systems.

In conclusion, this approach overcomes the limitations of traditional numerical methods and data-driven techniques, offering a solution that is both computationally

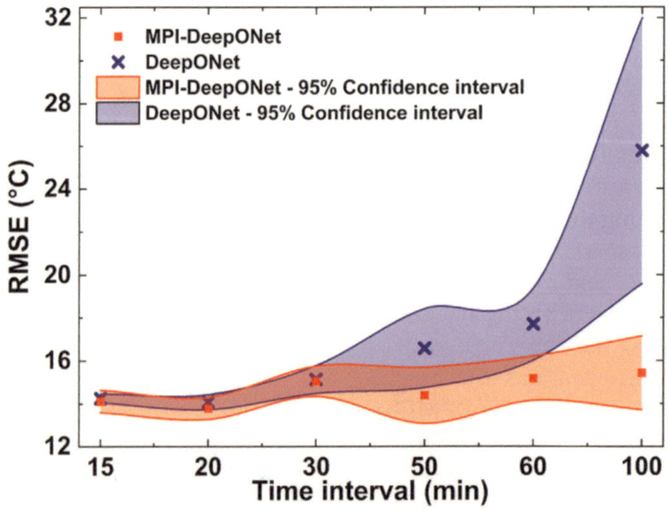

Figure 11.
Temperature RMSE of MPI-DON and DON across various time interval of the data collocation points [37].

efficient and highly accurate. The proposed neural network offers indispensable data for sophisticated thermal battery management systems, thereby improving the reliability and safety of LIBs. This advancement propels the development of digital twins for electric transport systems through artificial intelligence transformation. Additionally, beyond addressing the TR phenomenon, this approach can be implemented in various systems, furthering the impact of artificial intelligence transformation across various domains.

5. Conclusion

This chapter delved into the potential of artificial intelligence, particularly focusing on PINN, which are adept at handling complex and nonlinear systems in real-world engineering. PINN effectively addresses challenges such as data scarcity and imbalance by integrating physics and fundamental principles during the training phase. PINN ensures predictions adhere to physical laws, even when data is sparse, by embedding governing equations as constraints within the loss function. However, incorporating physical constraints into neural networks increases the training complexity, necessitating appropriate strategies for optimal performance. Especially, strategies to address complexity become crucial when applying PINN to multiphysics systems, where multiple physics are coupled. Therefore, this chapter also introduced various strategies for applying PINN to mechatronic systems such as motor and battery. The principles of PINN summarized and the introduced framework for applying PINN to multiphysics systems will be crucial in advancing technological innovation, ensuring system reliability, and influencing the future of engineering and applied sciences.

Acknowledgements

This work was supported by the Air Force Office of Scientific Research under award number FA2386-23-1-4094, by the National Research Foundation of Korea (NRF) grant funded by the Korean government (MSIT) [grant number 2020R1C1C1003829], by the Korea Institute of Machinery and Materials [grant No. NK250B].

Nomenclature

DNN	deep neural network
DeepONet	deep operator network
FEM	finite element model
LIB	lithium-ion battery
MLP	multi-layer perceptron
MPI-DeepONet	multiphysics-informed deep operator network
MSE	mean squared error
NTK	neural tangent kernel
PDE	partial differential equation
PHM	prognostics and health management
PINN	physics informed neural network

RMSE	root mean squared error
SEI	solid electrolyte interphase
TR	thermal runaway

Symbols

$\boldsymbol{B}$	magnetic flux density
$\boldsymbol{b}_*^{(l)}$	bias of the lth hidden layer
c_e	value of electrolyte
c_{ne}	value of negative electrode
c_{pe}	value of positive electrode
c_{SEI}	value of SEI
$\boldsymbol{f}$	final output of the neural network
$\mathbf{F}^{\mathbf{i}}$	Fourier feature mapping matrix for the i-th embedding
G_*	operator output
$\boldsymbol{H}_*^{(\mathrm{l})}$	output of the lth hidden layer
H^{NTK}	NTK matrix
$\boldsymbol{I}$	indicator function
L	total loss function
N_*	number of collocation points
$\boldsymbol{O}_*$	final output
$\boldsymbol{\Phi}$	Fourier feature mapping of input
Res_*	residual of governing equation
T	time span
L_*	loss term
$\boldsymbol{W}$	weight for each loss function
$\boldsymbol{W}_*^{(l)}$	weight of the lth hidden layer

Greek letters

λ_*	adaptive weights
θ	trainable parameters
u	reference solution of the PDE

Subscripts

0	initial value
BC	boundary condition
D	data fitting
I	initial condition
P	physics
q	subdomain
u	branch network
y	trunk network

Superscripts

$\hat{}$	predicted solution of neural network

DOI: http://dx.doi.org/10.5772/intechopen.1006130

Author details

Seho Son[1], Jinho Jeong[1], Dayeon Jeong[1], Kyung ho Sun[2] and Ki-Yong Oh[1,3]*

1 Department of Mechanical Convergence Engineering, Hanyang University, Seoul, Republic of Korea

2 Virtual Engineering Research Center, Korea Institute of Machinery and Materials, Daejeon, Republic of Korea

3 School of Mechanical Engineering, Hanyang University, Seoul, Republic of Korea

*Address all correspondence to: kiyongoh@hanyang.ac.kr

References

[1] Vaswani A, Shazeer N, Parmar N, Uszkoreit J, Jones L, Gomez AN, et al. Attention is all you need. Advances in Neural Information Processing Systems. 2017;**30**. DOI: 10.48550/arXiv.1706.03762

[2] Devlin J, Chang M-W, Lee K, Toutanova K. Bert: Pre-Training of Deep Bidirectional Transformers for Language Understanding. arXiv preprint arXiv:1810.04805. 2018. DOI: 10.48550/arXiv.1810.04805

[3] Lei S, Yi W, Ying C, Ruibin W. Review of attention mechanism in natural language processing. Data Analysis and Knowledge Discovery. 2020;**4**:1-14. DOI: 10.11925/infotech.2096-3467.2019.1317

[4] Krizhevsky A, Sutskever I, Hinton GE. Imagenet classification with deep convolutional neural networks. Communications of the ACM. 2012;**60**:84-90. DOI: 10.1145/3065386

[5] Redmon J, Divvala S, Girshick R, Farhadi A. You only look once: Unified, real-time object detection. Proceedings of the IEEE Conference on Computer Vision and Pattern Recognition. 2016:779-788

[6] Yin Y, Li H, Fu W. Faster-YOLO: An accurate and faster object detection method. Digital Signal Processing. 2020;**102**:102756. DOI: 10.1016/j.dsp.2020.102756

[7] Kim D, Kim S, Jeong S, Ham JW, Son S, Moon J, et al. Rotational multipyramid network with bounding-box transformation for object detection. International Journal of Intelligent Systems. 2021;**36**:5307-5338. DOI: 10.1002/int.22513

[8] Moon J, Jeon M, Jeong S, RoMP-transformer K-YO. Rotational bounding box with multi-level feature pyramid transformer for object detection. Pattern Recognition. 2024;**147**:110067. DOI: 10.1016/j.patcog.2023.110067

[9] Zhang S, Zhang S, Wang B, Habetler TG. Deep learning algorithms for bearing fault diagnostics—A comprehensive review. IEEE Access. 2020;**8**:29857-29881. DOI: 10.1109/ACCESS.2020.2972859

[10] Çınar ZM, Abdussalam Nuhu A, Zeeshan Q, Korhan O, Asmael M, Safaei B. Machine learning in predictive maintenance towards sustainable smart manufacturing in industry 4.0. Sustainability. 2020;**12**:8211. DOI: 10.3390/su12198211

[11] Jeong Y. Digitalization in production logistics: How AI, digital twins, and simulation are driving the shift from model-based to data-driven approaches. International Journal of Precision Engineering and Manufacturing-Smart Technology. 2023;**1**:187-200. DOI: 10.57062/ijpem-st.2023.0052

[12] Kim M, Son S, Oh K-Y. Margin-maximized hyperspace for fault detection and prediction: A case study with an elevator door. IEEE Access. 2023;**11**:128580-128595. DOI: 10.1109/ACCESS.2023.3330137

[13] Son S, Oh K-Y. Integrated framework for estimating remaining useful lifetime through a deep neural network. Applied Soft Computing. 2022;**122**:108879. DOI: 10.1016/j.asoc.2022.108879

[14] Hornik K, Stinchcombe M, White H. Multilayer feedforward networks are universal approximators. Neural

Networks. 1989;**2**:359-366. DOI: 10.1016/0893-6080(89)90020-8

[15] Huang Z, Shen Y, Li J, Fey M, Brecher C. A survey on AI-driven digital twins in industry 4.0: Smart manufacturing and advanced robotics. Sensors. 2021;**21**:6340. DOI: 10.3390/s21196340

[16] Wang J, Li Y, Gao RX, Zhang F. Hybrid physics-based and data-driven models for smart manufacturing: Modelling, simulation, and explainability. Journal of Manufacturing Systems. 2022;**63**:381-391. DOI: 10.1016/j.jmsy.2022.04.004

[17] Rai R, Sahu CK. Driven by data or derived through physics? A review of hybrid physics guided machine learning techniques with cyber-physical system (cps) focus. IEEE Access. 2020;**8**: 71050-71073. DOI: 10.1109/ACCESS.2020.2987324

[18] Chen H, Lou S, Lv C. Hybrid physics-data-driven online modelling: Framework, methodology and application to electric vehicles. Mechanical Systems and Signal Processing. 2023;**185**:109791. DOI: 10.1016/j.ymssp.2022.109791

[19] Son S, Jeong S, Kwak E, Kim J-H, Oh K-Y. Integrated framework for SOH estimation of lithium-ion batteries using multiphysics features. Energy. 2022;**238**:121712. DOI: 10.1016/j.energy.2021.121712

[20] Kumar K, Choi Y. Accelerating particle and fluid simulations with differentiable graph networks for solving forward and inverse problems. Proceedings of the SC'23 Workshops of the International Conference on High Performance Computing, Network, Storage, and Analysis. 2023. pp. 60-65

[21] Raissi M, Perdikaris P, Karniadakis GE. Physics-informed neural networks: A deep learning framework for solving forward and inverse problems involving nonlinear partial differential equations. Journal of Computational Physics. 2019;**378**: 686-707. DOI: 10.1016/j.jcp.2018.10.045

[22] Tartakovsky AM, Marrero CO, Perdikaris P, Tartakovsky GD, Barajas-Solano D. Physics-informed deep neural networks for learning parameters and constitutive relationships in subsurface flow problems. Water Resources Research. 2020;**56**:e2019WR026731. DOI: 10.1029/2019WR026731

[23] Cao Y, Fang Z, Wu Y, Zhou D-X, Gu Q. Towards Understanding the Spectral Bias of Deep Learning. arXiv preprint arXiv:1912.01198. 2019. DOI: 10.48550/arXiv.1912.01198

[24] Wang S, Sankaran S, Perdikaris P. Respecting Causality is All You Need for Training Physics-Informed Neural Networks. arXiv preprint arXiv: 2203.07404. 2022. DOI: 10.48550/arXiv.2203.07404

[25] Bischof R, Kraus M. Multi-Objective Loss Balancing for Physics-Informed Deep Learning. arXiv preprint arXiv: 2110.09813. 2021. DOI: 10.48550/arXiv.2110.09813

[26] McClenny LD, Braga-Neto UM. Self-adaptive physics-informed neural networks. Journal of Computational Physics. 2023;**474**:111722. DOI: 10.1016/j.jcp.2022.111722

[27] Krishnapriyan A, Gholami A, Zhe S, Kirby R, Mahoney MW. Characterizing possible failure modes in physics-informed neural networks. Advances in Neural Information Processing Systems. 2021;**34**:26548-26560. DOI: 10.48550/arXiv.2109.01050

[28] Wang S, Teng Y, Perdikaris P. Understanding and mitigating gradient flow pathologies in physics-informed neural networks. SIAM Journal on Scientific Computing. 2021;**43**:A3055-A3081. DOI: 10.1137/20M1318043

[29] Jagtap AD, Kharazmi E, Karniadakis GE. Conservative physics-informed neural networks on discrete domains for conservation laws: Applications to forward and inverse problems. Computer Methods in Applied Mechanics and Engineering. 2020;**365**: 113028. DOI: 10.1016/j.cma.2020.113028

[30] Kharazmi E, Zhang Z, Karniadakis GE. hp-VPINNs: Variational physics-informed neural networks with domain decomposition. Computer Methods in Applied Mechanics and Engineering. 2021;**374**:113547. DOI: 10.1016/j.cma.2020.113547

[31] Lu L, Jin P, Pang G, Zhang Z, Karniadakis GE. Learning nonlinear operators via DeepONet based on the universal approximation theorem of operators. Nature Machine Intelligence. 2021;**3**:218-229. DOI: 10.1038/s42256-021-00302-5

[32] Li Z, Kovachki N, Azizzadenesheli K, Liu B, Bhattacharya K, Stuart A, et al. Fourier Neural Operator for Parametric Partial Differential Equations. arXiv preprint arXiv:2010.08895. 2020. DOI: 10.48550/arXiv.2010.08895

[33] Tancik M, Srinivasan P, Mildenhall B, Fridovich-Keil S, Raghavan N, Singhal U, et al. Fourier features let networks learn high frequency functions in low dimensional domains. Advances in Neural Information Processing Systems. 2020; **33**:7537-7547. DOI: 10.48550/arXiv.2006.10739

[34] Basri R, Galun M, Geifman A, Jacobs D, Kasten Y, Kritchman S. Frequency bias in neural networks for input of non-uniform density. International Conference on Machine Learning. PMLR; 2020. pp. 685-694

[35] Niaki SA, Haghighat E, Campbell T, Poursartip A, Vaziri R. Physics-informed neural network for modelling the thermochemical curing process of composite-tool systems during manufacture. Computer Methods in Applied Mechanics and Engineering. 2021;**384**:113959. DOI: 10.1016/j.cma.2021.113959

[36] Cai S, Wang Z, Wang S, Perdikaris P, Karniadakis GE. Physics-informed neural networks for heat transfer problems. Journal of Heat Transfer. 2021;**143**:060801. DOI: 10.1115/1.4050542

[37] Jeong J, Kwak E, Kim J-H, Oh K-Y. Prediction of thermal runaway for a lithium-ion battery through multiphysics-informed DeepONet with virtual data. eTransportation. 2024;**21**: 100337. DOI: 10.1016/j.etran.2024.100337

[38] Mao Z, Jagtap AD, Karniadakis GE. Physics-informed neural networks for high-speed flows. Computer Methods in Applied Mechanics and Engineering. 2020;**360**:112789. DOI: 10.1016/j.cma.2019.112789

[39] Cai S, Mao Z, Wang Z, Yin M, Karniadakis GE. Physics-informed neural networks (PINNs) for fluid mechanics: A review. Acta Mechanica Sinica. 2021;**37**:1727-1738. DOI: 10.1007/s10409-021-01148-1

[40] Son S, Lee H, Jeong D, Oh K-Y, Sun KH. A novel physics-informed neural network for modeling electromagnetism of a permanent

magnet synchronous motor. Advanced Engineering Informatics. 2023;**57**: 102035. DOI: 10.1016/j.aei.2023.102035

[41] Kollmannsberger S, D'Angella D, Jokeit M, Herrmann L. Deep Learning in Computational Mechanics. Springer International Publishing; 2021. DOI: 10.1007/978-3-030-76587-3

[42] Diao Y, Yang J, Zhang Y, Zhang D, Du Y. Solving multi-material problems in solid mechanics using physics-informed neural networks based on domain decomposition technology. Computer Methods in Applied Mechanics and Engineering. 2023;**413**: 116120. DOI: 10.1016/j.cma.2023.116120

[43] Faroughi SA, Pawar NM, Fernandes C, Raissi M, Das S, Kalantari NK, et al. Physics-guided, physics-informed, and physics-encoded neural networks and operators in scientific computing: Fluid and solid mechanics. Journal of Computing and Information Science in Engineering. 2024;**24**:040802. DOI: 10.1115/1.4064449

[44] Zhang E, Dao M, Karniadakis GE, Suresh S. Analyses of internal structures and defects in materials using physics-informed neural networks. Science Advances. 2022;**8**:eabk0644. DOI: 10.1126/sciadv.abk0644

[45] Lou Q, Meng X, Karniadakis GE. Physics-informed neural networks for solving forward and inverse flow problems via the Boltzmann-BGK formulation. Journal of Computational Physics. 2021;**447**:110676. DOI: 10.1016/j.jcp.2021.110676

[46] Raissi M. Forward–backward stochastic neural networks: Deep learning of high-dimensional partial differential equations. Peter Carr Gedenkschrift: Research Advances in Mathematical Finance. World Scientific; 2024. pp. 637-655

[47] Sirignano J, Spiliopoulos K. DGM: A deep learning algorithm for solving partial differential equations. Journal of Computational Physics. 2018;**375**: 1339-1364. DOI: 10.1016/j.jcp.2018.08.029

[48] Jagtap AD, Karniadakis GE. Extended physics-informed neural networks (XPINNs): A generalized space-time domain decomposition based deep learning framework for nonlinear partial differential equations. Communications in Computational Physics. 2020;**28**:5. DOI: 10.4208/cicp.oa-2020-0164

[49] Shukla K, Jagtap AD, Karniadakis GE. Parallel physics-informed neural networks via domain decomposition. Journal of Computational Physics. 2021;**447**: 110683. DOI: 10.1016/j.jcp.2021.110683

[50] Wang S, Yu X, Perdikaris P. When and why PINNs fail to train: A neural tangent kernel perspective. Journal of Computational Physics. 2022;**449**: 110768. DOI: 10.1016/j.jcp.2021.110768

[51] Guan H, Dong J, Lee W-N. Towards Real-time Training of Physics-informed Neural Networks: Applications in Ultrafast Ultrasound Blood Flow Imaging. arXiv preprint arXiv: 2309.04755. 2023. DOI: 10.48550/arXiv.2309.04755

[52] He J, Koric S, Kushwaha S, Park J, Abueidda D, Jasiuk I. Novel DeepONet architecture to predict stresses in elastoplastic structures with variable complex geometries and loads. Computer Methods in Applied Mechanics and Engineering. 2023; **415**:116277. DOI: 10.1016/j.cma.2023.116277

[53] Koric S, Abueidda DW. Data-driven and physics-informed deep learning operators for solution of heat conduction equation with parametric heat source. International Journal of Heat and Mass Transfer. 2023;**203**:123809. DOI: 10.1016/j.ijheatmasstransfer.2022.123809

[54] Goswami S, Yin M, Yu Y, Karniadakis GE. A physics-informed variational DeepONet for predicting crack path in quasi-brittle materials. Computer Methods in Applied Mechanics and Engineering. 2022;**391**: 114587. DOI: 10.1016/j.cma.2022.114587

[55] Wang S, Wang H, Perdikaris P. Improved architectures and training algorithms for deep operator networks. Journal of Scientific Computing. 2022;**92**:35. DOI: 10.1007/s10915-022-01881-0

[56] He J, Kushwaha S, Park J, Koric S, Abueidda D, Jasiuk I. Sequential deep operator networks (S-DeepONet) for predicting full-field solutions under time-dependent loads. Engineering Applications of Artificial Intelligence. 2024;**127**:107258. DOI: 10.1016/j.engappai.2023.107258

[57] Rahaman N, Baratin A, Arpit D, Draxler F, Lin M, Hamprecht F, et al. On the spectral bias of neural networks. International Conference on Machine Learning. PMLR; 2019. pp. 5301-5310

[58] Wang S, Wang H, Perdikaris P. On the eigenvector bias of Fourier feature networks: From regression to solving multi-scale PDEs with physics-informed neural networks. Computer Methods in Applied Mechanics and Engineering. 2021;**384**:113938. DOI: 10.1016/j.cma.2021.113938

[59] Hesthaven JS, Gottlieb S, Gottlieb D. Spectral Methods for Time-Dependent Problems. Cambridge University Press; 2007;**21**. DOI: 10.1017/CBO9780511618352

[60] Jabbar M, Liu Z, Dong J. Time-stepping finite-element analysis for the dynamic performance of a permanent magnet synchronous motor. IEEE Transactions on Magnetics. 2003;**39**: 2621-2623. DOI: 10.1109/TMAG.2003.816500

[61] Gherabi Z, Toumi D, Benouzza N, Boudinar AH, Koura MB. Discrimination between demagnetization and eccentricity faults in PMSMs using real and imaginary components of stator current spectral analysis. Journal of Power Electronics. 2021;**21**:153-163. DOI: 10.1007/s43236-020-00169-6

[62] Hyunseung Lee SS, Jeong D, Sun KH, Jeon BC, Ki-Yong O. High-fidelity multiphysics model of a permanent magnet synchronous motor for fault data generation. Journal of Sound and Vibration. 2024;**589**:118573. DOI:10.1016/j.jsv.2024.118573

[63] Lee H, Son S, Jeong D, Sun KH, Jeon BC, Oh K-Y. A Finite Element Model of an Electric Motor with an Unbalanced Rotor for Vibration Data Generation. International Journal of Precision Engineering and Manufacturing-Smart Technology. 2024;**2**(1):47-56. DOI: 10.57062/ijpem-st.2023.0122

[64] Kwak E, Kim J-H, Jeong J, Oh K-Y. Multiphysics-informed thermal runaway model for estimating the pressure evolution induced by the gas formation in a lithium-ion battery. Applied Thermal Engineering. 2024;**246**:122941. DOI: 10.1016/j.applthermaleng.2024.122941

[65] Guo G, Long B, Cheng B, Zhou S, Xu P, Cao B. Three-dimensional thermal finite element modeling of lithium-ion

battery in thermal abuse application. Journal of Power Sources. 2010;**195**: 2393-2398. DOI: 10.1016/j.jpowsour.2009.10.090

[66] Liu B, Jia Y, Yuan C, Wang L, Gao X, Yin S, et al. Safety issues and mechanisms of lithium-ion battery cell upon mechanical abusive loading: A review. Energy Storage Materials. 2020; **24**:85-112. DOI: 10.1016/j.ensm.2019.06.036

Chapter 5

FPGA-Based Spiking Neural Networks

Ali Mehrabi and André van Schaik

Abstract

This chapter explores the development and application of Spiking Neural Networks (SNNs) on Field-Programmable Gate Arrays (FPGAs), tracing their evolution since the debut of FPGAs in mid-1980s. It begins by examining the historical growth of FPGAs, emphasizing their role in developing complex neural network architectures. The narrative then charts the advancement of SNN designs on FPGAs, from early experiments to modern-day applications, spotlighting significant technological milestones and breakthroughs. The main emphasis is on the design and implementation strategies for SNNs on FPGAs, incorporating the latest research aimed at optimizing hardware use and computational efficiency. The chapter outlines effective techniques for mapping SNN models onto FPGA resources. Discussions include computational models of biological neurons on FPGAs, designing SNN accelerators to harness FPGA's parallel processing capabilities, implementing SNN simulators, time-multiplexed neuronal networks, large SNN architectures on FPGA, and self-trainable neural architectures. This comprehensive blend of concepts and practical methodologies sets the foundation for designing modern SNNs that can be adapted for a range of advanced applications.

Keywords: neuromorphic computing, FPGA, Spiking Neural Networks, system on chip, network on chip, reconfigurable hardware

1. Introduction

Field-Programmable Gate Arrays (FPGAs) have undergone a remarkable transformation since their inception, evolving from simple configurable logic fabrics to sophisticated System on Chips (SoCs) capable of tackling a broad spectrum of advanced computing challenges. This evolution has been driven by persistent advancements in Moore's Law [1], continuous refinement of fabrication processes, and a series of significant architectural innovations. Moore's Law's impact is vividly demonstrated in the exponential growth observed in FPGA logic capacity. This is illustrated by the dramatic increase in the number of logic elements (LEs) available in commercial FPGA products from leading manufacturers like Altera (now part of Intel) and Xilinx (now part of AMD), from just a few in their initial offerings to millions in today's high-end devices (as depicted in **Figure 1**). Initially, FPGAs in the mid-1980s were limited to thousands of logic elements, constraining their use to relatively simple combinatorial and sequential functions. In contrast, modern high-end FPGAs

Figure 1.
Increase in reconfigurable logic FPGA products Altera and Xilinx products from 1984 to date.

routinely boast millions of logic elements, enabling them to handle the realization of highly complex digital subsystems or even entire standalone systems within a single device. Fundamentally, early FPGAs primarily utilized Look-Up Tables (LUTs) as their configurable building block. While LUTs are versatile, they have limitations in the complexity of logic functions they can express within a given area. The introduction of Adaptive LUTs (ALUTs) marked a significant advancement, allowing for more efficient mapping of a broader range of logic circuits onto FPGAs. This enhancement significantly improved FPGA usability in the design of complex finite-state machines, control logic, and data paths. Recognizing the performance bottlenecks and specialized needs of certain industry segments, FPGA architectures have expanded to include dedicated hardware blocks integrated directly into the programmable fabric. Examples include Digital Signal Processing (DSP) blocks optimized for mathematical operations commonly found in communications, image, and video processing systems. Modern FPGAs often incorporate numerous DSP blocks, enabling designers to efficiently implement complex signal processing algorithms. Furthermore, the integration of high-speed transceivers, which support multi-gigabit communication protocols, has propelled FPGAs into a pivotal role within data-intensive networking, telecommunications, and high-performance computing (HPC) platforms. Arguably, the most transformative architectural shift has been the emergence of Programmable Systems-on-Chip (SoC) [2]. These devices integrate large amounts of programmable logic with embedded processors (both soft-core and hard-core), internal memory hierarchies, and a rich assortment of analog and digital peripherals. This paradigm shift has redefined the concept of FPGAs. What were once platforms for configurable logic are now highly capable heterogeneous computing engines, blurring the traditional lines between FPGAs, embedded processors, and even general-purpose computing systems. This relentless advancement in architecture is supported by remarkable improvements in semiconductor manufacturing processes. From technology nodes in the multiple micrometers range decades ago, persistent adherence to Moore's Law has driven a dramatic scaling down of transistor feature sizes. Contemporary FPGAs use manufacturing processes at the 10 nm scale, and researchers are pushing into even smaller realms, exploring techniques as fine as 5 nm and smaller. The impact of this miniaturization is significant. The density of logic circuits on a chip skyrockets, the fastest speeds that FPGAs can operate increase, and, importantly, they use much less power. This dramatic improvement in efficiency and performance makes it possible to use FPGAs in situations where heat, power availability, and environmental conditions were once limiting factors—applications previously thought to be out of reach.

1.1 FPGAs from configurable logic to neuromorphic architectures

The interest in Spiking Neural Networks (SNNs) is rapidly growing due to their potential for energy-efficient computing that resembles the functioning of the human brain. Inspired by the brain's remarkably efficient communication and power usage, SNNs could fundamentally transform the way we process large datasets and recognize complex patterns. However, implementing them is challenging. Their event-driven nature and complex neuronal interactions pose significant obstacles. This is where FPGAs excel. Their adaptability, finely-tuned parallel processing capabilities, and seamless hardware-software integration make them an ideal fit for SNNs.

1.1.1 The FPGA advantage: flexibility, parallelism, and event-driven design

The strengths of FPGAs in the context of SNNs lie in three core areas:

- Tailored architectures: unlike CPUs and GPUs, whose fixed hardware excels within established computational paradigms, FPGAs provide a blank canvas for hardware design. Researchers can escape traditional computation models and instead craft architectures closely mirrored to the specific structure, dynamics, and connectivity of SNNs. This customization translates directly into superior performance and power efficiency gains compared to conventional computing platforms.

- True parallelism: the massive parallelism inherent in neural networks well aligns with the programmable fabric of FPGAs. FPGAs excel at implementing numerous neuron and synapse models concurrently. This allows for the exploration of SNNs at scales difficult to achieve with traditional sequential or vector-based processors.

- Embracing spikes: FPGAs offer a unique advantage for handling the fundamental characteristic of SNNs—their spike-driven communication model. The fine-grained control over clocking mechanisms, logic resources, and I/O within FPGAs enables the design of systems that are inherently event-driven. This compatibility minimizes overhead and maximizes accuracy in representing spiking behavior, an area where CPUs and GPUs can introduce timing distortions and inefficiencies.

1.1.2 Key considerations for SNN implementation on FPGAs

While FPGAs provide compelling advantages, the successful implementation of SNNs necessitates a careful balance between biological realism and hardware efficiency. Key considerations include:

- Neuron design: implementing biologically plausible neuron models that fit efficiently into the FPGAs is favorable, yet the realization of these models on a digital platform can be complex and may not always be resource-efficient. Researchers often face trade-offs between the complexity of neuronal dynamics, such as choosing between simpler models like Leaky Integrate-and-Fire (LIF) [3] or more complex ones like Hodgkin-Huxley [4], and the constraints imposed by available hardware resources. This balancing act is crucial to optimizing both the performance and the feasibility of implementing these models on FPGAs.

- Synaptic representation: the choice of memory structures to store and manage synaptic connectivity and weights has profound implications for the scalability, speed, and power consumption of the SNN. Both FPGA on-chip memory resources (e.g., BRAM) and external (off-chip) memory may be utilized, often in a hierarchical fashion to balance capacity and access speeds.

- Learning mechanisms: the implementation of on-chip learning algorithms tailored to FPGAs is an active and exciting area of research. On-chip learning provides flexibility and the potential for real-time adaptation, key requirements for autonomous and embedded systems. FPGA implementations need to address the efficient implementation of algorithms such as Spike-Timing-Dependent Plasticity (STDP) and its variants.

- Communication and spike encoding/decoding: Spiking Neural Networks (SNNs) uniquely process spatio-temporal information, known as "spikes." For SNNs to function, traditional data types must be converted into spikes. This transformation involves various methods for encoding and decoding spikes [5], which are crucial to the architectural design of the SNN. The chosen method for spike encoding/decoding directly influences how the network is structured and operates. Efficient and high-speed communication with the external world, alongside robust spike coding and decoding, are vital elements in the design of SNNs, impacting their overall performance and effectiveness.

- Modularity and expandability: designing an SNN in a modular fashion allows for easier expansion and upgrading of the network. Modularity ensures that different parts of the network can be independently developed, tested, and optimized. This approach supports scalable solutions that can grow in complexity and size as needed without requiring a complete redesign.

2. Early implementations of SNNs on FPGA

The mid-1990s marked an important era for the application of Field-Programmable Gate Arrays (FPGAs) in modeling biological neurons. In 1996, a study by Rossmann et al. [6] made notable progress by implementing a Hebbian learning algorithm [7] on a Xilinx XC3090 FPGA as depicted in **Figure 2**. This effort was among the first to realize such an algorithm in hardware, with the complexity of each neuron requiring a dedicated FPGA. The researchers built a system consisting of 18 individual neurons, each connected to five sensory synapses. Distributed across multiple FPGAs operating at 5 MHz, the system achieved an update rate of 333 kCUPS (Kilo Connection Updates Per Second). Notably, this design was successfully applied in an autonomous vehicle (Wheelchair), enabling it to learn and navigate obstacles. Building on their earlier achievements, Rossmann et al. continued to refine their work in [8], implementing a neuron model with Hebbian learning (**Figure 3**) using a more advanced Xilinx FPGA, XC4028. This iteration featured a modular system that could accommodate up to eight units, each equipped with an FPGA and additional RAM. These units were linked through a backplane, which allowed for effective communication across the system. Within each module, individual neurons were tasked with autonomously computing their assigned portion of the neural network. Dedicated RAM served the purpose of storing input/output signals and internal register values. The neuronal architecture comprised various fundamental building blocks such as adders, multipliers, and non-linear low-pass elements. The Xilinx XC4028 FPGAs, connected to a global bus, provided access to synaptic weights and local registers' information from a central controller. This setup allowed for a flexible connection strategy between neurons, where the output from one neuron could directly feed into another. The flexibility of this system made it suitable for a variety of practical applications. For instance, it was used in autonomous robots, and in developing adaptive velocity controllers for slot car racing. The system's ability to

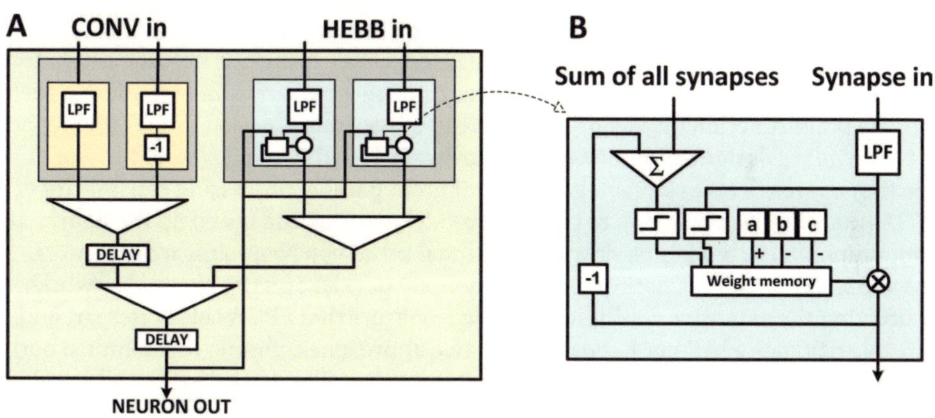

Figure 2.
Neuron architecture in [6]. A: a four synapse neuron with conventional excitatory and inhibitory synapses with fixed positive and negative weights and two Hebbian learning synapses. B: structure of Hebbian learning synapse including short-term memories at the input of each synapse realized by a digital LPF with a non-linear characteristic, threshold elements determining the different learning- and forgetting-modes, weight memories for each adaptable synapse. Adapted from [6].

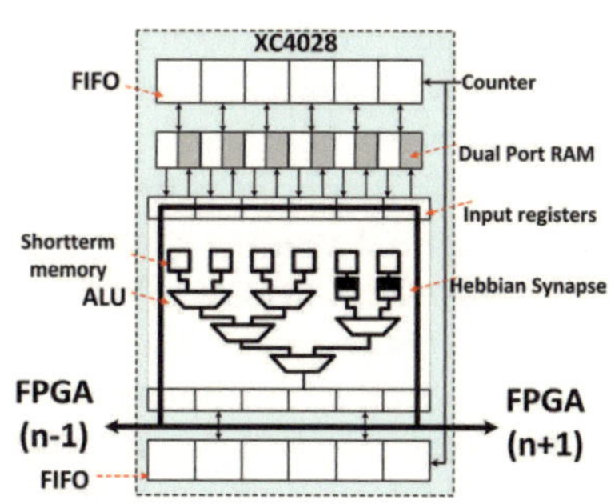

Figure 3.
Neuronal computation module architecture consisting of a neuron and input/output memory. Adapted from [8].

receive sensor inputs also enhanced its capability to interact with and respond to its environment, making it a powerful tool for real-world applications. The FPGA implementation exhibited high-speed computation capabilities, with a single input/output operation taking only 212 ns. However, the internal clock frequency was limited to around 5 MHz. Despite achieving impressive individual module performance (198 MCPS and 66 MCUPS), the overall system encountered challenges inherent to discrete hardware implementations, i.e., the impact of the FPGA's propagation delay on overall computation speed.

3. FPGA evolution and impacts on SNN designs

In the early 2000s, as the capacity of FPGAs approached the threshold of millions of configurable logics. Computational elements, i.e., DSP modules, and block memories were integrated into FPGA fabrics. Partial configuration capabilities and soft-processor IPs added to FPGA design tools. Research on reconfigurable hardware gained significant attention during this period. An influential paper, "CAM-brain Machine" by de Garis [9], presented ideas on reconfigurable neural networks and the implementation of high-density neurons on FPGA chips. The CAM project, in particular, achieved a breakthrough by realizing a modular design comprising 75.4 million neurons using 72 Xilinx's XC6264 FPGAs. Unlike previous approaches that relied on time-multiplexed utilization of neurons, these efforts aimed to more closely emulate brain functionality using a large array of neurons. This led to the emergence of two primary design methodologies in hardware-based Spiking Neural Networks. The first approach takes advantage of the inherent parallel processing capabilities of FPGAs and time multiplexing to precisely model neurons and speed up the neuronal computations that tend to be slow in traditional serial von Neumann architectures. The second approach focuses on building densely packed Spiking Neural Networks by utilizing the extensive configurable logic resources that FPGAs offer. Researchers typically navigate a balance between these two approaches, aiming to maximize both the size of the network and the speed of computations. This balancing act allows them to draw on the advantages of each method, enhancing both the performance and the scalability of neural network implementations on FPGAs.

Upegui et al. [10] proposed a functional spiking neuron model designed specifically for efficient hardware implementation. While this model simplifies many biological and software-based neuron characteristics, it retains functionality and tackles complex tasks like temporal pattern recognition. To compensate for the limited representational power of individual simplified neurons, the model utilizes a larger number of neurons. This trade-off between neuron complexity and network size becomes advantageous in hardware contexts due to the model's architectural simplicity. The model captures key elements of spiking neurons, including membrane potential, resting potential, threshold potential, post-synaptic response, and after-spike response. The membrane potential acts as a counter, accumulating (or subtracting) a specific value upon receiving excitatory (or inhibitory) synaptic inputs. This potential gradually decays toward a resting state. If an input arrives while a previous post-synaptic response is ongoing, its effect is summed with the existing potential. When the threshold is reached, the neuron fires a spike, resets its membrane potential to a dedicated after-spike potential, and enters a refractory period. During this refractory period, the neuron recovers from firing, with its membrane potential

DOI: http://dx.doi.org/10.5772/intechopen.1006168

returning to its resting state. Two types of refractoriness, absolute and partial, were implemented. Absolute refractoriness completely ignores incoming spikes, while partial refractoriness weakens their influence by a constant factor. The model uses a Moore finite-state machine (FSM), which is a basic but powerful hardware design tool for outlining sequential operations. It functions in two main states: operational and refractory (see **Figure 4**). In the operational state, the neuron processes and integrates incoming spikes, which affects its membrane potential. Once the membrane potential crosses a specific threshold, the neuron activates, fires a spike, and enters a hyperpolarized after-spike state before moving into the refractory phase. This refractory period essentially serves as a cooldown during which the neuron's activity is paused, allowing its membrane potential to return to a resting state. After this, the neuron switches back to the operational state, ready to process new spikes. This architecture was implemented in a multi-layered setup and showed promise in solving pattern recognition problems. However, due to the simplified nature of the neuron model, the limited computational capabilities of individual neurons had to be compensated for by increasing the number of neurons. This trade-off in hardware resources is considered acceptable for less complex pattern recognition tasks, where a larger network of simpler neurons can still achieve effective results.

The mid-2000s marked a significant era in FPGA development, known as the age of accumulation [2], characterized by the emergence of SoC (System on Chip) FPGAs and a paradigm shift in FPGA manufacturing. SoC FPGAs integrate high-density reconfigurable logic elements, DSP units, and block memories alongside hard-processor units. These systems also typically include Physical layers (PHY) that support a variety of standard interface peripherals, such as DRAM and SRAM controllers, as well as high-speed Ethernet, I2C, SPI, UART, PCI, and USB interfaces, providing a robust platform for mixed hardware-software system design. During these years, researchers focused on harnessing the potential of reconfigurable and highly interconnected arrays of neural network elements within hardware to create powerful signal processing units. To accomplish this, they explored various architectures for Spiking Neural Networks across different platforms, ranging from multiprocessor software-based systems to analog/mixed-signal implementations. Notably, FPGA-based architectures stood out for their exceptional flexibility in system design, positioning them as a preferred choice for implementing complex computational models. For instance, the processor-based SpiNNaker project [11] aims to develop a

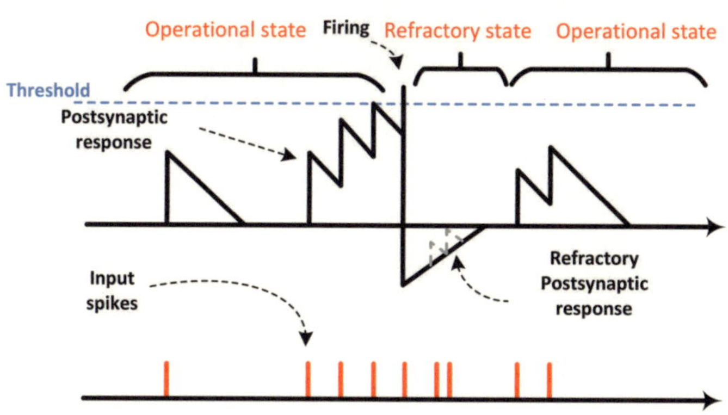

Figure 4.
Demonstration of refractory and operational states in neuron model proposed by Upegui et al. [10].

massively parallel computer capable of simulating SNNs of various sizes and topologies, with programmable neuron models. While this approach provides the flexibility necessary for modeling complex SNN computations, due to its size, cost, and power requirements, SpiNNaker does not target embedded systems applications, highlighting the need for more scalable and energy-efficient solutions.

Upegui et al. [12] enhanced their previous work by introducing an SNN platform comprising three key components: a hardware substrate, a computation engine, and an adaptation mechanism. The hardware substrate supports the computation engine also, offers the flexibility required for the adaptation mechanism to modify the engine. Taking advantage of the latest features in Xilinx FPGAs, such as Dynamic Partial Reconfiguration (DPR) [13], the authors utilized independent design (ID) partial reconfiguration flexibility in their platform. The computation engine, serving as the problem solver of the platform, is centered around the functional neuronal model introduced in their earlier work [10]. Meanwhile, the adaptation mechanism enables modifications to the function described by the computational part. This encompasses synaptic weight learning, which involves altering only the contents of memory, as well as module-restricted growing and pruning techniques where neurons may be enabled or disabled. The design integrates a simplified version of the Hebbian learning rule, which is well-suited for hardware implementation. The neural network is implemented in the reconfigurable section of the FPGA (refer to **Figure 5B**), and a Genetic search algorithm is employed to find the optimal configuration for the network. Thanks to the inclusion of the PowerPC hard-processor as a new feature in Xilinx Virtex II Pro devices, the genetic algorithm can be executed on the hard-processor on the fixed logic section of the FPGA. While this approach presents a trade-off between flexibility and performance through reconfigurable computing, it is important to note that the basic genetic algorithm [14], used to optimize connection weights during simulations, is computationally expensive and memory-intensive. Additionally, the authors' experiments showed that it does not consider certain information that could be valuable for optimizing the network, such as the direction of the error, making it unsuitable for hardware implementation due to the hardware's limited on-chip memory resources. Therefore, the development of a new learning

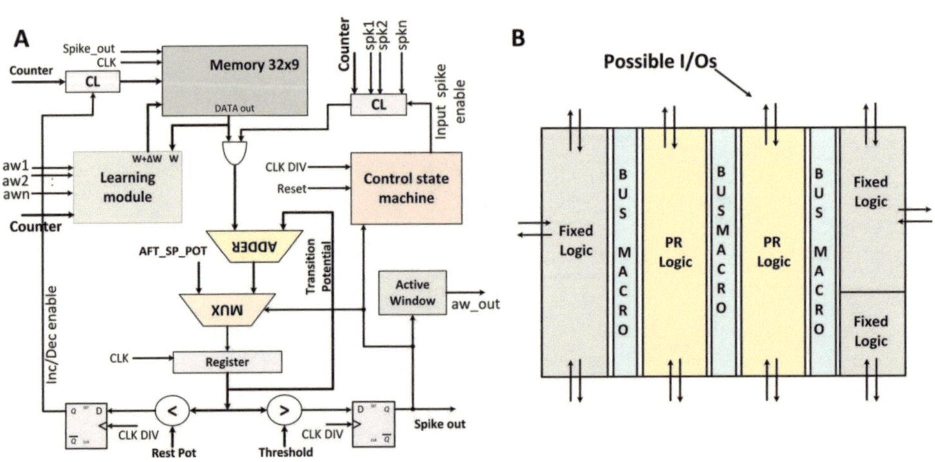

Figure 5.
A: neuronal computation module architecture consisting of a neuron and input/output memory and B: design layout with partially re-configurable modules and fixed modules. Adapted from [12].

algorithm specifically designed for online and on-chip implementation on FPGAs remains an open challenge.

Hellmich and Klar [15] developed the Spiking Neural Network Emulation Engine (SEE), a multi-FPGA platform designed to overcome the challenge of memory bandwidth during the simulation of large-scale neural networks. SEE efficiently manages millions of neurons and over 800,000 synaptic weights. It features a flexible architecture that supports both sparse and dense connection schemes for neuron state calculations. The SEE architecture comprises three FPGAs, each dedicated to specific simulation tasks. The first FPGA used for simulation control employs two PowerPC (PPC) processors, a feature introduced in Xilinx Virtex II Pro devices, which handle simulation control tasks including initial network configuration, real-time monitoring, and management of event lists that track neuronal activity. This setup is shown in (**Figure 6A**). The second FPGA focuses on network topology computation (NTC), dynamically determining the impact of firing events on neurons and updating neuron states within event lists to maintain simulation accuracy and responsiveness, as depicted in (**Figure 6B**). The third FPGA, dedicated to neuron state computation (NSC), updates neuron states using numerical integration methods and manages synaptic weight updates for dynamic synapses, as illustrated in (**Figure 6C**). SEE's distributed memory architecture allows for parallel access to event lists, tag fields, and weight memories, enhancing the system's performance. The flexibility and modular design of SEE make it particularly effective for studying the intricate architectures found in biological neural systems, offering a robust platform for large-scale neural network simulations. The distributed memory architecture, coupled with its task-tailored FPGAs in SEE, provides significant performance enhancements. This setup allows for parallel memory access, a crucial feature when handling the typically large datasets in complex SNN simulations. The modular nature of SEE also boosts its utility, enabling the neuron state calculation module to be reconfigured to support diverse SNN models with varying connectivity patterns. SEE emphasizes

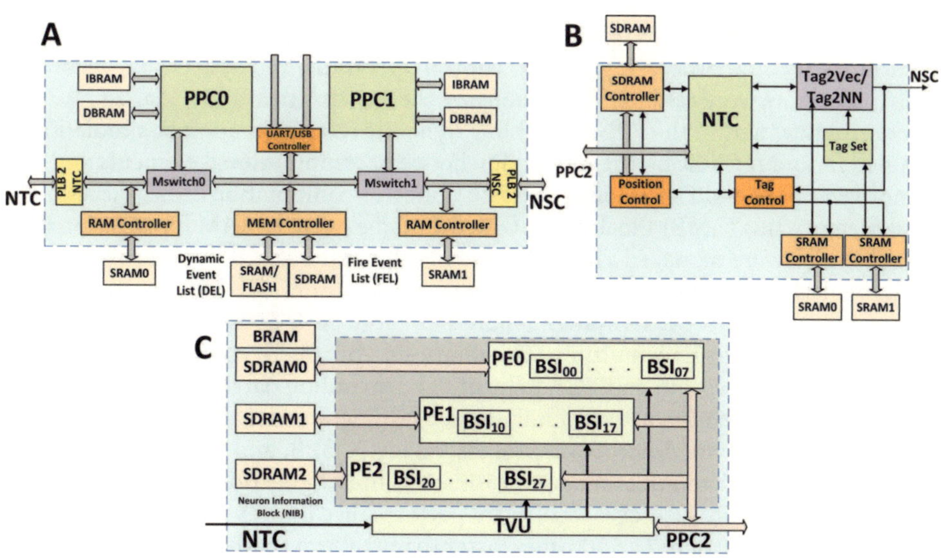

Figure 6.
SEE architecture across 3 Virtex-II pro FPGAs. A: simulation control by 2 embedded PowerPCs, B: network topology computation module, C: reconfigurable neuron state computation module. Adapted from [15].

numerical accuracy by utilizing the Bulirsch-Stoer integration method, ensuring that the simulated network dynamics closely mirror those observed in real-world SNN behavior. This approach helps avoid synchronization issues that might arise from simpler integration methods or analytical approximations. However, while SEE's advanced design provides numerous advantages, it also introduces potential challenges. The complexity of its multi-FPGA setup and the blend of hardware and software components increase the intricacy of system setup, configuration, and debugging. Additionally, while SEE significantly enhances memory bandwidth, potential bottlenecks in memory access could still appear as SNNs scale to even larger sizes. Moreover, achieving real-time simulation for exceptionally large and complex networks within SEE's design environment requires careful consideration and planning.

Glackin et al. [16] developed a similar strategy to tackle the challenges of deploying large-scale Spiking Neural Networks (SNNs) on FPGAs. They chose to use the Integrate-and-Fire (I and F) conductance model to navigate the intricate logic demands that make fully parallel implementations impractical for expansive networks. Their approach cleverly balanced computational speed with efficient resource utilization by incorporating time multiplexing. This technique enhances the simulation capabilities of broad network topologies without overloading the FPGA hardware. At the heart of their method was a significant adaptation of the traditional FPGA-based neural network architecture to support the larger scale and complexity of SNNs by involving several key components. Firstly, the Integrate-and-Fire model was used to simplify the dynamic representation of neurons, significantly reducing the computational overhead compared to more complex models like Hodgkin-Huxley. This simplification made it more efficient to use hardware resources. Moreover, time multiplexing was implemented to address the limitations of FPGA resources by cycling through neuron simulations in distinct time slots. This allowed for the simulation of a larger network than would be possible at any single instance, effectively scaling up the network size through dynamic resource reuse. Another crucial element of their strategy was the integration of hybrid parallel processing and memory management. Multiple MicroBlaze soft-processors were employed to manage tasks requiring sequential processing, such as control operations and system management. These processors were essential for enhancing the system's flexibility, managing the control flow within the FPGA, enabling dynamic reconfiguration of simulation parameters, and facilitating the interaction between computational elements and memory components. The architecture also utilized a combination of fast-access Local Memory Bus (LMB) Block RAM (BRAM) and external SRAM for additional storage, which were managed via the On-chip Peripheral Bus (OPB) and controlled by External Memory Controllers (EMC). **Figure** 7 illustrates Glackin et al.'s intricate multi-processor, multi-FPGA system tailored for large-scale SNN implementations. This schematic details how multiple MicroBlaze soft-processor cores are configured and interconnected within an FPGA to meet the demanding parallel processing requirements of extensive neural simulations. The diagram visually illustrates the complex setup involving MicroBlaze processors, LMB, OPB, and EMC, highlighting the sophisticated architecture and its intricate interconnections. Glackin et al.'s design implementation achieves significant performance improvements, executing real-time operations up to 12,500 times faster than real time and demonstrating the system's ability to manage complex SNNs unmanageable on less dynamic platforms. However, the system faces several challenges. These mainly include the complexity of the setup, involving time multiplexing and multiple MicroBlaze processors, which

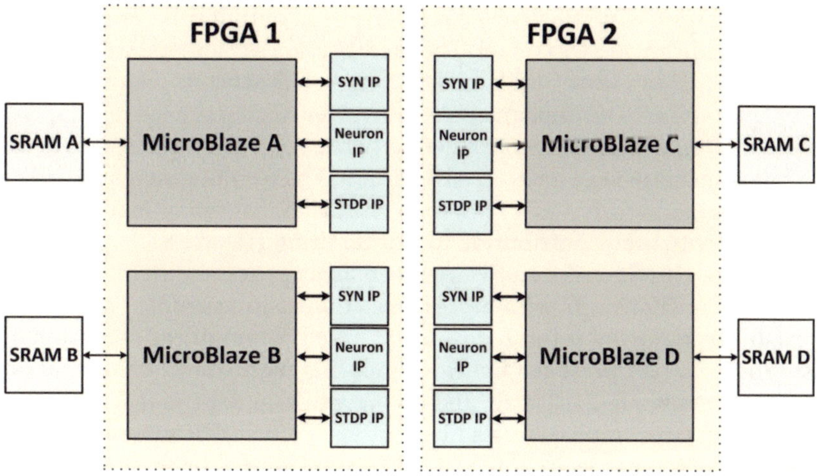

Figure 7.
Architecture of FPGA-based multi-processor system for Spiking Neural Networks. This diagram depicts the sophisticated arrangement of multiple MicroBlaze soft-processor cores interconnected within an FPGA environment, showcasing the system's capability to handle large-scale neural simulations. Adapted from [16].

adds significant complexity in system configuration and management. While time multiplexing permits larger networks, the absolute scale of implementable networks remains confined by the physical resources available on the FPGA. The performance is also dependent on the specifications of the FPGA used, potentially limiting the system's application to high-end FPGA platforms.

Cassidy et al. [17] introduced an FPGA-based neural array employing Address Event Representation (AER) to interconnect neuromorphic sensors, such as event-based cameras and cochleas. Their design illustrated in **Figure 8**, utilized a simplified LIF neuron model, strategically selected for its balance between biological realism and computational feasibility. This system architecture not only supports the efficient simulation of neural dynamics but also enhances the array's capability to interface seamlessly with various sensory inputs, providing a robust platform for studying and implementing Spiking Neural Networks. The neural array incorporates 32 identical LIF neurons arranged to exchange spikes via a multiplexer and demultiplexer configuration connected to a shared AER bus. This setup facilitates dynamic interaction across the neural network, supported by an AER mapper block that establishes extensive connectivity among neurons. Each neuron within the array operates on the LIF model, implemented using a 16-bit digital accumulator to manage the membrane potential. When this accumulator's value exceeds a predefined threshold, it triggers a spike output and subsequently resets. The process resumes after an absolute refractory period during which the neuron is unresponsive to further inputs. This model also includes programmable parameters that define the relative refractory period and the exponential decay of the membrane potential, emulating a biological neuron's leak current. Moreover, each neuron possesses 128 8-bit synaptic weights, capable of modeling both excitatory and inhibitory synapses. Synapses additionally incorporate a delay mechanism modeled as a circular, dual-port buffer to emulate the time delay caused by the neuron's dendritic tree, with a maximum per-synapse delay of 128 clock cycles. The architecture integrates the Spike-Time-Dependent Plasticity (STDP) learning rule, essential for facilitating online learning within the neural network. STDP adjusts synaptic weights based on the timing of pre- and post-synaptic spikes.

Specifically, synapses that effectively contribute to an output spike are strengthened, while those that do not are weakened. The modification of synaptic weights according to STDP is depicted in a function that shows weight adjustments relative to the timing of pre-synaptic spikes. The implementation involves storing pre-synaptic spike times in a circular buffer, which are then compared to the times of output spikes to calculate synaptic adjustments using a look-up table (LUT). The resulting weight change (ΔW) is applied via a read-modify-write operation, ensuring that synaptic strengths are updated in line with their contribution to neuron firing (**Figure 8**).

Pearson et al. [18] describe an FPGA-based array processor architecture capable of simulating large networks with more than a thousand neurons. This architecture's scalability, however, is limited by a bus-based communication protocol. In contrast, Ros et al. [19] present a hybrid computing platform where the neuron model is implemented in hardware, and the network model and learning are managed in software, emphasizing a blend of execution environments. However, for large-scale SNNs, hardware interconnect poses significant challenges due to the high levels of required inter-neuron connectivity, often limiting the number of neurons that can be realized in hardware. The direct neuron-to-neuron interconnection also leads to non-linear growth in switching requirements as network size increases.

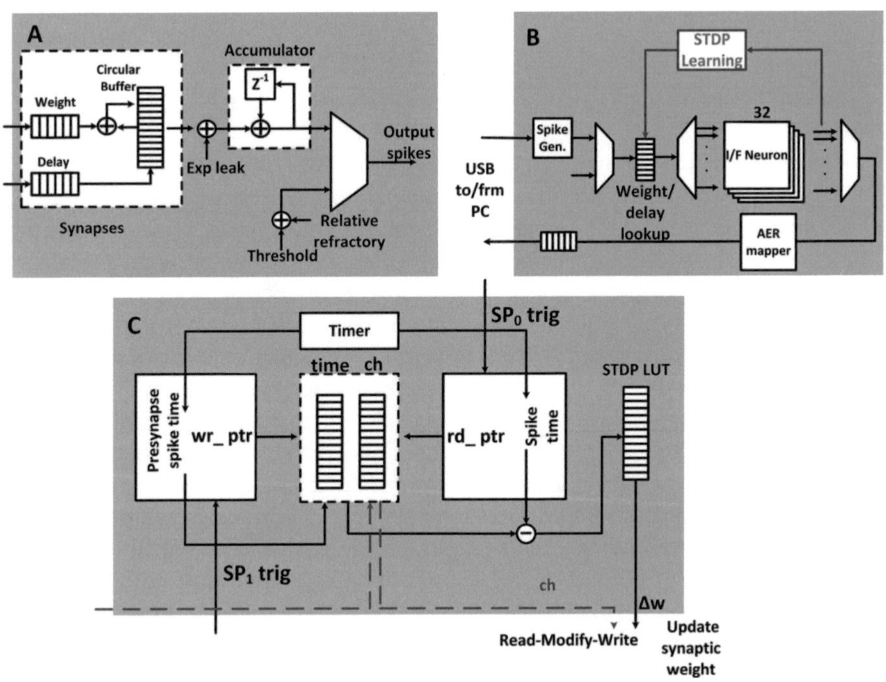

Figure 8.
Overview of the FPGA-based neuron array design by Cassidy et al. [17]. A: details the individual neuron architecture featuring components such as the synapses, delay mechanisms, a circular buffer for synaptic inputs, and an accumulator for integrating the inputs to trigger output spikes based on a threshold influenced by the exponential leak and relative refractory periods. B: shows the overall network architecture including interfaces for spike generation, AER mapping, and interfaces for USB communication with a PC. This section emphasizes the integration of the 32 I and F neuron model with system-wide components that manage the input, processing, and learning phases. C: implementation of STDP, illustrating the flow from spike timing to synaptic weight adjustment through a LUT. This block diagram displays the process of reading pre-synaptic spike times, determining synaptic weight adjustments, and applying these modifications to synapses in real time.

4. Advanced SNN architectures

Since the late 2000s, there has been a significant paradigm shift in designing Spiking Neural Networks (SNNs) on FPGAs, driven by the quest to develop neuromorphic computing systems capable of processing complex tasks. Central to this shift has been the focus on designing extra-large SNNs and simplifying neuron models. This has necessitated the adoption of alternative communication frameworks, such as Network-on-chip (NoC) technology, along with techniques like time multiplexing and leveraging off-chip memory access. The late 2000s witnessed the rise of Network-on-chip (NoC) technology in System on Chip (SoC) FPGAs, which became a game-changer for designing high-density SNNs. NoCs offer a scalable and efficient way to handle the complex communication needs of large-scale SNNs, which traditional bus-based systems cannot manage. Incorporating NoCs into SoC FPGAs has enabled the creation of highly interconnected and reconfigurable neural networks that significantly boost scalability and performance. This advancement allows for the real-time simulation of vast neural networks, closely mimicking the intricate connectivity and dynamics of biological systems. The flexibility of NoCs also allows for the dynamic reconfiguration of neural network parameters, making these systems more adaptive and efficient. Overall, the integration of NoC technology into SoC FPGAs has revolutionized the design of high-density SNNs, opening up new possibilities in neuromorphic computing and bringing neural networks closer to operating like the human brain.

In this context, the EMBRACE-FPGA architecture presented by Morgan-Cawley et al. [20, 21] is notable. The EMBRACE (Embedded Multicore Building Blocks for Reconfigurable Architecture Computational Emulation) project focuses on developing a scalable and flexible FPGA-based platform for emulating Spiking Neural Networks (SNNs). Rather than employing traditional analog neurons, EMBRACE models these neurons using soft-processors on the FPGA, facilitating a novel approach to neural computation that leverages the reconfigurability of digital systems. EMBRACE-FPGA architecture illustrated in **Figure 9A** features a 2-dimensional $N \times M$ array of interconnected SNN neural tiles, each linked in the North, East, South, and West directions to facilitate nearest-neighbor connections. The neural tile depicted in **Figure 9B** comprises critical elements like the NoC router (zoomed in **Figure 9C**) and neural cell components—neurons and synapses. Communication across these tiles is conducted through these cardinal direction ports, where the NoC router's configuration memory stores vital information about the SNN topology, synaptic weights, and neuron firing thresholds. Each neural cell within the EMBRACE-FPGA can contain up to 32 synapses and a neuron, which are managed using a picoBlaze soft-processor. This setup enhances the SNN's flexibility and functionality, supporting a wide range of applications by enabling the evolution and reconfigurability of the network's architecture. The NoC routers manage data flow within the system; they use a round-robin arbitration policy to handle spike packet generation and routing, ensuring efficient communication between the neural tiles. Furthermore, the NoC supports dynamic SNN configuration changes, including adjusting synaptic connections and neuron thresholds. This reconfigurability helps adapt to different computational requirements and environmental changes. The routers enable spike packets to be routed from their source to the appropriate destination synapse through time-multiplexed connections, integrating sophisticated packet handling protocols to ensure that data reaches its target effectively. The NoC router's finite-state machine (FSM) oversees packet routing based on the neuron's activity—firing spikes when the

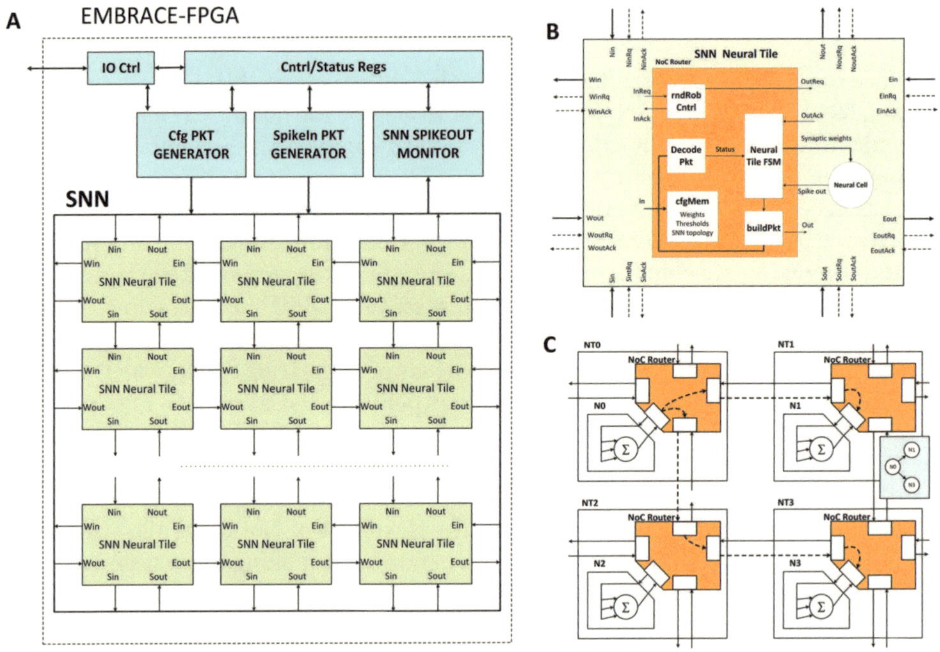

Figure 9.
A: EMBRACE-FPGA Platform, which features a two-dimensional $N \times M$ *array of interconnected SNN neural tiles. Each tile in this array is connected in the north, east, south, and west directions. B: SNN neural tile block diagram. C: EMBRACE NoC. Illustrating a packet routing example (neuron connectivity inset). Adapted from [21].*

neuron's output, or when incoming spike packets are received. This system's flexibility is further demonstrated by its ability to configure SNN parameters through NoC configuration packets, which carry information about the destination neural tile and the specific synaptic or neuron adjustments needed. The EMBRACE-FPGA architecture thus not only provides a robust platform for simulating neural activities and interactions but also facilitates complex network evolutions and configurations. This capability is essential for developing adaptive neural networks that can efficiently process information and respond to changes, making EMBRACE-FPGA a powerful tool in the field of neuromorphic computing. Carrillo et al. [22] introduced a hierarchical Network-on-Chip (H-NoC) architecture aimed at resolving scalability challenges in hardware implementations of SNNs. The H-NoC architecture employs a multi-level hierarchical structure comprising neuron facilities, tile facilities, and cluster facilities, each with specialized NoC routers to efficiently manage both local and global neuron connectivity. The architecture leverages a combination of star and mesh topologies, which significantly enhances scalability by allowing seamless expansion through the addition of more clusters without incurring substantial communication delays. Implemented on an FPGA, the architecture was tested using a 3 × 3 array of cluster facilities, demonstrating its high-throughput capability of handling up to 3.33 billion spikes per second and low-power consumption of 13.16 mW per cluster facility, thus validating its practical feasibility and efficiency for large-scale SNN applications. One of the standout features of this architecture is the spike traffic compression technique, which reduces data packet volume, thereby improving throughput and reducing power consumption. The hierarchical design introduces complexity, particularly in managing routing and traffic across different levels, and the system's effectiveness is highly dependent on specific traffic patterns of the SNN, which may vary across applications. Moreover, while the FPGA implementation offers practical insights, much of the performance validation is based on simulations, which may not fully capture real-world conditions.

A Polychronous Spiking Neural Network (PSNN) is an advanced form of neural network that utilizes the process of polychronization. In this process, spikes from different neurons travel down axons with precise delays, arriving at a target neuron simultaneously and causing it to fire, even though the source neurons fire asynchronously. This mechanism allows PSNNs to store and recognize complex spatio-temporal patterns, known as polychronous groups. The introduction of adaptive delay mechanisms allows these networks to modify synaptic delays dynamically, enhancing their ability to learn temporal patterns. According to Izhikevich [23], these networks can form more groups than there are neurons, suggesting a vast memory capacity. This feature is particularly important for implementing short-term memory in cognitive systems, as it enables the network to handle a large variety of behaviors and patterns. In essence, PSNNs are ideal for applications that require the recognition and storage of intricate temporal sequences, mimicking the sophisticated processing capabilities of the human brain. Wang et al. in their paper [24] argued that FPGAs are ideally suited for this implementation due to their reconfigurability and parallel processing capabilities, which can efficiently handle the complex computations required by PSNNs. Their proposed architecture primarily consists of spiking neurons interconnected through synapses capable of delay adaptation. The key innovation in this architecture lies in its ability to dynamically adjust synaptic delays based on the timing of spikes, which is a critical factor for learning temporal patterns. Each neuron in the network is modeled to emit a spike when its membrane potential exceeds a certain threshold. The neuron model typically integrates input spikes using a LIF model, a common approach in Spiking Neural Networks. This integration respects the timing and delay of each input spike, which can vary as the network operates and learns. The synapses are modeled not only to transmit spikes between neurons but also to adjust the transmission delay of these spikes. The delay adaptation mechanism is central to the architecture. Each synapse includes a delay line that can be dynamically adjusted. These delay lines are implemented using shift registers in the FPGA, allowing for the precise control of spike timing. Accompanying each synaptic unit is adaptation logic that modifies the delay based on the temporal patterns of activity observed. This adaptation is driven by a set of rules and algorithms that determine how and when to adjust the delay based on the network's performance and learning progress. Each neuron and its associated synapses are implemented as a processing element (PE) on the FPGA. These PEs are capable of processing spikes independently, allowing for parallel processing across the network. The FPGA's memory resources are utilized to store the state of each neuron, the synaptic weights, and the configuration of the delay lines. An on-chip communication infrastructure facilitates the transmission of spikes between neurons. This infrastructure must handle the variable delays introduced by the synaptic models, ensuring that spikes are delivered at the correct times. The network's learning and adaptation capabilities are enhanced by plasticity mechanisms integrated into the neuron and synapse models. Synaptic weights and delays are dynamically adjusted through local learning rules, which are hard-coded into the hardware to function in real time. These rules account for the timing and sequence of spikes, optimizing the network's structure to more accurately encode temporal patterns. The architecture is designed to be both scalable and modular, employing time multiplexing to support up to 1.15 million axons. This enables the network to comprehensively store and recall spatial-temporal patterns. The innovative deployment of a multiplexed neuron array, which simulates 4000 virtual neurons using only 128 physical neurons, showcases efficient resource utilization and scalability. **Figure 10A** illustrates the PSNN design communicating via AER protocol. In their later work, Wang et al. [25] presented a systematic approach to FPGA-based SNN implementation that significantly improves upon prior methodologies by incorporating memory management techniques, parallel processing, and modular design principles. They introduced a robust FPGA design framework tailored for large-scale Spiking Neural Networks, especially those characterized by high-density or all-to-all synaptic connections. This framework leverages a reconfigurable neural layer implemented through a time-multiplexing strategy, enabling the simulation of up to 200 K virtual neurons with a single physical neuron (compared to 4 K virtual neurons in their previous work). This approach utilizes only a minimal portion of the hardware resources available on commercial FPGAs, including entry-level models. Unlike traditional methods that rely on mathematical computational models, the physical neuron in this architecture is realized using a conductance-based model with randomized parameters across neurons, mimicking the natural variability found in biological neurons. Additionally, it incorporates a novel time-multiplexed reconfigurable neural layer equipped with an address buffer. This buffer dynamically generates fixed random weights for each synaptic connection as spikes arrive, significantly reducing memory usage. They showcased a network comprising 23 of these neural layers. Each layer hosts 64 k neurons, culminating in a network with 1.5 million neurons and 92 billion synapses. This configuration achieved a total spike throughput of 1.2 trillion spikes per second, operating in real time on a Virtex 6 FPGA, demonstrating the framework's scalability and efficiency and its potential to handle extraordinarily large neural networks with reduced hardware demand. The real bottleneck of this design is the limited on-chip memory while the use of off-chip memory is limited by the communication bandwidth and significant increase in hardware complexity due to the off-chip memory interface requirements. **Figure 10B** shows the architecture of a Neural layer in [25].

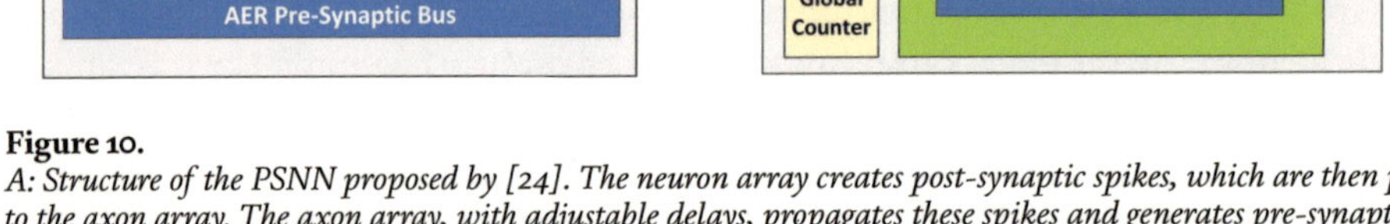

Figure 10.
A: Structure of the PSNN proposed by [24]. The neuron array creates post-synaptic spikes, which are then passed to the axon array. The axon array, with adjustable delays, propagates these spikes and generates pre-synaptic spikes at the axon terminals. These pre-synaptic spikes are then fed back into the neuron array, potentially triggering neurons to fire. Both the connectivity and delay within the axon array are programmable, allowing for flexible network configurations. B: A neuron soma equipped with a single post-synaptic current generator (PSC_Gen) capable of producing both excitatory and inhibitory post-synaptic currents, modulated by synaptic weights from the address buffer. Linear summation of currents requiring only one generator per neuron in this model. The soma integrates these currents in a leaky manner to compute the membrane potential. Upon reaching a threshold, it generates a spike and resets the potential, entering a refractory period. Membrane potential values are read from and written back to on-chip SRAM at each cycle. Adapted from [25].

Neil et al. [26] introduced Minitaur, an event-driven Spiking Neural Network (SNN) accelerator designed to process data dynamically, making it particularly efficient for handling sporadic or bursting input patterns. Minitaur achieves significant computational efficiency, managing 19 million post-synaptic currents per second while consuming only 1.5 W of power. It supports up to 65,536 neurons per board, showcasing its capability for large-scale neural network tasks. In practical applications, Minitaur demonstrated impressive performance, achieving 92% accuracy on the MNIST handwritten digit classification and 71% on the 20 newsgroups text classification dataset. Minitaur addresses some of the challenges in training and implementing SNNs on FPGA platforms. One significant challenge is the difference in dynamics between spiking neurons and traditional artificial neurons, which complicates the training process. Minitaur mitigates this issue by utilizing rule-based connections that follow predictable patterns common in artificial neural networks like deep belief networks (DBNs), autoencoders, and multi-layer perceptrons. These rules allow connections to be defined in a ranged-rule format, simplifying storage and retrieval by only requiring start and end addresses for both source (SRC) and destination (DEST) neurons within each layer. This method reduces the complexity of connection lookups, decreases storage demands, and speeds up the processing of post-synaptic currents (PSCs) by retrieving destination addresses only when necessary, after the axonal delay. To optimize memory usage and processing efficiency, Minitaur stores spikes according to their source addresses rather than destination addresses. This approach significantly reduces the storage requirements and allows the system to process post-synaptic currents more efficiently. The cache locality is another critical aspect of Minitaur's design. By exploiting patterns in the input data and assigning neuron IDs to specific computational cores, Minitaur ensures that each core handles a subset of neurons, thereby reducing contention and improving access times for neuron weights and state information. Additionally, Minitaur's architecture integrates several design principles to enhance performance. It uses a simplified LIF neuron model, which balances biological realism with computational efficiency. The system employs an event-driven processing model, where computation occurs only upon receiving input events, thereby minimizing unnecessary processing and reducing power consumption. The FPGA implementation leverages the inherent parallelism of the hardware, with 32 parallel cores, and dedicated memory caches for neuron state and weight storage. This configuration allows Minitaur to handle a high volume of post-synaptic currents efficiently. **Figure 11** demonstrates a simplified diagram of Minitaur architecture.

Wang et al. [27] presented a massively parallel neuromorphic cortex simulator that was a significant achievement in the field of neuromorphic engineering, particularly in simulating SNNs on a large scale. This highly scalable and flexible architecture (**Figure 12**) can be deployed on both single and multiple FPGA boards, enabling the simulation of neural networks ranging from 20 million to 2.6 billion neurons in real time. This massive scale is achieved with remarkable energy efficiency, with the system consuming only about 1.62 μW per neuron. The architecture effectively mimics the hierarchical and localized connectivity of biological neural networks through its innovative use of minicolumns and hypercolumns as functional units, which are not direct replicas of biological structures but serve to enhance computational efficiency and parallelism. They introduced a sophisticated memory management system that utilizes both on-chip and off-chip memory to handle the extensive data throughput required by such large-scale simulations. Furthermore, the system's ability to dynamically assign computational resources based on neuronal activity helps

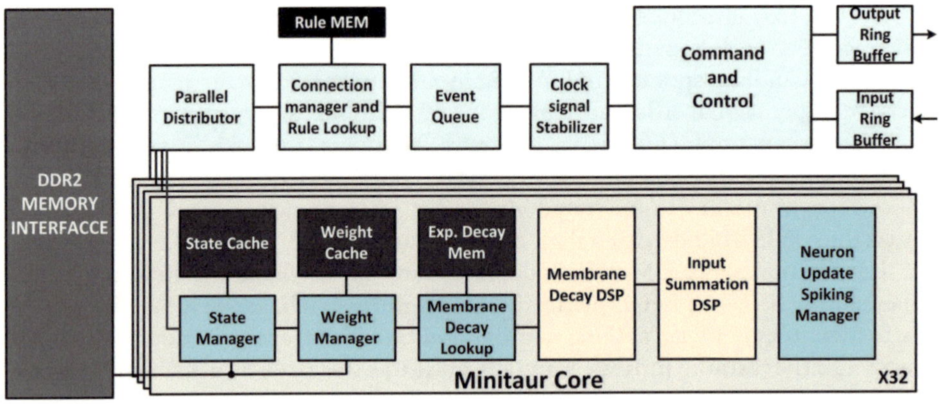

Figure 11.
The simplified structure of the Minitaur system, featuring 32 parallel cores and 128 MB of DDR2 main memory. Each core is equipped with 2 MB of state cache and 8 MB of weight cache, alongside two DSP units for fixed-point mathematical operations—one for decay multiplication and another for summing input currents. Additionally, 2 MB of RAM is utilized for exponential decay lookup, preloaded, and functioning as ROM. Adapted from [26].

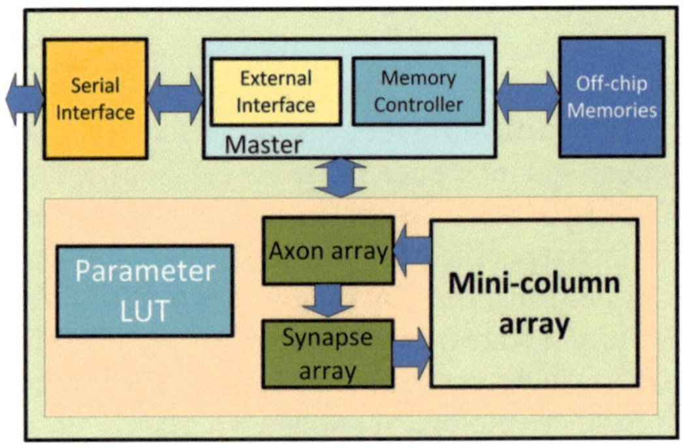

Figure 12.
Architecture of the cortex simulator. This system includes a neural engine, a master controller, off-chip memory, and a serial interface. The neural engine mimics biological neural system structures, facilitating the simulation of their functions. The master controller manages data flow between the neural engine and off-chip memories, which are used for storing neural states and event data. Additionally, the serial interface facilitates communication with additional FPGAs and external controllers such as PCs. Adapted from [27].

in optimizing power consumption and processing speed, making it a groundbreaking tool for real-time applications in computational neuroscience and potentially in other areas like robotics and artificial intelligence. The architecture of the neuromorphic cortex simulator, as depicted in **Figure 13**, is structured around a neural engine core that operates in conjunction with a master control unit, off-chip memories, and a high-speed serial interface. The neural engine itself is subdivided into three primary components: the minicolumn array, the synapse array, and the axon array. The minicolumn array hosts time-multiplexed minicolumns which simulate the neurons' behavior, integrating inputs to generate spiking events. These events are then passed to the axon array, which is responsible for propagating the events with specific axonal delays to the synapse array. Here, events are modulated based on synaptic weights and routed to their intended destinations across the neural network. The entire process is underpinned by a parameter look-up table (LUT), which stores crucial information on neuron parameters and connection rules, facilitating the dynamic configuration

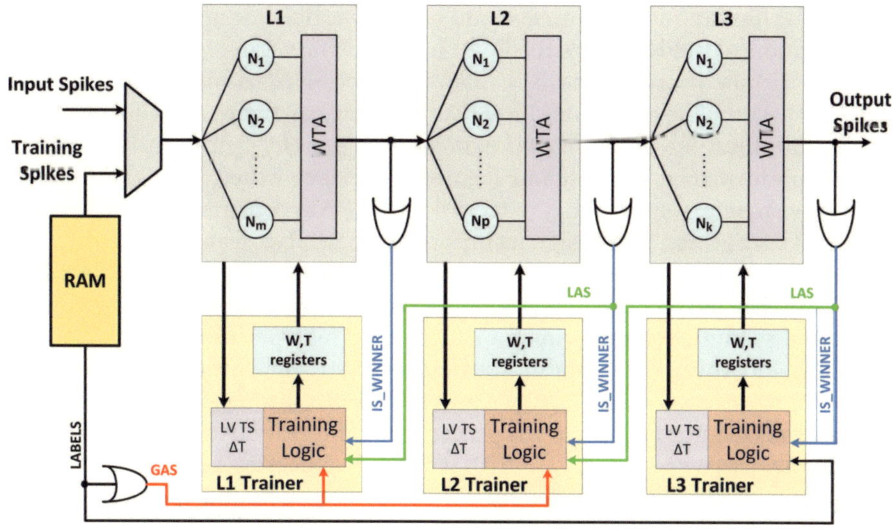

Figure 13.
Diagram of the ODESA network. This illustration showcases the neuron layers, the dedicated training hardware modules, and the interconnections between them. Each layer is equipped with its own training module, enabling dynamic online adjustments to neuron weights and thresholds.

and flexibility required for simulating different neural network models. This architecture is designed to ensure that each component efficiently manages data flow and computation, directed by the master control unit which coordinates the interaction between the neural engine and the external memories. This setup supports a seamless and scalable emulation of complex neural dynamics, emphasizing real-time processing capabilities necessary for interactive applications. This design has been adapted by the authors in 2023 to create, a Neuromorphic Supercomputer that will come online in 2024 using 96 Stratix 10 MX boards [28]. This computer will be the first to simulate the same number of neurons with the same number of synaptic operations per second as a human brain. The system will be made available online for researchers worldwide to investigate SNNs at massive scales. The performance and scalability of this simulator are highly dependent on the underlying FPGA hardware. This means that the performance of the system will improve as FPGA technology improves over time, but it also makes it a costly endeavor as it requires high-end, often expensive FPGA boards to function optimally. While the system is designed to be flexible and can be adapted to different types of neural networks, neuron models, learning rules, or other specific experimental setups, doing so could require extensive reconfiguration and reprogramming, and would thus require significant effort.

Recent research has increasingly focused on SNN architectures suitable for edge computing, particularly in areas like Intelligent Internet of Things (IoT) and autonomous systems. These applications benefit from the low-power consumption and high-speed processing capabilities of FPGAs. Moreover, the scalability of FPGA platforms allows for the deployment of complex SNN models that can be dynamically reconfigured as per the application's requirements. This adaptability, combined with the inherent advantages of SNNs, such as their event-driven nature and potential for low-power operation, positions FPGA-based SNNs as a promising technology for advancing edge computing applications across various sectors. FireFly is a high-throughput hardware accelerator for Spiking Neural Networks introduced by Li et al. [29] aimed to address the limitations in arithmetic and memory efficiency often found in FPGA implementations. FireFly utilizes the DSP blocks in Xilinx Zynq Ultrascale FPGAs to enhance arithmetic operations. By generalizing the SNN arithmetic operation to a multiplex-accumulate operation, FireFly utilizes the capabilities of DSP blocks for efficient multiplication, addition, and data routing, thereby significantly boosting arithmetic performance. To overcome memory efficiency issues, FireFly introduces an innovative memory system that reduces on-chip RAM consumption while ensuring efficient data access. The design incorporates a partial sum and membrane voltage (Psum-Vmem) unified buffer, which balances off-chip memory access bandwidth with on-chip data buffering. This system supports the extensive parallel processing of spikes and synaptic weights, vital for maintaining high performance in real-world applications. Moreover, the use of line buffers and a stream width upsizer in the design minimizes data transfer latencies and maximizes throughput, further enhancing the system's memory efficiency. Together, these innovations allow FireFly to operate on edge devices with limited resources while still delivering peak performance and maintaining the adaptability needed for various SNN models and applications. This robust architecture not only advances the computational capabilities of neuromorphic hardware but also pushes the boundaries of what can be achieved in terms of power and area efficiency on FPGA platforms. FireFly architecture is designed to be scalable, supporting large SNN models with millions of neurons and synaptic connections, particularly when deployed on larger FPGA devices.

In a transformative approach, Mehrabi et al. [30] introduced the Optimized Deep Event-driven Spiking Neural Network (ODESA), a novel SNN architecture optimized for computational efficiency on FPGA-based systems and capable of online, local supervised training. This multi-layered architecture employs a gradient-free, threshold-based learning algorithm that dynamically adjusts synaptic weights and neuronal thresholds based on local synaptic activities and a Winner-Takes-All (WTA) mechanism. This design simplifies the learning process by eliminating the need for complex backpropagation calculations. Each neuron in ODESA operates in an event-driven manner, processing inputs as discrete binary spikes, significantly reducing power consumption and processing requirements. The system is engineered for real-time learning and adaptation, with an efficient communication method between layers that uses direct spike transmission. This approach not only emulates the operational principles of biological neural networks but also leverages the inherent strengths of FPGA technology, such as parallel processing capabilities and reconfigurability. Notably, the architecture avoids time multiplexing, yet its reduced computational complexity allows the implementation of up to 95 K physical neurons on a Stratix FPGA family [31]. Each neuronal layer includes a trainer module that adapts neurons' weights and thresholds during the online training phase, enhancing the system's adaptability. This portability feature extends beyond specific FPGA overlays, making ODESA particularly suitable for real-time pattern recognition tasks, such as anomaly and intrusion detection.

5. Applications of FPGA-based SNNs

FPGA-based Spiking Neural Networks have been increasingly utilized across a diverse range of fields. The following are some prominent applications where FPGA-based SNNs have demonstrated significant potential:

5.1 Robotics and control

FPGA-based Spiking Neural Networks (SNNs) have found diverse applications in robotics, taking advantage of their unique capabilities for real-time control and adaptive behavior. As robots become increasingly integrated into various societal functions, they benefit significantly from SNNs' ability to model and control complex behaviors. In locomotion systems, SNNs serve as Central Pattern Generators (CPGs) for multi-legged robots. Studies using Spartan 6 FPGAs have developed compact and programmable architectures for bipedal, quadrupedal, and hexapodal locomotion [32]. Furthermore, advancements in hardware SNN models, such as pyramidal neurons inspired by hippocampal functions, have been pivotal for autonomous navigation tasks, enhancing robotic spatial awareness and decision-making [33]. The application of Dynamic Adaptive Neural Network Arrays (DANNA) further exemplifies FPGA-based SNNs' utility in robotic navigation by facilitating configurable neuromorphic computing elements that mimic neuronal connectivity crucial for adaptive navigation strategies [34]. Additionally, FPGA-based implementations of SNNs have been integral in obstacle avoidance tasks [6], utilizing runtime reconfigurable connectivity within 2D arrays of spiking neurons to enable real-time decision-making and path planning in autonomous robots [35]. SNNs implemented on FPGAs have been utilized in robotic applications such as obstacle avoidance. These networks help in real-time decision-making and sensory processing, which are crucial for autonomous navigation and interaction with dynamic environments. Pearson et al. [18] designed a Neuro-processor on FPGA to be used as part of the closed-loop system of a feedback controller.

5.2 Signal processing

The implementation of SNNs on FPGAs has shown considerable promise in the field of real-time signal processing. Applications in audio and speech processing benefit from the event-driven nature of spiking neurons [36], which are adept at handling complex, time-varying signals. This capability is crucial for tasks such as speech recognition and audio filtering, where the ability to process signals in real time is paramount. FPGA-based SNNs have also been instrumental in edge detection tasks, offering scalable solutions to reduce computation times and enhance performance [37]. Moreover, They have been applied in image segmentation and sound source separation using algorithms like the Oscillatory Dynamic Link Matcher (ODLM), underscoring their versatility and effectiveness in complex signal processing applications [38]. As an example, Iakymchuk [39] introduced an SNN architecture on FPGA to perform simple image transforms such as edge detection, spot detection or removal, and Gabor-like filtering without any further computation requirements.

5.3 Pattern recognition, anomaly detection

FPGA-based Spiking Neural Networks (SNNs) are utilized in various pattern recognition tasks, including image and speech recognition. The event-driven nature of spiking neurons makes them well-suited for efficiently detecting and processing patterns in large datasets. Examples of such implementations can be found in [40, 41], as well as fault detection and prediction in industrial applications proposed in [42, 43]. In the realm of cybersecurity, FPGA-based SNNs have been employed for detecting intrusions and abnormal network activities. Neuromorphic implementations of deep learning networks often provide accuracy comparable to that of full-precision models while significantly reducing power consumption and cost [44]. Additionally, FPGA-based SNNs have extensive applications in the biomedical field. Recent research by Scrugli et al. [45] highlights the use of a customized FPGA-based SNN for the real-time detection of arrhythmia, demonstrating the expanding scope of FPGA-accelerated neural network applications in biomedical signal processing.

5.4 Neuromorphic computing

One of the primary applications of FPGA-based SNNs is in the development of neuromorphic computing systems. These systems aim to replicate the architecture and functionality of the human brain, providing insights into brain function and potential advancements in artificial intelligence. A notable example of this application is the DeepSouth [28].

6. Challenges in implementing FPGA-based SNNs

Implementing Spiking Neural Networks (SNNs) on Field-Programmable Gate Arrays (FPGAs) presents several significant challenges. One primary issue is the inherent complexity of SNN models, which require precise temporal dynamics and event-driven processing, making it difficult to map these biological computations onto the general-purpose logic blocks of FPGAs. This often leads to inefficient utilization of hardware resources, increased area size, and higher power consumption. Additionally, the von Neumann bottleneck poses a substantial challenge as the bandwidth limitations of modern memory systems cannot keep pace with the big data requirements of SNNs. Scalability and interconnectivity also pose significant obstacles. As SNN's neuron density increases, the interconnect complexity grows non-linearly, exacerbating routing latency and performance issues. Current FPGA routing structures struggle to support the high levels of inter-neuron connectivity required by large-scale SNNs, often resulting in limited network sizes and sub-optimal performance. Another challenge is the limited on-chip memory of FPGAs, which often necessitates the use of external memory, increasing power consumption and latency. Efficient memory management and innovative data storage solutions are crucial to address this limitation. Interconnectivity challenges in FPGAs significantly impact the performance of Spiking Neural Networks (SNNs) by limiting their scalability, increasing latency, and reducing overall efficiency. As the density of neurons in an SNN increases, the interconnect complexity grows non-linearly. For example, a two-layered feed-forward network with m neurons per layer has an interconnect density of m^2. This rapid increase in interconnect requirements can overwhelm the routing resources of an FPGA, leading to congestion and increased signal propagation delays. Current FPGA architectures typically employ diagonal, segmented, or hierarchical two-dimensional routing structures, which are not optimized for the dense and dynamic connectivity patterns characteristic of SNNs. This inadequacy results in inefficient routing and higher switching requirements, further increasing latency and diminishing the performance of the implemented SNN. The challenge is even more pronounced in large-scale implementations, where high levels of inter-neuron connectivity are essential for accurate and efficient neural processing.

Moreover, the non-linear growth in routing complexity leads to increased power consumption as more resources are dedicated to maintaining the connectivity between neurons. This increased power demand can negate the inherent energy efficiency advantages of using SNNs, making FPGA implementations less attractive for applications requiring low-power consumption.

To mitigate these issues, as detailed in Section 4, researchers are exploring various routing optimizations and topologies. Techniques such as Network-on-Chip (NoC) architectures, which offer scalable and efficient interconnectivity, have shown promise in addressing the connectivity problems in FPGA-based SNNs. NoC topologies can provide higher levels of connectivity without excessive interconnect-to-device area ratios, thereby improving performance and scalability. Despite these advancements, achieving efficient and scalable interconnectivity in FPGA-based SNNs remains a significant challenge that requires ongoing research and innovation. Addressing memory bandwidth limitations in FPGA-based Spiking Neural Networks (SNNs) is critical for improving performance and scalability. Several solutions have been proposed to mitigate these limitations:

- *High Bandwidth Memory (HBM):* HBM is a stacked DRAM integrated with the processing elements through a silicon interposer, offering significantly higher bandwidth compared to traditional memory technologies. For example, a single HBM2 block can provide a bandwidth of 256 GB/s, and a stack with four HBM blocks can reach up to 1 TB/s. Using HBM in FPGA-based SNN implementations can help alleviate the memory bandwidth bottleneck by enabling faster data transfer rates, which is essential for handling the large volumes of data processed by SNNs.

- *In-Memory Computing (IMC):* IMC involves moving computational logic into the memory itself, thereby reducing the need to transfer data back and forth between the memory and the processing units. This approach is particularly effective for SNNs, as it can significantly reduce latency and power consumption associated with memory access [46]. IMC allows for parallel processing of memory cells, enhancing the overall throughput of the system.

- *Model Compression Techniques:* Techniques such as model compression [47], pruning, and quantization reduce the amount of data that needs to be processed and stored. Model compression involves simplifying the neural network model without significantly impacting its performance. Pruning removes redundant or less significant neurons and synapses, while quantization reduces the precision of the weights and activations. These techniques help in lowering the memory bandwidth requirements and improve the efficiency of data transfer and storage.

- *Efficient Memory Management:* Implementing efficient memory management strategies can help optimize the use of available memory resources. Techniques such as memory partitioning, caching, and pipelining can improve data access patterns and reduce memory contention. Effective management of on-chip and off-chip memory resources ensures that critical data is readily accessible, minimizing delays caused by memory bottlenecks.

- *Emerging Memory Technologies:* Researchers are exploring the use of emerging memory technologies such as Phase Change Memory (PCM) [48],

Spin-Torque-Transfer Magnetoresistive RAM (STT-MRAM), and Resistive RAM (ReRAM). These technologies offer advantages in terms of speed, power consumption, and density, which can help address the memory bandwidth limitations in SNN implementations.

Moreover, the development of SNNs on FPGAs requires sophisticated toolchains that can handle both hardware and neural network algorithm complexities. Existing high-level synthesis tools are not fully optimized for SNN development, requiring significant expertise to achieve efficient implementations. Power consumption remains a critical issue, with FPGAs typically consuming more power than application-specific integrated circuits (ASICs) for similar tasks. Techniques such as probabilistic spike propagation [49, 50] and event-driven processing have been proposed to mitigate this, but they add to the design complexity. Lastly, the evolving landscape of AI hardware, with emerging technologies like Phase Change Memories (PCM) and Spin-Torque-Transfer Magnetoresistive RAM (STT-MRAM), presents both opportunities and challenges for integrating these novel memory technologies into FPGA-based SNNs, necessitating continuous research and adaptation.

7. Conclusion

This chapter on FPGA-Based Spiking Neural Networks offers a thorough review of how Spiking Neural Network designs on FPGAs have evolved since the advent of FPGAs. Starting with the foundational designs of SNNs on FPGAs, the narrative progresses to elaborate on sophisticated architectures that aim to model and understand the intricate computational processes of neurons. It highlights the pivotal transformations brought about by FPGAs in neuromorphic computing, tracing the trajectory from basic implementations to the complex systems capable of simulating extensive neural networks today. A significant portion of the chapter is dedicated to exploring various architectures that have been developed, including everything from basic neuron models like integrate-and-fire, to more advanced setups that integrate dynamic learning capabilities and adaptability—a standout feature enabled by the reconfigurability of FPGAs. The discussion of SNN accelerators is particularly notable. These systems utilize the parallel processing capabilities of FPGAs to enhance neural computation speed and efficiency significantly. Over time, these accelerators have incorporated soft-processors and SoC capabilities on FPGAs, which manage more complex control flows and integrate learning algorithms directly into the hardware, showcasing the versatile applications of FPGAs in building more intelligent systems. Time-multiplexed designs also receive significant attention. These innovative designs allow for the simulation of large-scale neural networks by efficiently cycling through neuron simulations, thus offering a way to study complex neural behaviors within limited hardware scopes. Moreover, the chapter covers the development of self-trainable SNNs. These networks adjust and learn in real time, illustrating the potential of FPGAs to support systems that learn autonomously. This capability not only makes neural networks more adaptable but also opens up new avenues for real-world applications where learning on-the-fly is crucial. In conclusion, the chapter reflects on the promising future of FPGA-based SNNs given the continuous advancements in FPGA technology and ongoing research into neural networks. As hardware continues to shrink in size and grow in capability, and as FPGA designs become increasingly sophisticated, the potential for enhancing SNN capabilities seems limitless. The merging of FPGA flexibility, growing computational power, and advanced neural modeling techniques is likely to have a profound impact across various fields such as robotics, AI, and Neuromorphic computing, potentially leading to innovative approaches in the design and implementation of intelligent systems.

Authors contribution

Ali Mehrabi collected and reviewed the information and drafted the documents. André van Schaik provided feedback, edits, and additional opinions and interpretations.

Author details

Ali Mehrabi and André van Schaik*
International Centre for Neuromorphic Systems, MARCS Institute of Brain and Behaviour, Western Sydney University, Sydney, Australia

*Address all correspondence to: a.mehrabi@westernsydney.edu.au

References

[1] Moore GE. Cramming more components onto integrated circuits. Proceedings of the IEEE. 1998;**86**(1):82-85

[2] Trimberger SM. Three ages of FPGAS: A retrospective on the first thirty years of FPGA technology. IEEE Solid-State Circuits Magazine. 2018;**10**(2):16-29

[3] Gerstner W, Kistler WM. Spiking Neuron Models: Single Neurons, Populations, Plasticity. Cambridge, UK: Cambridge University Press; 2002

[4] Hodgkin AL, Huxley AF. A quantitative description of membrane current and its application to conduction and excitation in nerve. Bulletin of Mathematical Biology. 1990;**52**:25-71. DOI: 10.1007/BF02459568 [Accessed: April 12, 2024]

[5] Guo W, Fouda ME, Eltawil AM, Salama KN. Neural coding in spiking neural networks: A comparative study for robust neuromorphic systems. Frontiers in Neuroscience. 4 Mar 2021;**15**:638474, p. 21

[6] Rossmann M, Hesse B, Goser K, Buhlmeier A, Manteuffel G. Implementation of a biologically inspired neuron-model in FPGA. In: Proceedings of Fifth International Conference on Microelectronics for Neural Networks. Lausanne, Switzerland: IEEE; 1996. pp. 322-329

[7] Hebb D. The Organisation of Behaviour. NewYork, NY: John Wiley and Sons; 1949

[8] Rossmann M, Burwick C, Bühlmeier A, Manteuffel G, Goser K. Neural dynamics in real-time for large scale biomorphic neural networks. In: ICANN 98: Proceedings of the 8th International Conference on Artificial Neural Networks. Skövde, Sweden ICANN 1998. Perspectives in Neural Computing. London: Springer; 2-4 September 1998. pp. 481-486

[9] de Garis H, Korkin M, Fehr G. The CAM-brain machine (CBM): An FPGA based tool for evolving a 75 million neuron artificial brain to control a lifesized kitten robot. Autonomous Robots. 2001;**10**:235-249

[10] Upegui A, Peña-Reyes CA, Sanchez E. A functional spiking neuron hardware oriented model. In International Work-Conference on Artificial Neural Networks. Berlin, Heidelberg: Springer Berlin Heidelberg; 3 Jun 2003. pp. 136-143

[11] Ijaz Khan M, Lester DF, Plana LA, Rast A, Jin X, Painkras E, et al. SpiNNaker: Mapping Neural Networks onto a Massively-Parallel Chip Multiprocessor. 2008. DOI: 10.1109/ijcnn.2008.4634199 [Accessed: April 12, 2024]

[12] Upegui A, Peña-Reyes CA, Sanchez E. An FPGA platform for on-line topology exploration of spiking neural networks. Microprocessors and Microsystems. 2005;**29**(5):211-223

[13] Lim D, Peattie M. Two flows for partial reconfiguration: Module based or small bit manipulations. Xilinx, Inc. 17 May 2002:2100

[14] Vose MD. The simple genetic algorithm: Foundations and theory. Massachusetts, USA: MIT Press; 1999

[15] Hellmich H, Klar H. An FPGA based simulation acceleration platform for

spiking neural networks. In: The 2004 47th Midwest Symposium on Circuits and Systems, 2004. MWSCAS'04. Vol. 2. Hiroshima, Japan: IEEE; 2004. pp. II-II

[16] Glackin B, McGinnity TM, Maguire LP, Wu QX, Belatreche A. A novel approach for the implementation of large scale spiking neural networks on FPGA hardware. In: Cabestany J, Prieto A, Sandoval F, editors. Computational Intelligence and Bioinspired Systems. Vilanova i la Geltrú, Barcelona, Spain: IWANN; 2005. DOI: 10.1007/11494669_68 [Accessed: April 12, 2024]

[17] Cassidy A, Denham S, Kanold P, Andreou A. FPGA based silicon spiking neural array. In: 2007 IEEE Biomedical Circuits and Systems Conference. Montreal, QC, Canada: IEEE; 2007

[18] Pearson MJ, Pipe AG, Mitchinson B, Gurney K, Melhuish C, Gilhespy I, et al. Implementing spiking neural networks for real-time signal-processing and control applications: A model-validated FPGA approach. IEEE Transactions on Neural Networks. 2007;**18**(5):1472-1487. DOI: 10.1109/tnn.2007.891203

[19] Ros E, Ortigosa EM, Agis R, Carrillo R, Arnold M. Real-time computing platform for spiking neurons (RT-spike). IEEE Transactions on Neural Networks. 2006;**17**(4):1050-1063. DOI: 10.1109/tnn.2006.875980 [Accessed: April 12, 2024]

[20] Morgan F, Cawley S, McGinley B, Pande S, McDaid LJ, Glackin B, et al. Exploring the Evolution of NoC-Based Spiking Neural Networks on FPGAs. 2009. DOI: 10.1109/fpt.2009.5377663 [Accessed: April 12, 2024]

[21] Cawley S, Morgan F, McGinley B, Pande S, McDaid LJ, Carrillo S, et al. Hardware spiking neural network prototyping and application. Genetic Programming and Evolvable Machines. 2011;**12**:257-280

[22] Carrillo S, Harkin J, McDaid LJ, Morgan F, Pande S, Cawley S, et al. Scalable hierarchical network-on-chip architecture for spiking neural network hardware implementations. IEEE Transactions on Parallel and Distributed Systems. 2013;**24**(12):2451-2461. DOI: 10.1109/tpds.2012.289 [Accessed: April 12, 2024]

[23] Izhikevich EM. Poly-chronization: Computation with spikes. Neural Computation. 2006;**18**:245-282

[24] Wang R, Cohen G, Stiefel KM, Hamilton TJ, Tapson J, van Schaik A. An FPGA implementation of a polychronous spiking neural network with delay adaptation. Frontiers in Neuroscience. 13 Feb 2013;**7**:14

[25] Wang R, Hamilton TJ, Tapson J, and van Schaik A. An FPGA Design Framework for Large-Scale Spiking Neural Networks. 2014 DOI: 10.1109/iscas.2014.6865169. [Accessed: April 12, 2024]

[26] Neil D, Liu SC. Minitaur, an event-driven FPGA-based spiking network accelerator. IEEE Transactions on Very Large Scale Integration (VLSI) Systems. 2014;**22**(12):2621-2628

[27] Wang RM, Thakur CS, Van Schaik A. An FPGA-based massively parallel neuromorphic cortex simulator. Frontiers in Neuroscience. 10 Apr 2018;**12**:213. DOI: 10.3389/fnins.2018.0021

[28] Deep South. Home [Internet]. Available from: https://www.deepsouth.org.au

[29] Li J, Shen G, Zhao D, Zhang QW, Zeng Y. FireFly: A high-throughput

hardware accelerator for spiking neural networks with efficient DSP and memory optimization. IEEE Transactions on Very Large Scale Integration Systems. 2023;**31**(8):1178-1191. DOI: 10.1109/tvlsi.2023.3279349 [Accessed: April 12, 2024]

[30] Mehrabi A, Bethi Y, van Schaik A, Wabnitz A, Afshar S. Efficient Implementation of a Multi-Layer Gradient-Free Online-Trainable Spiking Neural Network on FPGA. arXiv (Cornell University); 2023

[31] Mehrabi A, Bethi Y, van Schaik A, Afshar S. An optimized multi-layer spiking neural network implementation in FPGA without multipliers. Procedia Computer Science. 1 Jan 2023;**222**:407-414. DOI: 10.1016/j.procs.2023.08.179

[32] Guerra-Hernandez EI, Espinal A, Batres-Mendoza P, Garcia-Capulin CH, Romero-Troncoso RD, Rostro-Gonzalez H. A FPGA-based neuromorphic locomotion system for multi-legged robots. IEEE Access. 2017;**5**:8301-8312

[33] Mokhtar M, Halliday DM, Tyrrell AM. Autonomous navigational controller inspired by the hippocampus. In: 2007 International Joint Conference on Neural Networks. Orlando, FL, USA: IEEE; 2007. pp. 813-818

[34] Mitchell JP, Bruer G, Dean ME, Plank JS, Rose GS, Schuman CD. NeoN: Neuromorphic control for autonomous robotic navigation. In: 2017 IEEE International Symposium on Robotics and Intelligent Sensors (IRIS). Ottawa, ON, Canada: IEEE; 2017. pp. 136-142

[35] Roggen D, Hofmann S, Thoma Y, Floreano D. Hardware spiking neural network with run-time reconfigurable connectivity in an autonomous robot. In: NASA/DoD Conference on Evolvable Hardware, 2003. Proceedings. Chicago, IL, USA: IEEE; 2003. pp. 189-198

[36] Deng B, Fan Y, Wang J, Yang S. Auditory perception architecture with spiking neural network and implementation on FPGA. Neural Networks. 2023;**165**:31-42

[37] Glackin B, Harkin J, McGinnity TM, Maguire LP, Wu Q. Emulating spiking neural networks for edge detection on FPGA hardware. In: 2009 International Conference on Field Programmable Logic and Applications. Prague, Czech Republic: IEEE; 2009. pp. 670-673

[38] Caron LC, Mailhot F, Rouat J. FPGA implementation of a spiking neural network for pattern matching. In: 2011 IEEE International Symposium of Circuits and Systems (ISCAS). Rio de Janeiro, Brazil: IEEE; 2011. pp. 649-652

[39] Iakymchuk T, Rosado-Munoz A, Bataller-Mompean M, Guerrero-Martínez JF, Francés-Villora JV, Wegrzyn M, et al. Hardware-accelerated spike train generation for neuromorphic image and video processing. In: 2014 IX Southern Conference on Programmable Logic (SPL). Buenos Aires, Argentina: IEEE; 2014. pp. 1-6

[40] Paz IT, Hernández Gress N, González Mendoza M. Pattern recognition with spiking neural networks. In: Advances in Soft Computing and its Applications: 12th Mexican International Conference on Artificial Intelligence, MICAI 2013; November 24-30, 2013; Mexico City, Mexico, Proceedings, Part II 12. Berlin Heidelberg: Springer; 2013. pp. 279-288

[41] Lammie C, Hamilton T, Azghadi MR. Unsupervised character recognition with a simplified FPGA neuromorphic system. In: 2018 IEEE International Symposium on Circuits and Systems (ISCAS). Florence, Italy: IEEE; 2018. pp. 1-5

[42] Mehrabi A, Dennler N, Bethi Y, van Schaik A, Afshar S. Real-time anomaly detection using hardware-based unsupervised spiking neural network (TinySNN). In: 2024 IEEE 33rd International Symposium on Industrial Electronics (ISIE). Ulsan South Korea: IEEE; 18 Jun 2024. pp. 1-8

[43] Wang J, Li T, Sun C, Yan R, Chen X. Improved spiking neural network for intershaft bearing fault diagnosis. Journal of Manufacturing Systems. 2022;**65**:208-219

[44] Zahm W, Stern T, Bal M, Sengupta A, Jose A, Chelian S, et al. Cyber-neuro RT: Real-time neuromorphic cybersecurity. Procedia Computer Science. 2022;**213**:536-545

[45] Scrugli MA, Busia P, Leone G, Meloni P. On-FPGA spiking neural networks for integrated near-sensor ECG analysis. In: 2024 Design, Automation and Test in Europe Conference and Exhibition (DATE). Valencia, Spain: IEEE; 2024. pp. 1-6

[46] AlZaabi M, Halawani Y, Mohammad B. In-memory computing using phase change memory. In: In-Memory Computing Hardware Accelerators for Data-Intensive Applications. Cham: Springer Nature Switzerland; 2023. pp. 81-96

[47] Deng L, Li G, Han S, Shi L, Xie Y. Model compression and hardware acceleration for neural networks: A comprehensive survey. Proceedings of the IEEE. 2020;**108**(4):485-532

[48] Liu ZC, Wang L. Applications of phase change materials in electrical regime from conventional storage memory to novel neuromorphic computing. IEEE Access. 2020;**8**:76471-76499

[49] Zhu X, Yuan L, Wang D, Chen Y. FPGA implementation of a probabilistic neural network for spike sorting. In: 2010 2nd International Conference on Information Engineering and Computer Science. Wuhan, China: IEEE; 2010. pp. 1-4

[50] Nallathambi A, Chandrachoodan N. Probabilistic Spike Propagation for FPGA Implementation of Spiking Neural Networks. Online. arXiv preprint arXiv:2001.09725. 2020

Section 3

Edge Applications

Chapter 6

Exploring Associative Learning of Audio and Color Stimuli with Neuromorphic Robots in a T-Maze

Md Abu Bakr Siddique, Tianze Liu, Yan Zhang and Hongyu An

Abstract

Deep neural networks (DNNs) have achieved remarkable success in various cognitive tasks through training on extensive labeled datasets. However, the heavy reliance on these datasets poses challenges for DNNs in scenarios with energy constraints in particular scenarios, such as on the moon. On the contrary, animals exhibit a self-learning capability by interacting with their surroundings and memorizing concurrent events without annotated data—a process known as associative learning. A classic example of associative learning is when a rat memorizes desired and undesired stimuli while exploring a T-maze. The successful implementation of associative learning aims to replicate the self-learning mechanisms observed in animals, addressing challenges in data-constrained environments. While current implementations of associative learning are predominantly small scale and offline, this work pioneers associative learning in a robot equipped with a neuromorphic chip, specifically for online learning in a T-maze. The system successfully replicates classic associative learning observed in rodents, using neuromorphic robots as substitutes for rodents. The neuromorphic robot autonomously learns the cause-and-effect relationship between audio and visual stimuli.

Keywords: associative learning, Hebbian learning, neuromorphic computing, neuromorphic robot, neuromorphic chip

1. Introduction

Deep neural networks (DNNs) have demonstrated remarkable success across various cognitive tasks [1], primarily attributed to their training on extensive datasets. DNNs refine their accuracy during training by comparing predictions against labeled data and adjusting their weights through backpropagation algorithms. Generally, larger datasets and more intricate neural networks yield superior accuracy [1, 2], leading to a continual push for larger datasets and more complex architectures [1–5]. However, the increasing size of DNNs and dependence on labeled datasets bring significant challenges, including high power consumption, data scarcity, and limited flexibility in autonomous operations. These challenges render DNNs less ideal for applications with stringent size, weight, and power (SWaP) constraints [1, 2], such as planetary rovers that demand high adaptability and autonomy with minimal human oversight in energy-limited and communication-restricted environments [2].

To mitigate these issues, we aim to enhance the autonomous capabilities of intelligent robots by mimicking animal associative learning through neuromorphic systems. These systems provide a more energy-efficient approach to artificial intelligence by replicating brain functions. Associative learning, a prevalent self-learning mechanism in animals, allows them to adapt to their environment by remembering concurrent events through interaction [6–8]. A quintessential example of this learning process is seen in rodents navigating a T-maze, where they learn to associate specific stimuli with positive or negative outcomes through repeated exposures. For instance, one arm of the maze might lead to a reward like food, while the other might offer no reward or a mild aversive stimulus. This associative learning process can similarly empower robots to link information and experiences, enabling them to autonomously navigate and adapt in dynamic environments, such as those encountered on Mars.

Several studies have investigated associative learning [7, 9–15] but often face limitations such as small-scale neural networks, a preference for simulations over real-world experiments, and a lack of real-world robotic deployment for testing [11–15]. To address these limitations, we have taken a novel approach. We developed a large-scale associative learning system using a neuromorphic chip (the Xylo chip) and deployed it on a mobile robot for online learning through real-world interactions. This successful implementation of associative learning in a real-world robotic deployment reassures the practicality of our research. The robot, mimicking rodents in a T-maze, learns by associating audio and visual signals as conditional and unconditional stimuli.

Our research marks a significant advancement in artificial intelligence and robotics. By implementing classical T-maze associative learning on a mobile robot in real-world settings, we have not only enhanced our understanding of associative learning but also paved the way for developing more efficient and adaptable robots. The integration of the Xylo chip with mobile robots has notably improved their signal processing speed and energy efficiency, making them more viable for practical applications. This work inspires us to imagine a future where robots can navigate and adapt in dynamic environments, such as those encountered on Mars, with minimal human intervention. The improved signal processing speed and energy efficiency of robots integrated with the Xylo chip should make us all feel optimistic about the future of robotics.

In our experiments, the red color input is an unconditional and aversive stimulus, while audio signals function as conditional and neutral stimuli. The neuromorphic robot learns to avoid the arm presenting the red color in the T-maze, with distinct neural assemblies processing the color and auditory signals.

This chapter's contributions are as follows:

1. Replicating the classical rodent associative learning paradigm in a T-maze in real time, both in simulations and experimental settings.

2. Implementing a neural assembly designed as a decision-making component and applying it to the associative learning paradigm in the T-maze.

2. Background of rodents' associative learning in T-maze

The T-maze paradigm is a pivotal tool in the study of associative learning in rodents, particularly rats, which holds significant importance. It offers profound insights into spatial navigation and memory processes. The experimental setup, featuring a T-shaped maze with distinct arms and a decision point, presents a unique challenge to the rats, compelling them to navigate and make choices based on spatial cues.

Initially, rats display exploratory behavior, moving through the maze without a specific preference for either arm. As the experiments progress, their behavior changes markedly. Through repeated trials, the rats begin to form associations between particular stimuli or cues in the arms and the outcomes of their choices. This learning process becomes evident as the rats consistently favor one arm, driven by the expectation of a positive reward, such as food.

The adaptability of rats in T-maze experiments is a testament to the dynamic nature of associative learning. These rodents demonstrate remarkable cognitive flexibility, adjusting their arm choices in response to changing spatial cues or new stimuli. For instance, when the location of the reward is altered, rats undergo a learning phase to realign their choices with the new reward location, showcasing their ability to adapt to new contingencies.

The neural mechanisms driving associative learning in the T-maze are intricate and complex, involving a web of interactions within the rat's brain. Key brain regions involved in memory, spatial navigation, and reward processing play crucial roles. The T-maze paradigm serves as an invaluable tool for delving into the fundamental principles of cognitive processes and behavior in mammals, casting light on the underlying neural circuitry and its adaptability.

3. Associative learning with neuromorphic robots

Our associative learning system, with its two distinct signal pathways for processing auditory and visual inputs, as illustrated in **Figure 1**, has the potential to revolutionize the field. This configuration empowers the neuromorphic robot to handle auditory and visual stimuli simultaneously, thereby greatly improving its learning efficiency.

The auditory pathway is a key component of our system, which captures and decodes sound cues and enables the robot to interpret and learn from auditory signals in its environment. Meanwhile, the visual pathway processes visual data and allows the robot to identify and respond to visual stimuli essential for associative learning. Integrating these pathways enriches the robot's cognitive abilities, facilitating a deeper understanding of the cause-and-effect relationships between auditory and visual inputs.

3.1 Audio and visual perception using a neuromorphic system

Figure 2(a) depicts the architecture of the audio perception neural network. Auditory data is imported into 16 channels via a microphone, aligning with the capabilities of the Xylo chip, as shown in **Figure 2(b)**. For this study, we focused on a

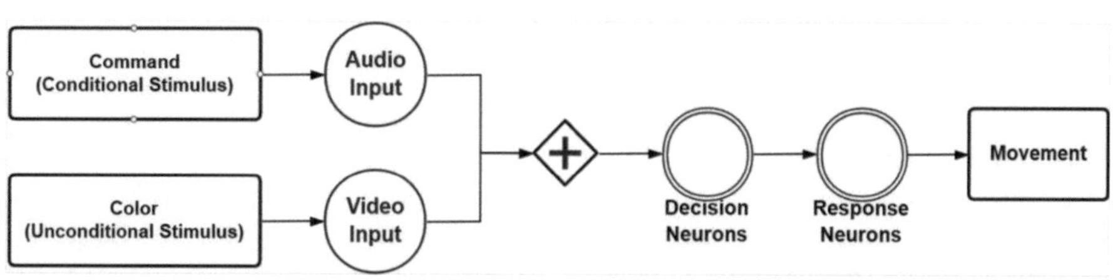

Figure 1.
Overall associative learning implementation.

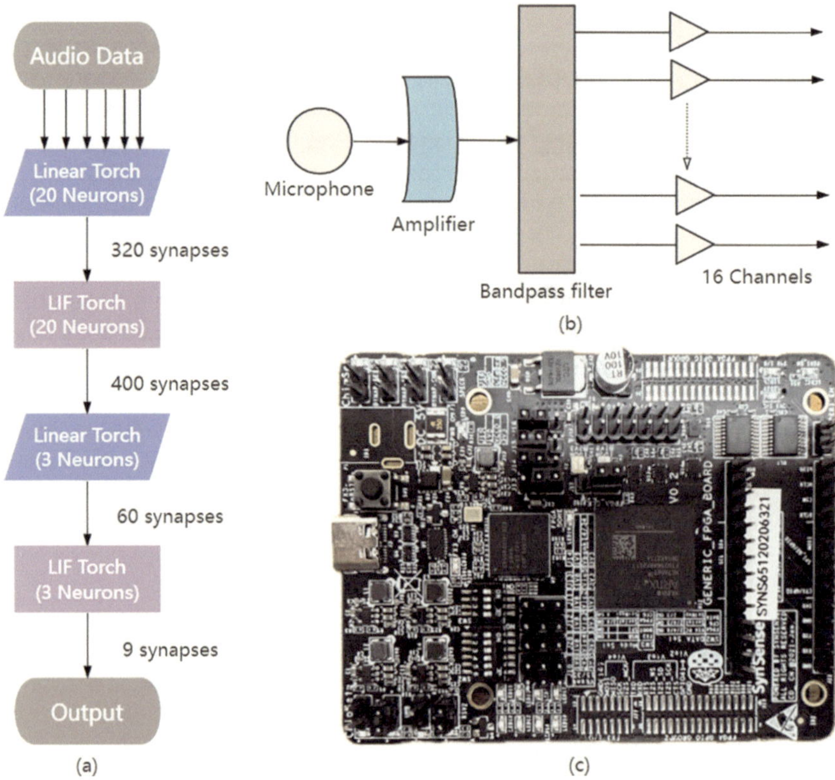

Figure 2.
(a) Audio perception neural network architecture. (b) Preprocessing module of Xylo neuromorphic chip. (c) XyloA2TestBoard for audio command detector model deployment.

subset of commands, specifically "left" and "right". The auditory data was reorganized by transforming events into frames. **Figure 2(c)** illustrates the Xylo neuromorphic chip processing audio perception.

The network architecture consists of an input layer with 16 channels, processed through a hidden layer containing 20 neurons. The final output layer produces 3 units. The simulations operate with a timestep of 10 milliseconds.

The input data was structured into tensors to seamlessly integrate with our model, enabling the generation of visual representations for the "left" and "right" audio commands. **Figures 3** and **4** illustrate the spiking signals for the "left" and "right" commands processed by the Xylo neuromorphic chips. The spiking neural networks (SNNs) underwent training for 17,500 epochs. Utilizing the Adam optimizer with a learning rate 1e-5, the model achieved a 92.

3.2 Power usage of Xylo neuromorphic chip

During the deployment of our trained SNNs on the Xylo neuromorphic chip, power consumption emerged as a crucial metric for assessing the system's efficiency in processing "left" and "right" audio commands. **Table 1** shows that the Logic component is the highest power consumer, drawing 1844.26 mW. The IO circuitry and the analog front-end (AFE) IO components consume 213.94 and 230.98 mW, respectively. Importantly, the Logic AFE component has high efficiency and

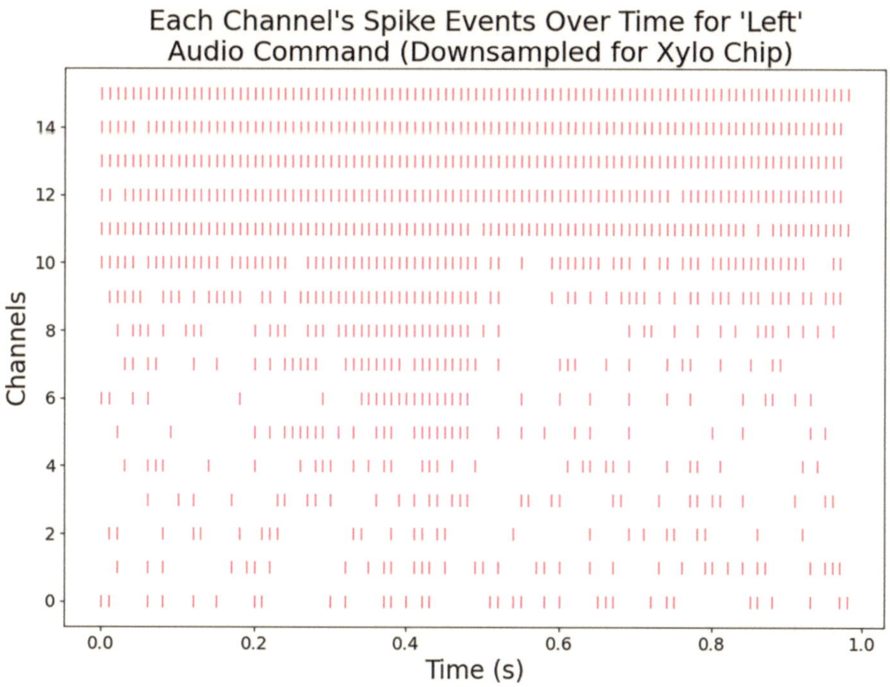

Figure 3.
Spike events for a left audio command.

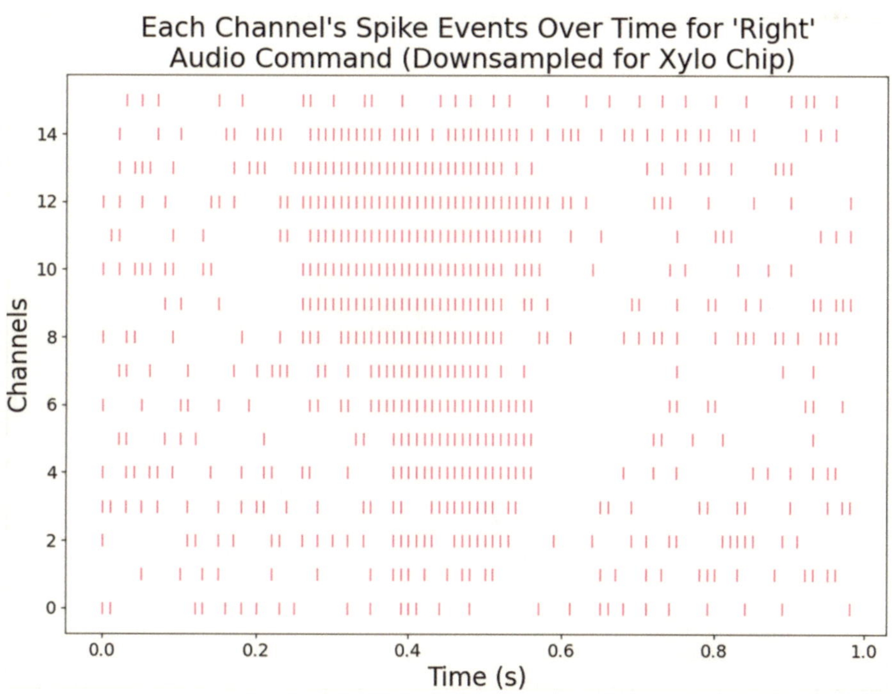

Figure 4.
Spike events for a down-sampled right audio command data.

Component	Power consumption (mW)
IO circuitry	213.94
Logic AFE	17.96
IO AFE	230.98
Logic	1844.26

Table 1.
Power consumption of Xylo neuromorphic chip.

consumption of only 17.96 mW, which provides reassurance about the chip's performance. These metrics underscore the feasibility and operational efficiency of implementing the associative learning system on the Xylo neuromorphic chip.

4. Simulations and experiments for associative learning in a T-maze using neuromorphic robot

In our system, detecting the red color is an unconditioned stimulus, while the audio command is a conditioned stimulus. When the robot detects the red color ahead, it stops and reverses direction, mimicking a rat's fear response. **Figure 5** depicts the experimental setup with our neuromorphic robot, and **Figure 6** illustrates the T-maze simulation and experimental scenarios. We developed specialized neuron models that convert audio commands and color data into spike signals to enable the robot to replicate a fear-conditioned response. Additionally, specific motion neurons are designed to control the robot's movements. These neurons are adaptations of the classic leaky integrate-and-fire (LIF) neurons, defined by the following equation:

$$C_m \frac{dV_m}{dt} = \frac{C_m}{\tau_{RC}}(E_L - V_m) + A \times I_{app}, \tag{1}$$

Figure 5.
Experimental setup of a mobile robot and Xylo neuromorphic chip.

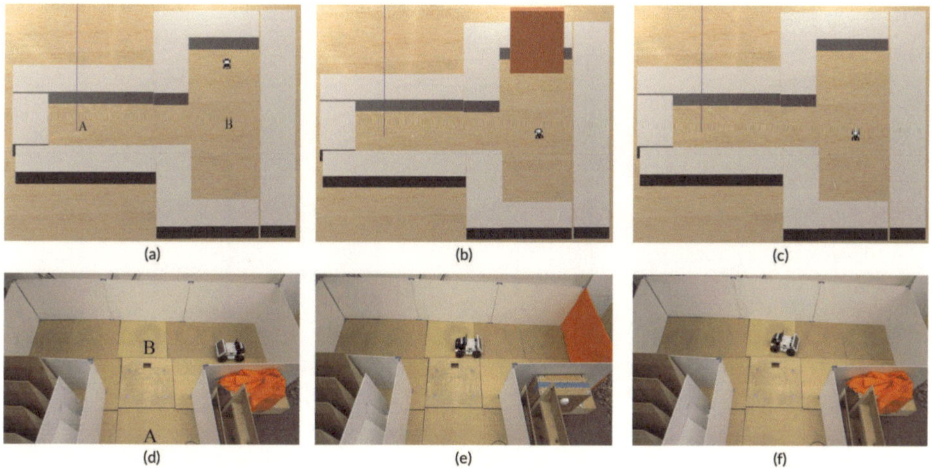

Figure 6.
Replicating Associative Learning in a T-Maze: Simulation and Experimental Exploration with a Neuromorphic Robot. (a) Gazebo simulation depicting the T-maze for robot navigation. (b) Detection of red color (US) input at position B. (c) The robot will learn to stop and turn to the arm with no red color presented. (d) The actual experimental setup of T-maze. (e) Detection of red color (US) input at position B in actual T-maze. (f) The robot will learn to stop and turn to the arm with no red color presented.

Neuron parameters	τ_{RC}	τ_{ref}	$V_{reset}(V)$	$V_{th}(V)$	**Gain (A)**
Color neuron	0.02	0.002	0.5	1.0	1.5
Command neuron	0.03	0.02	−0.5	0.9	1
Movement neuron	0.04	0.002	−0.1	0.8	1

Table 2.
LIF neuron parameters.

Where A denotes the input signal gain, is the membrane RC time constant, defines the membrane capacitance, and is the membrane potential leak potential (**Table 2**).

Table 2 lists the parameter values of the LIF neurons, which have been computed and refined to ensure they produce the desired experimental results. The gain and bias of the color-detecting neuron were determined empirically, ensuring it fires when detecting red stimuli but remains inactive for other colors.

The command neuron and LIF neurons calculate their gains and bias experimentally. The command neuron fires only when the aggregate output from the audio feature neurons is sufficiently high. The movement neuron fires whenever it receives continuous input spikes from the command or color neurons. The firing activations of these neurons are shown in **Figures 7–10**, respectively.

The XyloMonitor deployment tool facilitated real-time robot navigation via audio commands. This tool processes live audio inputs specifically in the “left” and “right” directions and predicts the robot’s intended direction. The XyloMonitor is configured to capture and process audio commands, with a brief waiting period mandated for the analog front-end (AFE) autocalibration, ensuring optimal and consistent audio data acquisition.

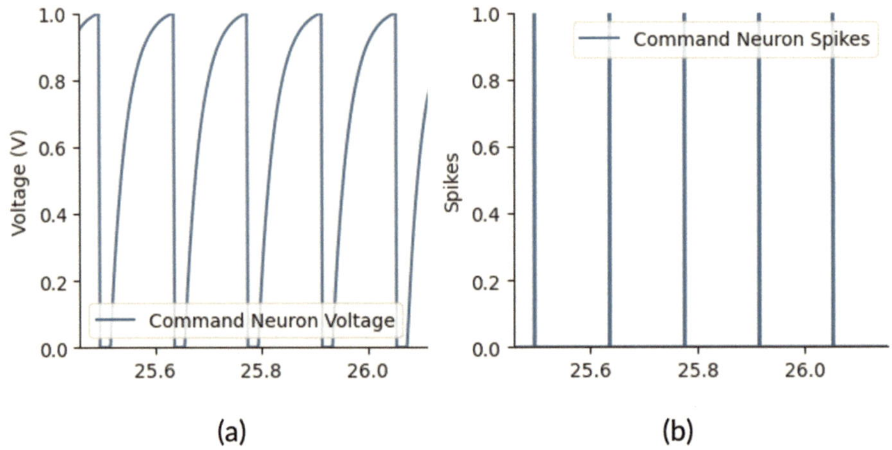

Figure 7.
Command neuron firing activity. (a) Membrane potential of command neuron (b) spiking activity of command neuron.

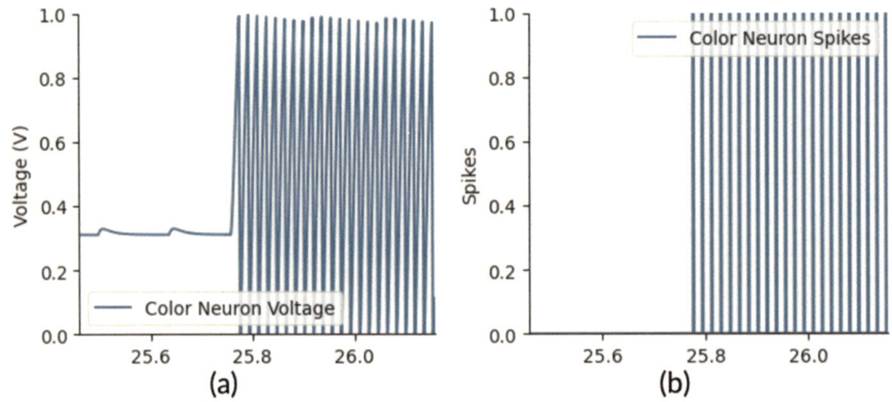

Figure 8.
Color neuron firing activity. (a) Membrane potential of color neuron (b) spiking activity of color neuron.

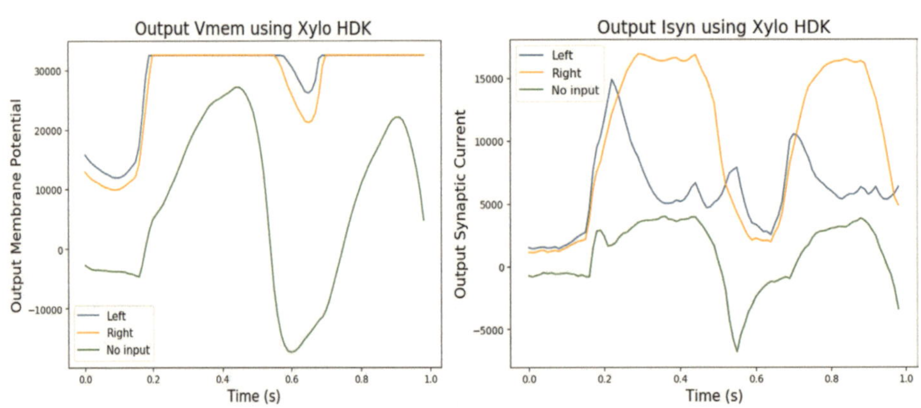

Figure 9.
Output membrane potentials and neuromorphic Xylo chip synaptic currents.

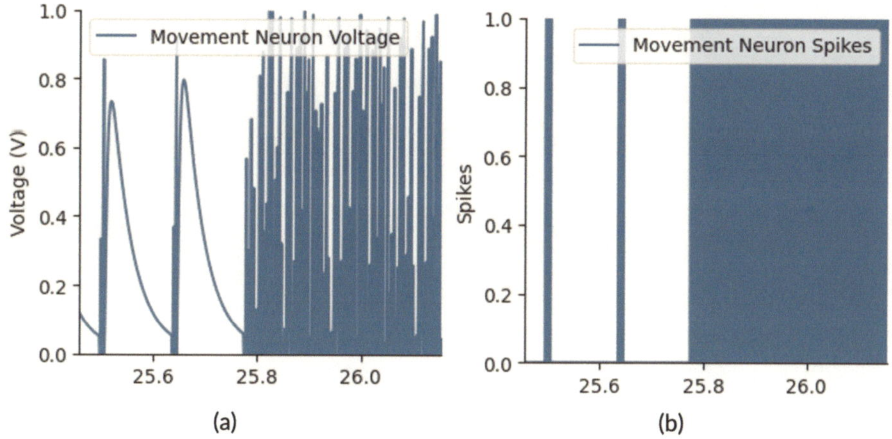

Figure 10.
Movement neuron firing activity. (a) Membrane potential of movement neuron (b) spiking activity of movement neuron.

Hebbian learning is utilized to adjust synaptic weights based on the principle that simultaneous activation of pre- and postsynaptic neurons strengthens their connection. The equation governing synaptic weight changes describes this adjustment. To manage variations in command delivery, such as differing volumes or distances from the microphone, the sensitivity of the audio capture system is increased using XyloMonitor, ensuring clear and accurate command recognition.

The Xylo neuromorphic chip processes incoming audio signals within a 250-millisecond time frame. The neuron's membrane potential, which indicates the received audio signal, determines the intended direction. If the membrane potential suggests "left," the robot turns left; if it suggests "right," the robot turns right. After processing, the determined direction is conveyed to the robot, directing its movement.

Figure 9 presents the membrane potential of audio neurons and the resulting synaptic currents on the Xylo neuromorphic chip in response to left and right audio commands.

Upon receiving a "left" or "right" command prediction from the Xylo neuromorphic chip, an additional neural network is deployed to control the robot's movement in the specified direction. This network includes ten LIF neurons specifically designed to ensure the robot steers accurately left or right.

The LIF neuron model is characterized by two key parameters: the membrane time constant and the refractory period. The refractory period is minimized to allow for rapid neuron firing following an output spike, enhancing the responsiveness of the robot's movements. Synaptic weights of the neurons are shown in **Table 3**.

The network receives a constant input, which generates a specific firing pattern when processed through the neurons with assigned synaptic weights. This pattern results in a mean firing probability, crucial for determining the robot's movement direction within the decision-making process. If the firing probability surpasses a threshold of 0.5, the neuromorphic robot turns left; if it falls below this threshold, then it turns right.

Specific synaptic weights and neuron properties are fixed to ensure the neuromorphic robot consistently turns left with a mean firing probability of 0.9. The following figure illustrates the firing probability of LIF neurons over time for the left turn. Neuron property are shown in **Table 4**.

Neuron index	Synaptic weights from input to neurons	Synaptic weights from neurons to output
1	45.0	9.0
2	−27.0	−18.0
3	72.0	27.0
4	−9.0	−36.0
5	63.0	45.0
6	−54.0	54.0
7	18.0	−63.0
8	81.0	72.0
9	−63.0	−81.0
10	9.0	9.0

Table 3.
Synaptic weights of the neurons for a left turn.

Parameter	Value
Membrane time constant	0.02
Refractory period	0.001
Seed	42

Table 4.
Neuron property for left turn.

Specific synaptic weights and neuron properties are established to guarantee that the neuromorphic robot consistently turns right with a mean firing probability of 0.2. **Table 5** illustrates the firing probability of LIF neurons over time for the right turn.

Neuron index	Synaptic weights from input to neurons	Synaptic weights from neurons to output
1	2.9	0.9
2	−0.5	−0.4
3	3.7	0.8
4	−0.3	−0.6
5	3.0	0.7
6	−0.6	0.8
7	0.8	−0.9
8	3.8	0.7
9	−0.7	−1.1
10	2.8	0.6

Table 5.
Synaptic weights of right-turning neurons.

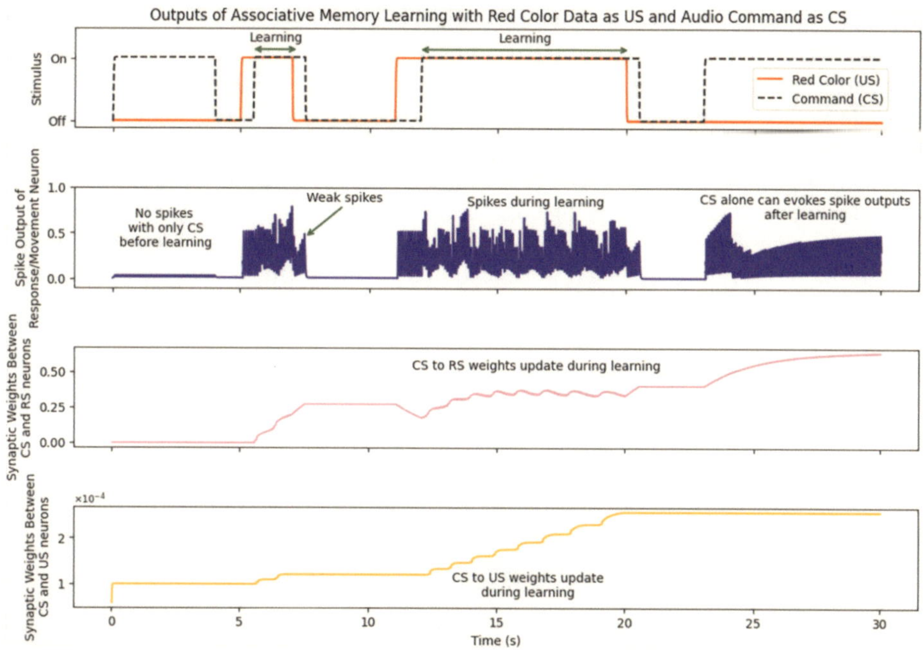

Figure 11.
Results of our associative learning.

The system's performance hinges on the pre- and postsynaptic neurons' learning and firing rates. In our experiment, the learning rate is set at 1e-4. **Figure 11** showcases the outcomes of our associative learning process.

Initially, the movement and audio command neurons (CS) possess low synaptic weights, preventing the movement neuron from responding to "left" and "right" auditory commands, resulting in no turns within the T-maze. Over time, associative learning updates the synaptic weights between the movement and audio command neurons. As a result, the movement neuron fires when the color-detection neuron detects red (US) through the camera. The activation of both command detection and movement neurons in response to combined color and audio stimuli strengthens the synaptic weights in the conditional signal pathway. **Figure 11** shows that the simultaneous application of red color and audio command stimuli enhances synaptic weights, though initially limited overlap leads to only moderate increases.

Insufficient overlap during the initial phase means that audio commands alone cannot trigger the movement neuron, as illustrated in **Figure 11**. However, with a more extended overlap period in the subsequent phase, there is a more significant increase in synaptic weights. Consequently, even without the red color input, the movement neuron will respond to auditory stimuli ("left" or "right" commands), demonstrating successful associative learning.

We replicated rat's associative learning experiments using a T-maze to evaluate and validate our associative learning system. **Figure 6** depicts both the simulation and experimental setups of our T-maze. In these setups, the red color functions as an unconditioned stimulus, while the audio commands act as conditioned stimuli.

Initially, the robot starts moving forward from the starting chamber, designated as position A and proceeds to the turning point, marked as position B. Upon reaching position B, the robot receives a "left" or "right" command and turns 90 degrees accordingly, moving into the corresponding arm of the T-maze, as shown in **Figure 6(a)**.

In our simulation, the red color is assigned as an aversive stimulus. The robot responds to this unpleasant stimulus by turning away from the red color and heading toward the arm without the red color.

During associative learning, the robot initially moves from position A to B, encountering simultaneous turning commands and red color stimuli. The color-detection neuron fires in response to red, prompting the robot to choose the arm without the red color, as depicted in **Figure 6(b)**. During this phase, synaptic weights between the audio signal and movement neurons increase due to the concurrent audio and color spikes.

After 2–3 trials, the neuromorphic robot strengthens the synaptic connections related to the red color and audio commands, effectively memorizing the association. Consequently, even without the red color, the robot will move toward the "safe" arm it memorized—the arm without the red stimulus. **Figure 6(c)** shows that when the robot reaches position B, it stops, reverses 180 degrees to the right, and proceeds into the arm it has learned to identify as "safe". The real-world T-maze experiments mirror this associative learning process, as **Figure 6(d–f)** illustrates.

$$\Delta w = \eta\left(xy - \beta w y^2\right), \tag{2}$$

Where η is the learning rate, x is the firing rate of the presynaptic neuron, y is the firing rate of the postsynaptic neuron, β is a constant that determines the strength of the normalization, and w is the current synaptic weight.

Parameter	Value
Membrane time constant	0.02
Refractory period	0.002
Seed	42

Table 6.
Neuron property for right turn.

	Neuron	Task	Learning methods	Validation
[12]	6	N/A	N/A	Simulation
[13]	3	N/A	N/A	Simulation
[14]	5	N/A	N/A	Simulation
[11]	3	N/A	N/A	Simulation
[16]	3	N/A	N/A	Simulation
[17]	3	N/A	N/A	Simulation
[9]	20	N/A	Pretraining	Simulation
[18, 19]	1419	Fear conditioning	No pretraining	Experiment
This work	259	Spatial learning and memory	Self-learning	Simulation & Experiment

Table 7.
Synaptic weights of right-turning neurons.

The term serves as a mechanism to prevent weights from growing without bounds. It functions as a subtractive normalization, adjusting the scale of weight changes based on the weight's size and the postsynaptic activity. This approach helps maintain stability and control in learning, ensuring synaptic weights do not undergo uncontrolled growth. **Table 6** shows the results of the associative memory learning result. Then we make the comparison of scale and association capability with other works in **Table** 7.

5. Conclusion

This study presents the implementation of rodent-like associative learning in a T-maze using neuromorphic robots. By integrating the Xylo neuromorphic chip into a mobile robot, our system replicates the classic T-maze experiments observed in rodents. The robot learns to associate the red color (unconditioned stimulus) with audio commands (conditioned stimulus) through Hebbian learning and LIF neurons. Our findings demonstrate real-time associative learning, highlighting potential applications for autonomous robots operating in energy-constrained and adaptive environments.

Acknowledgements

This work was supported by the Robust Intelligence program in the Directorate for Computer and Information Science and Engineering (CISE) of National Science Foundation under Award Number 2245712.

Author details

Md Abu Bakr Siddique[1], Tianze Liu[1], Yan Zhang[2] and Hongyu An[1*]

1 Department of Electrical and Computer Engineering, Michigan Technological University, Houghton, MI, USA

2 Department of Biological Sciences, Michigan Technological University, Houghton, MI, USA

*Address all correspondence to: hongyua@mtu.edu

References

[1] Goodfellow I, Bengio Y, Courville A. Deep Learning. Cambridge, MA: MIT Press; 2016. Available from: http://www.deeplearningbook.org

[2] Devlin J, et al. Bert: Pre-training of deep bidirectional transformers for language understanding. arXiv preprint arXiv:1810.04805. 2018

[3] Sun C et al. Revisiting unreasonable effectiveness of data in deep learning era. In: Proceedings of the IEEE International Conference on Computer Vision. New York City, U.S.: IEEE; 2017

[4] Sengupta S et al. A review of deep learning with special emphasis on architectures, applications and recent trends. Knowledge-Based Systems. 2020; **194**:105596

[5] An H et al. Robust deep reservoir computing through reliable memristor with improved heat dissipation capability. IEEE Transactions on Computer-Aided Design of Integrated Circuits and Systems. 2020;**40**(3): 574-583

[6] Kandel ER, Schwartz JH, Jessell TM, Siegelbaum S, Hudspeth AJ, Mack S. Principles of Neural Science. Vol. 4. New York: McGraw-Hill; 2000

[7] Sun J et al. Memristor-based neural network circuit of full-function pavlov associative memory with time delay and variable learning rate. IEEE Transactions on Cybernetics. 2019;**50**(7):2935-2945

[8] Kohonen T. Self-Organization and Associative Memory. Vol. 8. New York, NY, USA: Springer Science & Business Media; 2012

[9] An H, An Q, Yi Y. Realizing behavior level associative memory learning through three-dimensional memristor-based neuromorphic circuits. IEEE Transactions on Emerging Topics in Computational Intelligence. 2019;**5**(4): 668-678

[10] Hu SG et al. Associative memory realized by a reconfigurable memristive Hopfield neural network. Nature Communications. 2015;**6**(1):7522

[11] Moon K et al. Hardware implementation of associative memory characteristics with analogue-type resistive-switching device. Nanotechnology. 2014;**25**(49):495204

[12] Yang J et al. A novel memristive Hopfield neural network with application in associative memory. Neurocomputing. 2017;**227**:142-148

[13] Liu X, Zeng Z, Wen S. Implementation of memristive neural network with full-function pavlov associative memory. IEEE Transactions on Circuits and Systems I: Regular Papers. 2016;**63**(9):1454-1463

[14] Hu X et al. Modeling affections with memristor-based associative memory neural networks. Neurocomputing. 2017; **223**:129-137

[15] Eryilmaz SB et al. Brain-like associative learning using a nanoscale non-volatile phase change synaptic device array. Frontiers in Neuroscience. 2014;**8**:205

[16] Ziegler M et al. An electronic version of Pavlov's dog. Advanced Functional Materials. 2012;**22**(13):2744-2749

[17] Pershin YV, Di Ventra M. Experimental demonstration of associative memory with memristive neural networks. Neural Networks. 2010;**23**(7):881-886

[18] Engelbrecht A, An H, Yi YC. Neuromorphic Computing. BoD–Books on Demand. Norderstedt, Germany; 2023

[19] Zins N, An H. Reproducing fear conditioning of rats with unmanned ground vehicles and neuromorphic systems. In: 2023 24th International Symposium on Quality Electronic Design (ISQED). New York City, U.S.: IEEE; 2023

Chapter 7

Artificial Neural Network-Based Approach for Surface Energy Prediction

Fuming Lai and Shengfu Tong

Abstract

This chapter explores the utilization of artificial neural network (ANN) models in predicting surface energy values. ANN models are a type of machine learning (ML) algorithm inspired by the way the human brain processes information. The chapter delves into the theoretical foundations of ANN models and their application in modeling surface energy, a crucial parameter in various scientific and industrial processes. By training the ANN models with relevant datasets, researchers can develop a predictive model capable of estimating surface energy values with high accuracy. The chapter discusses the methodology, challenges, and potential benefits of using an ANN-based approach for surface energy prediction, offering insights into the intersection of artificial intelligence and materials science.

Keywords: ANN models, surface energy, predictive model, machine learning, material science

1. Introduction

The surface energy of a crystal, which is the excess energy at the surface compared to the bulk due to unbalanced interatomic forces, is a critical concept in materials science with wide-ranging applications [1–4]. It is fundamental to the processes of nucleation and crystal growth, influences the adhesion and wetting properties of materials, and is directly related to surface tension. Surface energy is also essential in the design of catalysts, where it affects reaction rates by altering the energy landscape at the reaction sites [5, 6]. Furthermore, it plays a role in enhancing the mechanical properties of materials through grain boundary formation and is crucial in the synthesis of nanoparticles with specific properties for various applications [7]. Surface energy calculations play a pivotal role in a multitude of applications across various scientific disciplines, providing critical insights into the behavior and properties of materials at the atomic level [8, 9]. Calculating the surface energy of a crystal is a complex and important task, as it involves the precise assessment of the unbalanced interatomic forces at the crystal surface [10–12]. The computation of surface energy must take into account not only the influence of atomic distances, temperature, and pressure but also the diversity of surface structures, such as terraces, kinks, and vacancies. Additionally, surface atoms may undergo reconstruction to form structures that are distinct from the bulk phase, as well as the impact of adsorbed atoms or molecules on the surface energy.

The evolution of surface energy calculation methods has mirrored the depth and breadth of research in this field, transitioning from early semiempirical models to contemporary first-principles calculations [13]. Each method has found its niche and limitations within the scope of material systems it can accurately represent. In the nascent stages of surface energy studies, researchers relied heavily on experimental data coupled with semiempirical models to estimate surface properties. The Embedded Atom Method (EAM), developed by Baskes, was a significant advancement that provided a quantum mechanical framework for predicting the properties of metals, including surface energy [14]. This method was particularly successful in capturing the many-body effects inherent in metallic bonding. Parallel to EAM, the Empirical Electron Surface Model (EESM) was utilized to calculate surface energies by considering the electron density associated with dangling bonds at the surface [15]. These semiempirical approaches were instrumental in laying the foundational understanding of surface phenomena in metals and alloys. However, the transformative shift in surface energy calculations came with the advent of Density Functional Theory (DFT), which emerged as a powerful tool for first-principles calculations [16]. DFT, as implemented in computational packages like VASP [17], allowed for the accurate determination of electronic structures and, consequently, surface energies. The method's ability to handle complex interactions in multicomponent systems and its versatility in studying a wide range of materials made it the de facto standard for surface energy calculations. DFT calculations have been extensively used to study the surface energy of various materials, including metals, semiconductors, and insulators. For instance, Lee et al. [18] and Vitos et al. [19] used DFT to establish a comprehensive database of surface energies for low-index surfaces of 60 metals, which has since been a valuable resource for surface science research. Despite the successes of DFT, the method also faces challenges, particularly when dealing with large systems or when high accuracy is required. To address these issues, researchers have developed various approximations and corrections to the exchange-correlation function, such as the Generalized Gradient Approximation (GGA), which improves the accuracy of DFT calculations [20]. Moreover, the computational cost of DFT calculations has led to the development of alternative methods, such as the GW approximation [21] for quasiparticle energies and time-dependent DFT (TDDFT) [22, 23] for excited states, which provide complementary information to standard DFT calculations. The development of high-throughput computational methods has further expanded the scope of surface energy calculations. These approaches, such as the one developed by Yalcin and Wolloch [24], allow for the rapid assessment of surface energies across a multitude of materials and crystal orientations, facilitating the discovery of new materials with desirable surface properties.

The development from semiempirical models to first-principles calculations has been marked by significant milestones that have progressively enhanced our ability to predict and understand surface energies [25, 26]. As computational resources continue to grow and theoretical models are refined, the accuracy and predictive power of surface energy calculations will undoubtedly continue to improve, enabling the design of materials with tailored surface properties for a wide array of applications. Accurate prediction of surface energy is crucial for understanding and designing new materials. However, calculating surface energy in crystals involves several challenges across theoretical, computational, and experimental domains. Theoretical models often simplify crystal structures and assume ideal conditions, potentially compromising accuracy. Computational methods like DFT can be computationally intensive and rely on approximations that may not capture complex interactions accurately. Experimental techniques such as contact angle measurements are sensitive to sample preparation and environmental conditions, which can introduce variability and affect measurement precision [27, 28]. Surface reconstruction in crystals alters surface atomic arrangements, complicating accurate energy determination. Temperature and pressure variations influence surface energy, requiring careful consideration in calculations. Nanoscale effects can lead to size-dependent deviations from bulk values, challenging accurate prediction. Material-specific considerations and limited data availability for some materials further constrain the reliability of calculated surface energies, underscoring the need for rigorous validation and complementary approaches to enhance accuracy in surface energy determination. In addition, surface energy values obtained using DFT and similar computational methods are typically derived under idealized vacuum conditions [29, 30]. In such situations, theoretical models neglect the presence of other molecules, solvents, or impurities that may exist in the environment and could influence surface energy. Consequently, computed surface energy values may deviate from those measured experimentally. Experimental measurements of surface energy are often conducted in liquids or gases, where molecular interactions and environmental effects significantly impact surface behavior. Therefore, theoretical calculations typically require experimental validation and correction to accurately reflect surface energy behavior under realistic conditions. Recently, ANN-based approaches have garnered attention due to their lower computational costs and satisfactory predictive performance. In the prediction of surface energy, ANN models typically receive specific characteristics of materials, such as atomic arrangement, chemical composition, and crystal structure, as inputs [31, 32]. Through training, they learn the relationships between these features and surface energy. ANN models are capable of handling complex nonlinear relationships and can provide highly accurate predictions for surface energy. Additionally, ANN models can process large volumes of data and offer rapid predictions, which aids in accelerating the discovery and design of materials.

In this chapter, we initially present an overview of the development and application of ANN models, with a particular focus on their advancements in predicting surface energies. Subsequently, we elaborate on the construction process of ANN predictive models and the assembly of datasets, which are crucial steps to ensure the models' accuracy in surface energy predictions. We then evaluate and compare the performance of these ANN models to ascertain their precision and reliability in forecasting surface energies. The discussion also encompasses the limitations of current models and explores the potential impact of these limitations on the accuracy of surface energy predictions. Finally, we provide a prospective outlook on future research directions in surface energy prediction models. This includes a discussion on enhancing the predictive accuracy through algorithmic improvements and the expansion of dataset diversity, as well as the potential positive implications of these research efforts on material design and application.

2. Development and application of ANN models

The ANN models, drawing inspiration from biological neural networks, stand as a cornerstone in the realm of ML, offering a robust framework for diverse computational tasks [33]. As depicted in **Figure 1**, the orange neurons therein constitute a

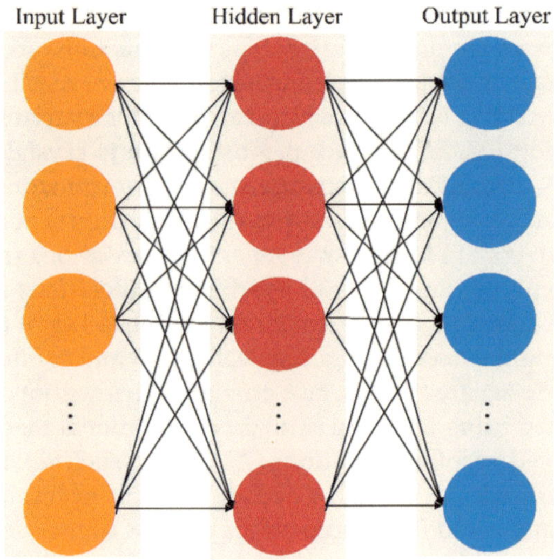

Figure 1.
ANN architecture.

layer, denoted as the first layer of the network, through which input data are propagated. Similarly, the final layer is referred to as the output layer, as indicated by the blue color. The layers situated between the input and output layers are termed hidden layers. In this example, we have only one hidden layer, depicted in red. From fundamental Feedforward Neural Networks (FNN) [34–37] to intricate architectures like Recurrent Neural Networks (RNN) [38–40], Convolutional Neural Networks (CNN) [41, 42], Generative Adversarial Networks (GAN) [43, 44], and Autoencoders [45], ANN models present a spectrum of capabilities tailored to specific data types and tasks. As the field of materials science increasingly relies on predictive modeling for understanding and anticipating material properties, the integration of neural network methodologies has become pivotal. Particularly in domains such as predicting surface energy and adsorption energy, the rapid evolution of ML and AI technologies has empowered neural network models to offer precise insights and forecasts.

Understanding and predicting material properties are foundational pursuits within materials science, where the application of ML and artificial intelligence (AI) technologies, particularly neural network models, has emerged as transformative. ANN models, with their adaptability and capacity to discern intricate patterns within data, have become indispensable tools in this field. From elucidating fundamental relationships to enabling precise predictions of properties like surface energy and adsorption energy, ANN models have revolutionized the landscape of material characterization and design. This synergy between advanced computational techniques and materials science underscores the imperative of harnessing neural network methodologies for accelerating discoveries and innovations in material research. The core strength of neural network models lies in their ability to learn from vast amounts of data and extract useful features to predict material properties. Graph neural networks (GNNs) [46], for instance, are particularly suited for addressing materials science problems due to their capacity to process graph-structured data, which aligns well with the atomic structure representation of materials. GNNs can effectively predict electronic properties, surface chemical properties, and catalytic performance of materials by learning the graph representation of atomic structures (**Figure 2**) [47].

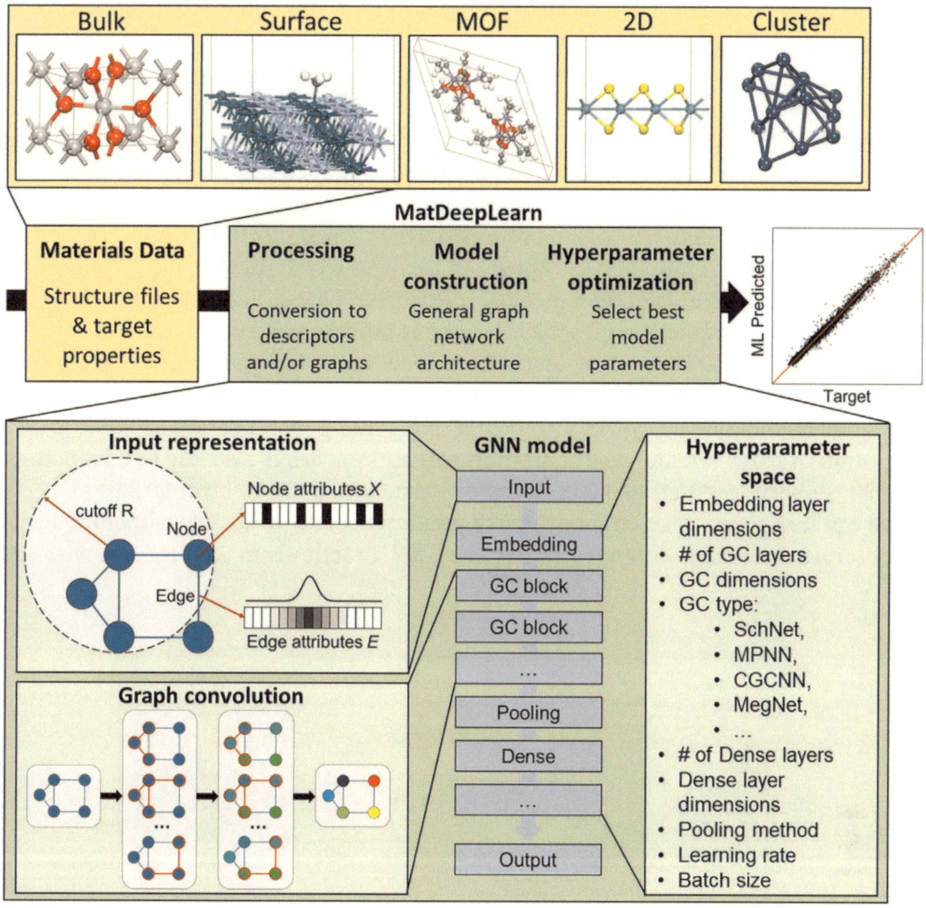

Figure 2.
Scheme of the GNN testing framework and workflow. Adapted with permission from Ref. [47]. Copyright 2021, Springer Nature Publishing Group.

In the domain of surface energy prediction, neural network models have achieved notable advancements. Surface energy, a pivotal parameter in material surface property characterization, influences the surface structure, relaxation, roughening, reconstruction, and the equilibrium shape of crystals. Traditional experimental techniques for measuring surface energy are subject to various limitations, including the complexity of experimental setups, measurement precision, and computational expenses. ML models, particularly Gaussian process regression (GPR), offer an efficient and cost-effective alternative for surface energy estimation. Zhang and Xu [48] developed a GPR model that predicts the surface energy of metals using physical parameters such as cohesive energy, lattice parameters, bulk modulus, and vacancy formation energy, enabling rapid estimation of surface energy for a variety of metals. When it comes to adsorption energy prediction, neural network models are equally instrumental. Adsorption energy is a critical metric for assessing catalyst activity and is vital for the discovery of novel catalysts. Li et al. [49] introduced a local environment pooling (LEPool) approach to enhance the predictive performance of GNNs for adsorption energy. By combining neural message passing with edge updates network

(NMPEU) and DimeNet++, they achieved high accuracy in predicting CO and H adsorption energies on transition metal catalyst surfaces.

These studies demonstrate the effectiveness of ANN models in predicting material properties, yet they also highlight some limitations. For instance, GNN models typically require a substantial amount of training data, and their performance may decline with smaller datasets. Additionally, the generalization ability of these models is a critical issue that needs further research to improve their performance across different datasets. To overcome these challenges, researchers are exploring various methods to refine neural network models. One approach involves hyperparameter optimization to adjust model parameters and enhance performance on specific datasets. Another method is transferring learning, which leverages models trained on one task to improve learning efficiency on a new task. Moreover, researchers are also investigating ways to integrate neural network models with physical principles and domain knowledge to enhance the models' interpretability and generalization capabilities. The integration of experimental and computational approaches is also key to advancing material property prediction. Combining experimental data with computational results can lead to more accurate property predictions and guide experimental design. For example, Lai and colleagues [31, 32] used ANN methods in conjunction with the

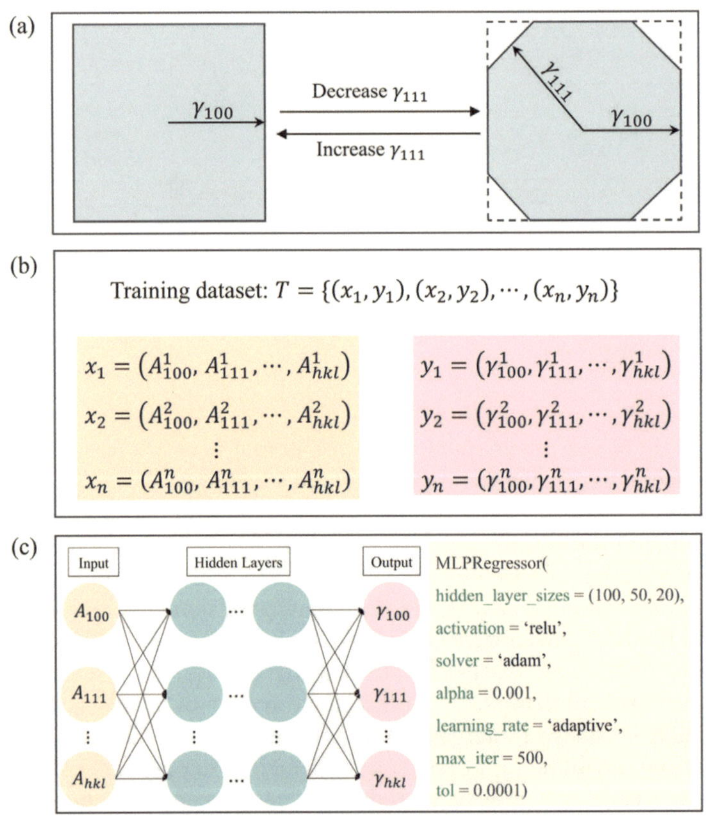

Figure 3.
(a) Morphological data generation using Wulff Construction for Cu_2O with {100} and {111} facets; (b) Feature vectors and instance classes of training dataset; and (c) ANN model training process and configuration for Cu_2O crystals. Adapted with permission from Ref. [32], Copyright 2023, MDPI Publications.

Wulff construction method to predict the surface energies of TiO_2 and Cu_2O crystals and validated the model's accuracy with experimental data.

The ANN utilized for machine learning-assisted facet design comprises an input layer, an output layer, and three hidden layers. To predict the surface energies of TiO_2, the input layer consists of three neurons corresponding to normalized elemental fractions summing to one. The three hidden layers each contain four neurons, ensuring sufficient depth for feature extraction and representation. The output layer is configured to normalize and output surface energies, also comprising three neurons [31]. In the case of predicting surface energies for Cu_2O crystals, the ANN model features three hidden layers with the following neuron configurations: the first hidden layer comprises 50 neurons, the second layer 30 neurons, and the third layer 20 neurons (**Figure 3**). This architecture enables comprehensive data processing and abstraction to effectively predict and analyze surface energies [32].

3. ANN prediction and dataset construction

The construction of databases is a pivotal step in understanding and predicting the properties of materials. These databases typically encompass a wealth of experimental data and theoretical calculations, serving as the foundation for ML models to train and validate their predictions. Initially, Palizhati et al. [8] focused on predicting the surface energy of inorganic crystals, particularly for complex intermetallic compounds. The challenge lay in the fact that existing predictive methods and datasets were predominantly geared toward monometallic crystals, with the surface properties of bimetallic or more intricate surfaces remaining largely unpredictable. To address this, the researchers developed a workflow that integrates high-throughput Density Functional Theory (DFT) calculations with an ML framework to predict the cleavage energies of alloys. This approach calculated the cleavage energy of 3033 intermetallic alloys across 36 elements and 47 space groups. The high-throughput nature of this workflow not only seeded a comprehensive database of cleavage energies but also facilitated the training of a Crystal Graph Convolutional Neural Network (CGCNN), as shown in **Figure 4**. The CGCNN model demonstrated accurate predictions of cleavage energy and qualitatively reproduced nanoparticle surface distributions, known as Wulff constructions. This workflow provided quantitative insights into uncharted chemical space, predicting which surfaces were relatively stable, thereby aiding in the selection of promising candidates for applications such as catalyst screening and nanomaterial synthesis.

In another study, Zhang and Xu [48] developed a Gaussian Process Regression (GPR) model to predict metal surface energy. The model was constructed based on several physical parameters, including cohesive energy, lattice parameters, bulk modulus, and vacancy formation energy, which are closely correlated with metal surface energy. The GPR model exhibited high accuracy and stability, offering a rapid, robust, and cost-effective tool for estimating the surface energy of various metals. The dataset included 43 metals with surface energies ranging from 0.10 to 3.68 Jm^{-2}, encompassing metals with face-centered cubic (FCC), body-centered cubic (BCC), and hexagonal close-packed (HCP) structures. The GPR model outperformed previous methods such as Support Vector Regression (SVR) and the Stabilized Jellium Model (SJM), demonstrating improved predictive capabilities. Furthermore, Liu et al. [50] focused on constructing a multiscale, multisource dataset of hydroxyapatite nanoparticles (HANPs) with varying morphologies and sizes. The dataset included experimental data such as TEM/SEM, XRD/crystallinity, reactive oxygen species

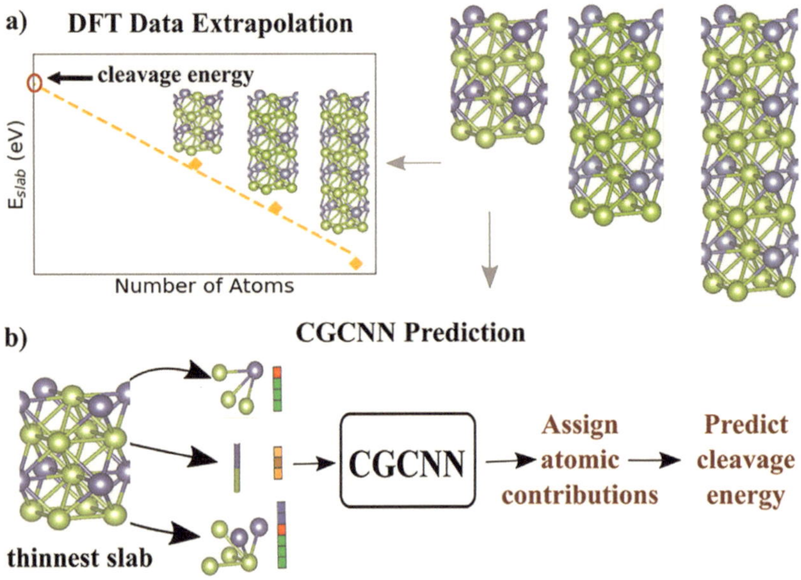

Figure 4.
(a) DFT calculation of cleavage energies, and (b) Predictions via CGCNN models. Adapted with permission from Ref. [8]. Copyright 2019, ACS Publications.

(ROS), antitumor effects, and zeta potential, as well as computational results from nanoparticles up to 9768 atoms in size, calculated using DFT, semiempirical DFTB, and force field methods (**Figure 5**). The researchers applied ML techniques to explore the correlation between surface energy and geometric features of HANPs. They also developed a graph convolutional neural network model to predict surface energy more accurately, without the need for predetermined features. The integration of image segmentation on experimental TEM images allowed for the reconstruction of 3D HANPs models, which were then used to simulate XRD patterns and crystallinity values that aligned well with experimental data.

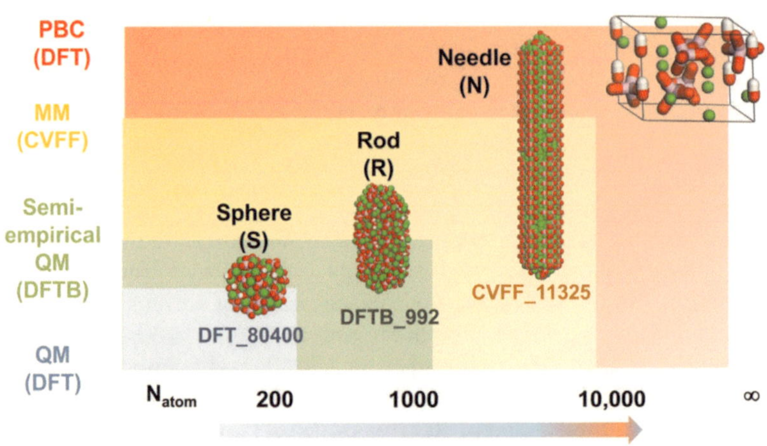

Figure 5.
Datasets of HANPs generated at various theoretical levels: DFT, Density Functional Tight Binding (DFTB), and Consistent Valence Force Field (CVFF). Adapted with permission from Ref. [50]. Copyright 2021, Springer Nature Publishing Group.

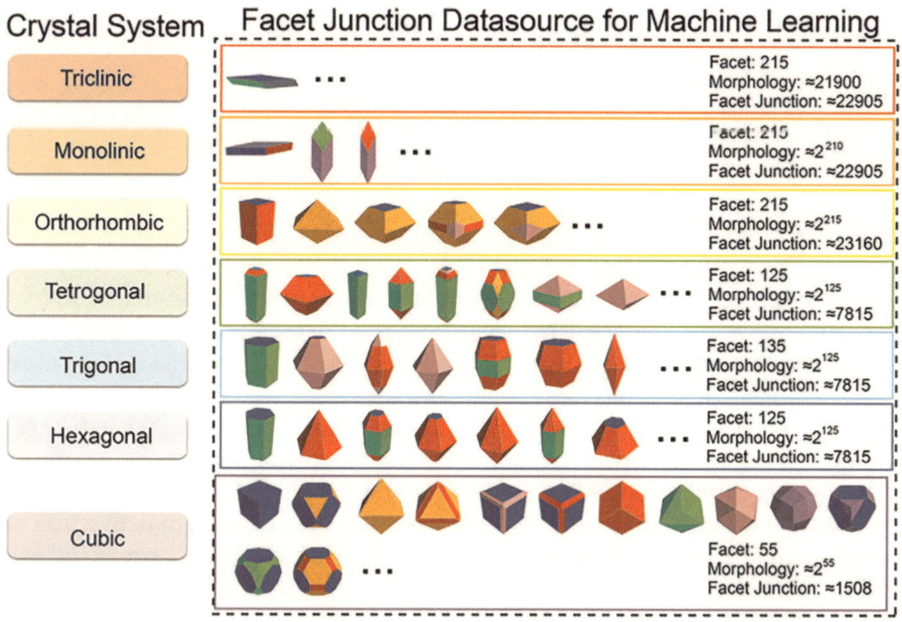

Figure 6.
The database of facet counts, morphologies, and junctions was constructed using the Wulff construction. Adapted with permission from Ref. [31] Copyright 2021, Wiley Publications.

Lai et al. [51] have undertaken a series of precise and systematic steps to construct databases of morphology and surface energy, which are crucial for understanding and predicting the crystalline shapes and surface characteristics of materials. This approach facilitated the acquisition of 1075 distinct facets across seven crystallographic systems, enabling the formulation of approximately 2251 potential morphologies and 92,033 diverse facet junctions (**Figure 6**) [31]. The dataset was further enriched by integrating surface energy and area data of these facets, derived from experimentally observed particle morphologies. To ensure the robustness of the ML model, a comprehensive training set was developed, employing an ANN that was rigorously trained and tested on a randomly distributed dataset comprising 1000 cases. The model's architecture was optimized with a hyperbolic tangent sigmoid transfer function across three hidden layers, with the input layer consisting of normalized elemental fractions. The dataset used in the study is made accessible through an open access link, ensuring reproducibility and facilitating further research in the domain.

4. Performance evaluation and comparison of ANN models

In the realm of ML, error metrics serve as pivotal instruments for quantifying the predictive performance of models. Here are several commonly used error measurement indicators:

$$\mathrm{MSE} = \frac{1}{n}\sum_{i=1}^{n}\left(y_i - \hat{y}_i\right)^2 \tag{1}$$

$$\text{RMSE} = \sqrt{\frac{1}{n}\sum_{i=1}^{n}\left(y_i - \hat{y}_i\right)^2} \tag{2}$$

$$\text{MAE} = \frac{1}{n}\sum_{i=1}^{n}\left|y_i - \hat{y}_i\right| \tag{3}$$

$$R^2 = 1 - \frac{\sum_{i=1}^{n}\left(y_i - \hat{y}_i\right)^2}{\sum_{i=1}^{n}\left(y_i - \bar{y}\right)^2} \tag{4}$$

where y_i is the ith observed value, $\bar{y}$ is the mean value of all observed values, $\hat{y}_i$ denotes the corresponding predicted value, and n is the total number of observations. These metrics provide a direct measure of accuracy by calculating the discrepancies between a model's predictions and the actual observed values. The selection of appropriate error metrics is contingent upon the characteristics of the data, the nature of the problem at hand, and the specific requirements of the researchers.

The mean squared error (MSE) and the root mean squared error (RMSE) are widely recognized error metrics. The MSE quantifies the average predictive bias of a model by computing the average of the squared differences between predicted and actual values. It assigns a greater weight to larger prediction errors, causing the MSE to increase significantly when the model exhibits substantial error for certain observations. This sensitivity makes the MSE an extremely responsive error metric, particularly suitable for applications with a low tolerance for large errors. However, a drawback of the MSE is that its units are squared, which can make the magnitude of the error less intuitive to interpret.

To address the MSE's unit discrepancy, the RMSE was introduced. The RMSE is the square root of the MSE and shares the same units as the original data, making the error magnitude more tangible. The RMSE offers a balanced measure of error, taking into account the magnitude of the error without disproportionately penalizing outliers. The mean absolute error (MAE) is another commonly used metric that assesses a model's predictive performance by calculating the average of the absolute differences between predictions and actual values. Unlike the MSE and RMSE, the MAE assigns equal weight to all errors, regardless of their magnitude. This characteristic renders the MAE more robust when dealing with data that includes outliers or follows a heavy-tailed distribution. Additionally, the MAE's intuitive nature and ease of interpretation make it highly favored in practical applications. In the study by Palizhati et al. [8], the MAE was utilized to measure the discrepancy between the cleavage energies predicted by the CGCNN model and those obtained from DFT calculations, achieving a value of 0.0071 eV/Å^2. This indicates that the CGCNN model is capable of predicting cleavage energies with a high degree of accuracy.

The R-squared (R^2) is an additional error measurement that complements the MSE, RMSE, and MAE in assessing the performance of predictive models. R^2 measures the proportion of the variance in the dependent variable that is predictable from the independent variables, and it is a common metric for assessing the fit of a model. R^2 provides a statistical measure of how close the data are to the fitted regression line, and it is a powerful tool for understanding the goodness of fit of a model. In contrast to other metrics that exclusively emphasize the size of the discrepancies between predicted and actual outcomes, R^2 also takes into account the variability of the data and the proportion of variance explained by the model.

In practical applications, the choice of the appropriate error metric requires a comprehensive consideration of various factors. While the MSE, RMSE, and MAE provide direct measures of prediction error, the R^2 metric offers a nuanced view of the model's ability to explain the response variable. It is a critical component in the comprehensive evaluation of model performance, especially when the goal is to understand the extent to which a model captures the complexity of the data. In the field of materials science, where the accurate prediction of surface energy is paramount, R^2 serves as a key indicator of model utility, guiding researchers in the selection and refinement of predictive tools that can inform the design and analysis of novel materials. Lai et al. [31] utilized a dataset comprising 1000 cases, which were randomly divided into training and testing sets with an 8:2 ratio to evaluate the performance of the ANN model in predicting the surface energy of TiO_2. The study found that the values predicted by the ANN model were highly congruent with those calculated using the inverse Wulff construction method, indicating a high degree of accuracy in the ML model's ability to predict the surface energy of crystal facet junctions. The model demonstrated low MAE and RMSE, both below 0.02 and 0.03, respectively, and a high R^2, above 0.95, which signifies a strong predictive performance and a reliable model for estimating surface energies in the context of TiO_2 crystal facets (**Figure 7(a–c)**). In the prediction of Cu_2O surface energy, the ANN model exhibited comparable MAE values between the training and testing sets, which ranged from 0.2 to 0.3. This indicates that the model has a low average absolute error in its predictions. Furthermore, the R^2 values for both sets were between 0.96 and 0.98, signifying the model's strong capacity to explain the variance in the target variable (**Figure 7(d–f)**). These findings suggest that the ANN model is effective in predicting material properties, offering automated feature learning and nonlinear modeling capabilities, which are crucial for the comprehensive understanding of Cu_2O crystals and their surface behavior.

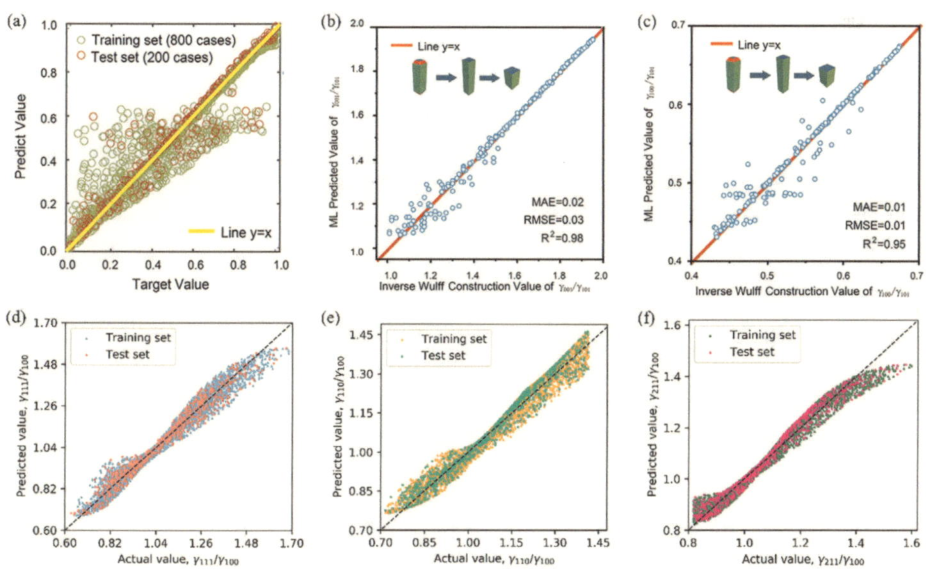

Figure 7.
(a) Evaluation of the ANN model's performance in predicting TiO_2 surface energy using a randomized 8:2 split of a 1000-case dataset; Comparison of surface energies for the: (a) {001}/{101}, and (b) {100}/{101} facet junctions calculated by inverse Wulff construction and predicted by ANN. Adapted with permission from Ref. [31] Copyright 2021, Wiley Publications. Surface energy predictions of the 50-facet polyhedron by the ANN model on both training and test sets: (d) $\gamma_{111}/\gamma_{100}$, (e) $\gamma_{110}/\gamma_{100}$, and (f) $\gamma_{112}/\gamma_{100}$. Adapted with permission from Ref. [32], Copyright 2023, MDPI Publications.

5. Conclusion

In summary, ANN models have shown great potential in predicting material properties, especially in the areas of surface energy and adsorption energy. As ML and AI technologies continue to advance, these models are expected to play an increasingly important role in material design and catalyst discovery. However, challenges remain, and future research directions should aim to address these issues to unlock the full potential of these models in material science. One significant challenge is the reliance on extensive training datasets, which can be costly and time-consuming to compile, particularly for less-studied materials. Additionally, the high computational demand associated with these models often necessitates powerful hardware, which may not be accessible to all research groups. Furthermore, the accuracy of surface energy predictions can be compromised by the models' generalization capabilities, particularly when extrapolating to materials or conditions beyond the scope of the training data. This limitation is exacerbated by the inherent complexity of surface phenomena, which can involve subtle interactions that are not easily captured by current ML frameworks. The interpretability of these models is also a concern, as the 'black box' nature of many neural network architectures makes it challenging to understand the underlying reasons for their predictions, which is crucial for scientific validation and trust.

Future research in surface energy prediction models should aim to address these limitations and enhance the models' predictive accuracy and reliability. There is a pressing need for the development of more efficient algorithms that can operate with reduced computational resources while maintaining or improving predictive performance. Innovations in transfer learning and few-shot learning could enable models to generalize better to new materials with limited data. Incorporating physical and chemical insights into the model development process may also improve the interpretability and reliability of predictions. Furthermore, the integration of multiscale modeling approaches that combine quantum mechanics, molecular dynamics, and ML could lead to a more nuanced understanding of surface phenomena. Finally, fostering open access to high-quality datasets and computational tools will be essential in democratizing the field and accelerating progress. The goal is to create models that are not only accurate but also transparent, efficient, and broadly applicable to a wide range of materials science problems.

Author details

Fuming Lai and Shengfu Tong*
School of Sustainable Energy and Materials Science, Jinhua Advanced Research Institute, Jinhua, China

*Address all correspondence to: shengfutong@gmail.com

References

[1] Wu Z-Z et al. Identification of Cu (100)/Cu(111) interfaces as superior active sites for CO dimerization during CO_2 Electroreduction. Journal of the American Chemical Society. 2021; **144**(1):259-269

[2] Wang Y et al. DNA origami single crystals with Wulff shapes. Nature Communications. 2021;**12**(1):3011

[3] Su H et al. Surface energy engineering of buried interface for highly stable perovskite solar cells with efficiency over 25%. Advanced Materials. 2024; **36**(2):2306724

[4] Xue-Guang Chen LL, Huang G-Y, Chen X-M, Li X-Z, Zhou Y-K, Zou Y, et al. Optofluidic crystallithography for directed growth of single-crystalline halide perovskites. Nature Communications. 2024;**15**:3677

[5] Zhang K et al. Surface energy mediated sulfur vacancy of $ZnIn_2S_4$ atomic layers for photocatalytic H_2O_2 production. Advanced Functional Materials. 2023;**33**(35):2302964

[6] Li H, Jiao Y, Davey K, Qiao SZ. Data-driven machine learning for understanding surface structures of heterogeneous catalysts. Angewandte Chemie International Edition. 2023; **62**(9):e202216383

[7] Zhu S, Xie K, Lin Q, Cao R, Qiu F. Experimental determination of surface energy for high-energy surface: A review. Advances in Colloid Interface Science. 2023;**315**:102905

[8] Palizhati A, Zhong W, Tran K, Back S, Ulissi ZW. Toward predicting Intermetallics surface properties with high-throughput DFT and convolutional neural networks. Journal of Chemical Information and Modeling. 2019;**59**(11): 4742-4749

[9] Shrestha A, Gao X, Hicks JC, Paolucci C. Nanoparticle size effects on phase stability for molybdenum and tungsten carbides. Chemistry of Materials. 2021;**33**(12):4606-4620

[10] Tran R et al. Surface energies of elemental crystals. Scientific Data. 2016; **3**:160080

[11] Lai F, Chen Y, Guo H. Inverse Wulff construction for surface energies of coexisting and missing surfaces of crystal particles. Journal of Crystal Growth. 2019;**508**:1-7

[12] Lai F, Chen Y, Guo H. Surface energies of non-centrosymmetric nanocrystals by the inverse Wulff construction method. Physical Chemistry Chemical Physics. 2019; **21**(30):16486-16496

[13] Barmparis GD, Lodziana Z, Lopez N, Remediakis IN. Nanoparticle shapes by using Wulff constructions and first-principles calculations. Beilstein Journal of Nanotechnology. 2015;**6**:361-368

[14] Baskes MI. Modified embedded-atom potentials for cubic materials and impurities. Physical Review B. 1992; **46**(5):2727-2742

[15] Fu B, Liu W, Li Z. Surface energy calculation of alkali metals with the empirical electron surface model. Materials Chemistry and Physics. 2010; **123**(2–3):658-665

[16] Kohn W, Becke AD, Parr RG. Density functional theory of electronic structure. Journal of Physical Chemistry. 1996;**100**:12974-12980

[17] Kresse G, Furthmüller J. Efficient iterative schemes for ab initio total-energy calculations using a plane-wave basis set. Physical Review B. 1996;**54** (16):11169-11186

[18] Lee JY et al. The surface energy and stress of metals. Surface Science. 2018; **674**:51-68

[19] Vitos L, Ruban AV, Skriver HL, Kollár J. The surface energy of metals. Surface Science. 1998;**411**(1–2):186-202

[20] Perdew JP, Burke K, Ernzerhof M. Generalized gradient approximation made simple. Physical Review Letters. 1996;**77**(18):3865-3868

[21] García-González P, Godby RW. GW self-energy calculations for surfaces and interfaces. Computer Physics Communications. 2001;**13**(1):108-122

[22] Burke K, Werschnik J, Gross EK. Time-dependent density functional theory: Past, present, and future. Journal of Chemical Physics. 2005;**123**(6):62206

[23] Adamo C, Jacquemin D. The calculations of excited-state properties with time-dependent density functional theory. Chemical Society Reviews. 2013; **42**(3):845-856

[24] Yalcin F, Wolloch M. SurfFlow: High-throughput surface energy calculations for arbitrary crystals. Computational Materials Science. 2024; **234**:112799

[25] Żenkiewicz M. Methods for the calculation of surface free energy of solids. Journal Of Achievements In Materials and Manufacturing Engineering. 2007;**24**(1):137-145

[26] Domińczuk J, Krawczuk A. Comparison of surface free energy calculation methods. Applied Mechanics and Materials. 2015;**791**:259-265

[27] Kwok DY, Neumann AW. Contact angle measurement and contact angle interpretation. Advances in Colloid and Interface Science. 1999;**81**:167-249

[28] Hoyt JJ, Asta M, Karma A. Method for computing the anisotropy of the solid-liquid interfacial free energy. Physical Review Letters. 2001;**86**(24): 5530-5533

[29] Ferrer MM, Gouveia AF, Gracia L, Longo E, Andrés J. A 3D platform for the morphology modulation of materials: First principles calculations on the thermodynamic stability and surface structure of metal oxides: Co_3O_4,α-Fe_2O_3, and In_2O_3. Modelling and Simulation in Materials Science and Engineering. 2016;**24**(2):025007

[30] Lai F, Luo R, Xie Y, Chen Y, Guo H. Modeling thermodynamic stability of morphologies and surfaces of YF_3. Surface Science. 2020;**700**:121674

[31] Lai F, Sun Z, Saji SE, He Y, Yu X, Zhao H, et al. Machine learning-aided crystal facet rational design with ionic liquid controllable synthesis. Small. 2021;**17**(12):2100024

[32] Shi Y, Wang M, Zhou Z, Zhao M, Hu Y, Yang J, et al. Artificial neural network-based prediction and morphological evolution of Cu_2O crystal surface energy. Coatings. 2023;**13**(9):1609

[33] Abiodun OI, Jantan A, Omolara AE, Dada KV, Mohamed NA, Arshad H. State-of-the-art in artificial neural network applications: A survey. Heliyon. 2018;**4**(11):13605-13635

[34] Eldan R, Shamir O. The power of depth for feedforward neural networks. In: 29th Annual Conference on Learning

Theory. Vol. 49. New York: PMLR; 2016. pp. 907-940

[35] Bebis G, Georgiopoulos M. Feed-forward neural networks. IEEE Potentials. 1994;**13**(4):27-31

[36] Sazlı MH. A brief review of feed-forward neural networks. Communications Faculty of Sciences University of Ankara Series A2-A3 Physical Sciences Engineering. 2006;**50**(1):11-17

[37] Svozil D, Kvasnicka V, Pospichal J. Introduction to multi-layer feed-forward neural networks. Chemometrics and Intelligent Laboratory Systems. 1997; **39**(1):43-62

[38] Schuster M, Paliwal KK. Bidirectional recurrent neural networks. IEEE Transactions on Signal Processing. 1997;**45**(11):2673-2681

[39] Medsker LR, Jain L. Recurrent neural networks. Design and Applications. 2001;**5**(64–67):2

[40] Pascanu R, Mikolov T, Bengio Y. On the difficulty of training recurrent neural networks. In: International Conference on Machine Learning. Atlanta: PMLR; 2013. pp. 1310-1318

[41] Gu J et al. Recent advances in convolutional neural networks. Pattern Recognition. 2018;**77**:354-377

[42] Li Z, Liu F, Yang W, Peng S, Zhou J. A survey of convolutional neural networks: Analysis, applications, and prospects. IEEE Transactions on Neural Networks Learning Systems. 2021; **33**(12):6999-7019

[43] Creswell A, White T, Dumoulin V, Arulkumaran K, Sengupta B, Bharath AA. Generative adversarial networks: An overview. IEEE Signal Processing Magazine. 2018;**35**(1): 53-65

[44] Goodfellow I et al. Generative adversarial networks. Communications of the ACM. 2020;**63**(11):139-144

[45] Baldi P. Autoencoders, unsupervised learning, and deep architectures. In: Proceedings of ICML Workshop on Unsupervised and Transfer Learning. Washington: JMLR Workshop and Conference Proceedings; 2012. pp. 37-49

[46] Reiser P et al. Graph neural networks for materials science and chemistry. Communications Materials. 2022;**3**(1):93

[47] Fung V, Zhang J, Juarez E, Sumpter BG. Benchmarking graph neural networks for materials chemistry. npj Computational Materials. 2021;**7**(1):84

[48] Zhang Y, Xu X. Machine learning modeling of metal surface energy. Materials Chemistry and Physics. 2021;**267**:124622

[49] Li X, Chiong R, Hu Z, Page AJ. A graph neural network model with local environment pooling for predicting adsorption energies. Computational and Theoretical Chemistry. 2023;**1226**: 114161

[50] Liu Z et al. Machine learning on properties of multiscale multisource hydroxyapatite nanoparticles datasets with different morphologies and sizes. npj Computational Materials. 2021;**7**(1): 142

[51] Lai F et al. Toward predicting surface energy of rutile TiO_2 with machine learning. CrystEngComm. 2023;**25**(2): 199-205